# CREATING GAMES WITH PYTHON, PYGAME AND RASBERRY PI

A Hands-On Guide to Interactive Game Development

FIRST EDITION

# Table of Contents

Table of Contents ...................................................................................................... 1
Preface ...................................................................................................................... 16
Chapter 1: Introduction to Game Development with Python and Raspberry Pi ............ 17
    What is Game Development? ................................................................................ 17
    Overview of Python and PyGame ........................................................................... 17
    Why Raspberry Pi for Game Development? ........................................................... 18
    Setting Up Your Development Environment ........................................................... 19
        Installing Python ................................................................................................ 19
        Installing PyGame ............................................................................................. 19
    Overview of Python and PyGame ........................................................................... 20
        Why Choose Python for Game Development? ................................................. 20
        Introduction to PyGame .................................................................................... 20
        Setting Up PyGame .......................................................................................... 21
        PyGame Architecture ........................................................................................ 21
        Drawing Graphics with PyGame ....................................................................... 23
        Adding Images and Sprites .............................................................................. 24
        Conclusion ........................................................................................................ 24
    Why Raspberry Pi for Game Development? ........................................................... 25
        1. Affordable and Accessible ........................................................................... 25
        2. Compact and Portable ................................................................................. 25
        3. Extensive GPIO Capabilities ....................................................................... 26
        4. Versatile Software Environment .................................................................. 27
        5. Active Community and Abundant Resources ............................................. 27
        6. Unique Project Opportunities ...................................................................... 28
        Conclusion ........................................................................................................ 28
    Setting Up Your Development Environment ........................................................... 28
        1. Preparing Your Raspberry Pi ....................................................................... 28
        2. Installing Python .......................................................................................... 29
        3. Setting Up PyGame ..................................................................................... 30
        4. Choosing an Integrated Development Environment (IDE) .......................... 30
        5. Configuring Your Raspberry Pi for Development ........................................ 30
        6. Creating a Virtual Environment .................................................................... 31
        7. Setting Up Version Control with Git ............................................................. 31

8. Setting Up Game Project Structure ..................................................................32
9. Creating a Basic Game Template ....................................................................32
   Conclusion ........................................................................................................33
**Chapter 2: Getting Started with Raspberry Pi and Python** ..........................35
   Introduction to Raspberry Pi ..............................................................................35
      What is the Raspberry Pi? ..............................................................................35
      Key Features of Raspberry Pi ........................................................................35
      Different Models of Raspberry Pi ..................................................................35
      Setting Up Your Raspberry Pi ........................................................................36
      Exploring the Raspberry Pi Desktop ..............................................................37
      Basic Linux Commands for Raspberry Pi ......................................................37
      Installing Python on Raspberry Pi ..................................................................38
      Using Python on the Raspberry Pi ..................................................................38
      Summary ........................................................................................................38
   Installing Python on Raspberry Pi .....................................................................39
      Checking the Current Python Installation ......................................................39
      Updating the System ......................................................................................39
      Installing Python ............................................................................................39
      Installing pip: The Python Package Manager ................................................40
      Using pip to Install Python Packages .............................................................40
      Setting Up a Python Virtual Environment .....................................................41
      Installing Development Tools ........................................................................42
      Installing PyGame ..........................................................................................42
      Testing Your Python and PyGame Installation ..............................................42
      Setting Python 3 as the Default Python .........................................................43
      Troubleshooting Common Issues ...................................................................44
      Summary ........................................................................................................44
   Basic Python Programming Refresher ...............................................................44
      Getting Started with Python ...........................................................................44
      Variables and Data Types ...............................................................................45
      Basic Arithmetic and Operators .....................................................................45
      Strings and String Manipulation .....................................................................46
      Lists and Tuples ..............................................................................................46
      Dictionaries ....................................................................................................47
      Conditional Statements ..................................................................................48
      Loops ..............................................................................................................48

- Functions ................................................................................. 49
- Exception Handling ................................................................ 49
- File Handling ......................................................................... 50
- Importing Modules ................................................................ 50
- Using Command-Line Arguments ........................................ 50
- Summary ............................................................................... 51
- Exploring GPIO Pins for Game Controls ................................. 51
  - What Are GPIO Pins? ........................................................... 51
  - Setting Up GPIO on Raspberry Pi ....................................... 52
  - Understanding the GPIO Pin Layout ................................... 52
  - Basic GPIO Setup with Python ............................................ 52
  - Using GPIO as Input: Reading Button Presses .................. 53
  - Debouncing Button Input .................................................... 54
  - Building a Basic Game Controller ....................................... 55
  - Using GPIO with PyGame .................................................... 56
  - Safety Tips for Working with GPIO ..................................... 56
  - Summary ............................................................................. 57
- Chapter 3: Introduction to PyGame: Building Your First Game ........ 58
  - Installing and Setting Up PyGame ......................................... 58
    - Why Use PyGame? ............................................................. 58
    - Setting Up Python and PyGame ........................................ 58
    - Creating a New PyGame Project ....................................... 59
    - Writing Your First PyGame Script ..................................... 59
    - Running the Game .............................................................. 60
    - Adding a Background Color .............................................. 61
    - Handling User Input ........................................................... 61
    - Creating a Moving Object .................................................. 62
    - Summary ............................................................................ 63
  - Understanding the PyGame Framework .............................. 64
    - Basic Structure of a PyGame Program ............................. 64
    - Understanding the Game Loop ......................................... 65
    - Event Handling ................................................................... 65
    - Game Clock and Frame Rate ............................................ 66
    - Using Sprites for Game Objects ....................................... 67
    - Handling Collisions ............................................................ 68
    - Conclusion .......................................................................... 69

Creating a Simple "Hello World" Game ...... 69
  Setting Up the Project ...... 69
  Importing PyGame and Initializing the Game ...... 70
  Rendering Text with PyGame ...... 70
  Main Game Loop ...... 71
  Adding User Interaction ...... 72
  Adding Simple Animation ...... 73
  Handling Mouse Events ...... 73
  Summary and Next Steps ...... 74
Game Loop: The Heart of Every Game ...... 74
  What is a Game Loop? ...... 74
  Anatomy of a Basic Game Loop ...... 75
  Managing Time in the Game Loop ...... 76
  Handling Input in the Game Loop ...... 77
  Different Types of Game Loops ...... 78
  Optimizing the Game Loop ...... 79
  Example: Putting It All Together ...... 79
  Summary ...... 80
Chapter 4: Game Elements: Graphics, Sound, and Animation ...... 81
  Working with Graphics in PyGame ...... 81
    1. Introduction to Surfaces ...... 81
    2. Drawing Basic Shapes ...... 82
    3. Loading and Displaying Images ...... 82
    4. Image Transformations ...... 83
    5. Using Transparency and Alpha Channels ...... 83
    6. Creating a Background ...... 84
    7. Handling Display Updates ...... 84
    8. Creating a Simple Animation ...... 84
    9. Tips for Optimizing Graphics Performance ...... 85
    Summary ...... 85
  Adding Sound Effects and Music ...... 86
    1. Initializing the Mixer ...... 86
    2. Loading Sound Effects ...... 86
    3. Using Music in PyGame ...... 87
    4. Handling Audio Events ...... 88
    5. Mixing Multiple Sounds ...... 88

- 6. Adding Audio Feedback to User Actions .......... 89
- 7. Fading In and Out .......... 89
- 8. Handling Audio Playback Errors .......... 90
- 9. Optimizing Audio Performance .......... 90
- Summary .......... 90

## Basic Animation Techniques .......... 91
- 1. Understanding the Game Loop and Frame Rate .......... 91
- 2. Frame-Based Animation .......... 92
- 3. Sprite-Based Animation .......... 93
- 4. Smooth Movement and Interpolation .......... 94
- 5. Easing Functions for Natural Animations .......... 95
- 6. Using Animated Sprites for Characters .......... 96
- Summary .......... 97

## Handling User Input and Events .......... 98
- 1. Introduction to Event Handling .......... 98
- 2. Handling Keyboard Input .......... 99
- 3. Handling Mouse Input .......... 99
- 4. Creating Clickable Buttons .......... 100
- 5. Handling Joystick and Gamepad Input .......... 101
- 6. Customizing User Input for Gameplay .......... 102
- 7. Handling Complex Input Sequences .......... 103
- Summary .......... 103

# Chapter 5: Building a Classic Arcade Game: Breakout .......... 105
## Game Design Overview: Breakout .......... 105
- Key Game Elements .......... 105
- Game Mechanics .......... 105
- Tools and Framework .......... 105
- Planning the Code Structure .......... 105
- Setting Up the Game .......... 106
- Creating the Paddle Class .......... 107
- Creating the Ball Class .......... 108
- Creating the Bricks .......... 108
- Main Game Loop .......... 109
- Conclusion .......... 110

## Setting Up the Game Screen and Paddle .......... 110
- Defining the Game Window .......... 110

Designing the Paddle ........................................................................................... 111
Handling User Input............................................................................................ 113
Fine-Tuning the Paddle Movement ................................................................. 113
Implementing Frame Rate Control ................................................................. 114
Testing the Paddle............................................................................................. 115
Customizing the Paddle ................................................................................... 115
Conclusion ......................................................................................................... 115

Adding Bricks and Collision Detection ............................................................. 116
Designing the Brick Structure ......................................................................... 116
Creating the Brick Class .................................................................................. 116
Generating the Brick Wall ................................................................................ 117
Drawing the Bricks ........................................................................................... 117
Implementing Ball Movement ......................................................................... 118
Detecting Collisions with Bricks ..................................................................... 119
Implementing a Scoring System .................................................................... 119
Handling Game Over ........................................................................................ 120
Enhancing Collision Detection ....................................................................... 120
Testing and Debugging ................................................................................... 120
Conclusion ......................................................................................................... 121

Scoring System and Game Over Conditions .................................................. 121
Designing the Scoring System ....................................................................... 121
Displaying the Score on the Screen .............................................................. 121
Implementing Lives .......................................................................................... 122
Displaying Lives ................................................................................................ 123
Handling Game Over ........................................................................................ 123
Restarting the Game......................................................................................... 124
Adding a High Score System........................................................................... 124
Adding Game Over Sound Effects ................................................................. 125
Enhancing the Game Over Screen ................................................................. 125
Testing the Scoring and Game Over System ............................................... 126
Conclusion ......................................................................................................... 126

Chapter 6: Implementing Game Physics and Enhancements ........................127
Understanding Game Physics and Mechanics................................................127
Physics Basics in Game Development ..........................................................127
Implementing Basic Physics in PyGame........................................................127
Explanation of the Code ..................................................................................129

Adding User Input for Movement ... 129
Enhancing Physics with Acceleration and Drag ... 130
Introducing Advanced Collision Response ... 130
Implementing Complex Physics: Simulating a Platform ... 130
Tips for Improving Game Physics ... 131
Adding Physics to the Ball Movement ... 131
Overview of Enhanced Ball Physics ... 131
Setting Up the Physics Engine ... 131
Understanding the Ball Class ... 133
Handling Collisions with the Ground ... 133
Improving Collision Response with Restitution ... 134
Simulating Rolling Friction ... 134
Adding User Control and Interaction ... 135
Advanced Physics: Simulating Angular Motion ... 135
Final Thoughts on Enhanced Ball Physics ... 136
Enhancing Gameplay with Power-Ups ... 136
Types of Power-Ups ... 136
Designing the Power-Up System ... 137
Integrating Power-Ups into the Game Loop ... 138
Adding Visual Feedback ... 139
Managing Power-Up Duration ... 139
Balancing Power-Ups ... 140
Example Game Loop with Power-Ups ... 140
Testing and Debugging Power-Ups ... 141
Conclusion ... 141
Improving User Experience with Smooth Animations ... 141
Understanding Animation Basics ... 141
Setting Up a Basic Animation Framework ... 142
Easing Functions for Smoother Transitions ... 143
Implementing a Fade-In Animation ... 143
Creating Smooth Movement with Interpolation ... 144
Implementing Sprite Animations ... 144
Adding Particle Effects ... 145
Best Practices for Smooth Animations ... 146
Conclusion ... 146
Chapter 7: Using Raspberry Pi's GPIO for Custom Game Controls ... 147

## Introduction to GPIO Programming .................................................. 147
### What Are GPIO Pins? .................................................. 147
### Setting Up the Development Environment .................................................. 147
### Configuring GPIO in Python .................................................. 148
### Example: Controlling an LED with a Button .................................................. 148
### Using Event Detection .................................................. 149
### Expanding the Example: Creating a Simple Game Controller .................................................. 150
### Summary .................................................. 151
## Connecting External Buttons and Joysticks .................................................. 152
### Understanding the Input Devices .................................................. 152
### Connecting Push Buttons to GPIO .................................................. 152
### Connecting a Digital Joystick .................................................. 153
### Connecting an Analog Joystick .................................................. 155
### Summary .................................................. 157
## Building a Custom Game Controller .................................................. 157
### Planning Your Game Controller .................................................. 157
### Components Needed .................................................. 157
### Setting Up the Hardware .................................................. 158
### Python Code for the Game Controller .................................................. 158
### Building an Enclosure .................................................. 160
### Integrating the Controller with PyGame .................................................. 160
### Summary .................................................. 162
## Integrating GPIO Input with PyGame .................................................. 162
### Setting Up the Project .................................................. 163
### Creating the Game Structure .................................................. 163
### Handling Input Debouncing .................................................. 166
### Enhancing User Feedback .................................................. 167
### Integrating with a More Complex Game .................................................. 167
### Summary .................................................. 167
# Chapter 8: Creating a Multiplayer Game with Raspberry Pi .................................................. 168
## Game Design for Multiplayer Experiences .................................................. 168
### Introduction to Multiplayer Game Design .................................................. 168
### Choosing the Right Game Type .................................................. 168
### Setting Up the Game Environment .................................................. 169
### Creating the Game Window .................................................. 169
### Implementing the Game Paddles .................................................. 170

Handling Player Input ... 170
Adding the Ball ... 171
Ball Movement and Collision Detection ... 171
Drawing Game Elements ... 172
Conclusion ... 172
**Setting Up Networked Games with Python** ... 172
Understanding Networking in Games ... 173
Setting Up the Server ... 173
Setting Up the Client ... 175
Testing the Connection ... 176
Handling Multiple Clients ... 176
Building a Simple Networked Game ... 177
Conclusion ... 179
**Coding a Simple Local Multiplayer Game** ... 179
Game Overview ... 179
Setting Up the Game Window ... 179
Creating the Game Elements ... 180
Handling Player Input ... 181
Ball Movement and Collision Detection ... 181
Scoring System ... 182
Resetting the Ball ... 183
Main Game Loop ... 183
Enhancing the Game ... 184
Conclusion ... 184
**Troubleshooting Common Network Issues** ... 184
1. Connectivity Issues ... 185
2. Socket Timeout Errors ... 186
3. Data Packet Loss ... 186
4. Lag and Latency Issues ... 187
5. Debugging Network Code ... 188
Conclusion ... 189
**Troubleshooting Common Network Issues** ... 189
Network Connectivity Problems ... 190
Socket Timeout Errors ... 191
Packet Loss and Data Corruption ... 191
High Latency and Lag ... 193

- Synchronization Issues ..................................................................................... 194
- Debugging Network Issues .............................................................................. 194
- Conclusion ........................................................................................................ 195

**Chapter 9: Advanced Graphics and Game Design with PyGame** ............. 196
- Introduction to Sprite Animation ........................................................................ 196
  - Understanding Sprites and Sprite Sheets .................................................... 196
  - Loading and Animating Sprites ..................................................................... 196
  - Creating a Basic Sprite Animation Class ..................................................... 197
  - Managing Sprite States ................................................................................. 199
  - Optimizing Sprite Performance .................................................................... 200
  - Conclusion ..................................................................................................... 201
- Creating Parallax Backgrounds ......................................................................... 201
  - Understanding Parallax Scrolling ................................................................. 201
  - Setting Up Multiple Background Layers ...................................................... 202
  - Coding a Basic Parallax Background System ............................................. 203
  - Implementing Parallax Scrolling in the Game Loop ................................... 204
  - Enhancing Parallax Effects .......................................................................... 205
  - Optimizing Parallax Performance ................................................................ 205
  - Conclusion ..................................................................................................... 205
- Implementing a Scoring and High-Score System ........................................... 206
  - Understanding Scoring Mechanics .............................................................. 206
  - Implementing a Basic Score Counter .......................................................... 206
  - Displaying the Score on the Screen ............................................................ 208
  - Saving and Loading High Scores ................................................................. 208
  - Displaying the High Score ............................................................................ 209
  - Enhancing the Scoring System with Multipliers and Bonuses .................. 210
  - Optimizing the Scoring System .................................................................... 211
  - Conclusion ..................................................................................................... 211
- Optimizing Game Performance .......................................................................... 211
  - Efficient Rendering and Blitting ................................................................... 211
  - Managing Game Loop Timing ...................................................................... 212
  - Memory Management and Asset Loading .................................................. 213
  - Collision Detection Optimizations ................................................................ 214
  - Leveraging PyGame's Sprite Groups for Performance ............................. 215
  - Avoiding Common Performance Pitfalls .................................................... 216
  - Conclusion ..................................................................................................... 217

## Chapter 10: Case Study: Creating a Raspberry Pi Arcade Console .......... 218
### Designing the Console Hardware .......... 218
#### Choosing the Raspberry Pi Model .......... 218
#### Selecting a Display Screen .......... 218
#### Choosing Controls: Buttons, Joysticks, and Wiring .......... 219
#### Designing the Arcade Console Frame .......... 219
#### Assembling the Components .......... 220
#### Wiring and Testing the Setup .......... 220
#### Finalizing and Refining the Console Design .......... 220
#### Coding and Testing Your Games on the Console .......... 221
#### Final Thoughts .......... 221
### Setting Up RetroPie for Classic Games .......... 221
#### Overview of RetroPie .......... 221
#### Installing RetroPie on the Raspberry Pi .......... 222
#### Initial Configuration and Controller Setup .......... 222
#### Updating RetroPie .......... 223
#### Adding Game ROMs to RetroPie .......... 223
#### Configuring Emulators and Video Settings .......... 223
#### Customizing the RetroPie Interface .......... 224
#### Configuring Controllers and Hotkeys .......... 225
#### Testing and Troubleshooting Common Issues .......... 225
#### Final Thoughts .......... 225
### Integrating Your Custom Games into RetroPie .......... 225
#### Preparing Your Custom Game Files .......... 226
#### Setting Up Python and PyGame on RetroPie .......... 226
#### Creating a Launch Script for Your Game .......... 227
#### Placing the Game in the Appropriate RetroPie Directory .......... 227
#### Adding Your Game to the RetroPie Menu .......... 228
#### Configuring Controller Support in PyGame .......... 229
#### Setting Up Game Metadata and Artwork .......... 230
#### Configuring Performance Settings .......... 230
#### Testing and Troubleshooting Your Custom Game .......... 231
#### Conclusion .......... 231
### Final Assembly and Testing .......... 231
#### Hardware Assembly .......... 231
#### Software Setup and Configuration .......... 233

Final Testing and Quality Checks ..................................................................... 234
Adding Final Customizations .......................................................................... 235
Troubleshooting Common Issues .................................................................... 236
Final Thoughts and Reflection ......................................................................... 236

Chapter 11: Publishing Your Game: From Raspberry Pi to the World .................. 237
Packaging Your Game for Distribution ................................................................ 237
Preparing Your Game Files ............................................................................. 237
Creating a README File ................................................................................ 238
Configuration .................................................................................................... 239
Contributing ...................................................................................................... 239
Sharing Your Game on Other Platforms ........................................................ 240
Marketing and Promoting Your Game ............................................................ 240
Legal Considerations and Licensing .............................................................. 241
Conclusion ..................................................................................................... 241
Uploading to GitHub and Sharing Code ............................................................. 241
Step 1: Setting Up Git Locally ........................................................................ 241
Step 2: Initializing a Local Repository ............................................................ 242
Step 3: Adding Files to the Repository ........................................................... 242
Step 4: Committing Changes ......................................................................... 243
Step 5: Creating a GitHub Repository ............................................................ 243
Step 6: Linking the Local Repository to GitHub ............................................. 243
Step 7: Pushing the Code to GitHub .............................................................. 243
Step 8: Writing a Comprehensive README ................................................. 244
License ............................................................................................................... 245
Step 11: Managing Your Repository with Issues and Pull Requests ............. 246
Step 12: Continuous Improvement with GitHub ............................................. 246
Conclusion ..................................................................................................... 247
Marketing and Sharing Your Game Online ........................................................ 247
Building a Game Website or Landing Page ................................................... 247
Social Media Marketing Strategies ................................................................. 248
Creating Promotional Materials ...................................................................... 248
Reaching Out to Influencers and Media Outlets ............................................ 249
Engaging with Gaming Communities ............................................................. 250
Leveraging Online Platforms for Distribution and Exposure ......................... 250
Analyzing Feedback and Adapting ................................................................. 251
Conclusion ..................................................................................................... 251

**Legal Considerations and Licensing** .................................................................. 251
   Copyright Basics .................................................................................................. 251
   Choosing the Right License for Your Game .................................................. 252
   End-User License Agreement (EULA) ............................................................. 253
   Protecting Your Game with Trademarks ........................................................ 254
   Handling Player Data and Privacy .................................................................... 255
   Conclusion ............................................................................................................. 256

**Chapter 12: Conclusion and Next Steps in Game Development** ............... 257
   Reflecting on What You've Learned ................................................................. 257
      Reviewing Your Progress ............................................................................. 257
      What Each Chapter Brought to Your Skillset .......................................... 258
      Key Takeaways for Continued Learning .................................................. 258
      Example Project Ideas .................................................................................. 259
      Code Example for a Final Reflection Project .......................................... 259
      Embracing the Community and Expanding Your Network ................. 261
   Exploring Advanced Game Development Topics ......................................... 261
      Advanced Game Physics ............................................................................. 261
      Artificial Intelligence (AI) in Games ......................................................... 264
      Procedural Generation ................................................................................ 265
      Conclusion ...................................................................................................... 266
   Joining the Game Development Community ................................................. 267
      The Benefits of Community Involvement ............................................... 267
      Online Communities and Forums ............................................................. 268
      Game Jams ..................................................................................................... 268
      Contributing to Open-Source Projects .................................................... 269
      Attending Conferences and Meetups ....................................................... 269
      Sharing Your Work ....................................................................................... 270
      Conclusion ...................................................................................................... 270
   Final Thoughts and Resources for Continued Learning .............................. 270
      Embrace a Growth Mindset ....................................................................... 270
      Keep Practicing and Building Projects .................................................... 271
      Learn New Tools and Technologies .......................................................... 271
      Utilize Online Learning Platforms ............................................................ 272
      Engage in Continuous Learning ................................................................ 272
      Code Example: Expanding Your Skills .................................................... 273
      Conclusion ...................................................................................................... 274

## Chapter 13: Appendices ............................................................................................. 275
### Glossary of Terms ................................................................................................. 275
#### Algorithm ............................................................................................................ 275
#### API (Application Programming Interface) ..................................................... 275
#### Argument ............................................................................................................ 275
#### Array .................................................................................................................... 275
#### Bit ......................................................................................................................... 276
#### Boolean ................................................................................................................ 276
#### Class .................................................................................................................... 276
#### Collision Detection ............................................................................................ 277
#### CPU (Central Processing Unit) ........................................................................ 277
#### Debugging ........................................................................................................... 277
#### Dictionary ........................................................................................................... 277
#### Event Loop ......................................................................................................... 278
#### FPS (Frames Per Second) .................................................................................. 279
#### GPIO (General-Purpose Input/Output) ........................................................... 279
#### Library ................................................................................................................. 279
#### Object .................................................................................................................. 279
#### Pixel ..................................................................................................................... 279
#### Python ................................................................................................................. 280
#### Sprite ................................................................................................................... 280
#### Variable ............................................................................................................... 280
#### Vector .................................................................................................................. 281
#### IDE (Integrated Development Environment) ................................................ 281
#### Loop ..................................................................................................................... 281
#### Module ................................................................................................................ 281
### Resources for Further Learning ......................................................................... 282
#### Books ................................................................................................................... 282
#### Online Courses .................................................................................................. 283
#### YouTube Channels ............................................................................................ 283
#### Tutorials and Blogs ........................................................................................... 283
#### Libraries and Tools ........................................................................................... 284
#### Communities and Forums ............................................................................... 286
#### Conferences and Events ................................................................................... 286
#### Final Tips for Continuous Learning ............................................................... 287
### Sample Projects and Code Snippets ................................................................... 287

Project 1: Simple Snake Game ..................................................................287
Project 2: Pong Game with Multiplayer Support .......................................290
GPIO-Controlled LED Game ....................................................................293
Final Thoughts ........................................................................................294
**Reference Guide** ......................................................................................294
Python Basics ..........................................................................................295
PyGame Reference ..................................................................................296
Raspberry Pi GPIO Reference .................................................................298
Troubleshooting Tips ................................................................................299
Python Modules and Libraries ..................................................................300
Game Design Tips ...................................................................................301
Final Reference .......................................................................................301
**Frequently Asked Questions** ...................................................................301
1. How do I install PyGame on my Raspberry Pi? ...................................302
2. How can I fix the 'display Surface quit' error in PyGame? ...................302
3. My game is running too fast or too slow. How do I control the frame rate?.....303
4. How do I handle keyboard input in PyGame? .....................................303
5. How do I connect a button to my Raspberry Pi for use in a game? ..................304
6. How can I optimize my game's performance in PyGame? ...................305
7. How do I play background music in PyGame?....................................305
8. My GPIO input is inconsistent. How do I handle button debouncing? ............306
9. How do I create an executable file from my Python game? ................307
10. Can I use a joystick with PyGame?....................................................307
11. How do I update PyGame to the latest version? ...............................308
12. Why isn't my game responding to events immediately?....................308
13. How can I handle multiple button presses in PyGame? ....................308
14. How do I resize the game window in PyGame?................................309
15. What is the best way to package and share my Python game?.......309

# Preface

The world of game development has undergone significant transformation in recent years, making it accessible to everyone, from hobbyists to professionals. In this book, we explore game development with an emphasis on Python and the Raspberry Pi, an affordable yet versatile platform that offers the opportunity to build exciting projects. By combining the Python programming language with the power of Raspberry Pi, you can create both simple and complex games while learning essential programming skills and electronics concepts.

The journey starts with an introduction to game development, focusing on setting up the development environment and understanding the tools you will use throughout the book. You will learn about Python, one of the most beginner-friendly programming languages, and PyGame, a popular library for creating games.

From there, you will dive into building your first game, mastering fundamental game elements like graphics, sound, and animation. Through practical examples, you will develop a classic arcade game, Breakout, enhancing it with game physics and additional features. You will also explore the use of Raspberry Pi's GPIO (General Purpose Input/Output) pins to create custom game controllers, expanding your hardware skills alongside your software development.

Multiplayer games bring an additional layer of complexity and excitement, and you will learn to implement local multiplayer games, handling network communication with Python. Advanced topics like sprite animation, parallax backgrounds, and performance optimization are covered to ensure your games look and feel polished.

A special case study guides you through building a full-fledged Raspberry Pi arcade console, complete with hardware design and RetroPie integration, allowing you to play both your own games and classic titles. Finally, you will learn how to publish your games, share them online, and navigate the legal considerations associated with game distribution.

This book concludes with appendices that provide additional resources, code snippets, and a reference guide to help you continue your journey in game development.

Whether you are a beginner or have some programming experience, this book aims to be a comprehensive guide, offering hands-on projects and valuable insights into the world of game development with Python and Raspberry Pi. Let's get started and turn your creative ideas into interactive games!

# Chapter 1: Introduction to Game Development with Python and Raspberry Pi

## What is Game Development?

Game development is the process of creating interactive entertainment experiences using computer software. It involves designing, programming, and testing games that can be played on various platforms such as computers, consoles, mobile devices, and even embedded systems like the Raspberry Pi. Whether it's a simple puzzle game or a complex 3D adventure, game development brings together creativity and technical skills to produce engaging experiences for players.

In the past, game development was a specialized field that required significant resources and expertise. However, with the rise of open-source software and affordable hardware, it has become accessible to a much wider audience. Python, known for its simplicity and readability, has become a popular choice for beginner game developers. Its extensive libraries and active community provide robust support for game creation. Combined with the Raspberry Pi, a low-cost microcomputer, you have a powerful setup for learning and experimentation.

Game development typically involves several key components:

1. **Game Design**: This is the initial stage where the concept of the game is developed. Game designers create storylines, characters, rules, and gameplay mechanics that will define the user experience.
2. **Programming**: This is the technical aspect of game development. Programmers write code that brings the game to life, handling everything from graphics rendering to user input.
3. **Art and Animation**: Visual elements like sprites, backgrounds, and animations are crucial for making the game visually appealing and immersive.
4. **Sound Design**: Sound effects and music are integral parts of the game experience, setting the tone and enhancing the player's engagement.
5. **Testing and Debugging**: Finally, the game needs to be thoroughly tested to identify and fix any issues, ensuring it runs smoothly for players.

With Python and the PyGame library, you can manage all these components effectively. Let's take a closer look at Python and PyGame in the next section.

## Overview of Python and PyGame

Python is a versatile, high-level programming language that is ideal for both beginners and experienced developers. It has a simple syntax that emphasizes readability, making it easy to learn. Python is widely used in various fields, including web development, data analysis, artificial intelligence, and, of course, game development.

**PyGame** is a set of Python modules designed for writing video games. It provides functionality for creating 2D games by handling tasks like rendering graphics, playing sound, and detecting user input. PyGame abstracts many of the complexities of game development, allowing you to focus on building the game itself rather than dealing with low-level details.

Here's an example of a simple PyGame program:

```
import pygame

# Initialize PyGame
pygame.init()

# Set up display
screen = pygame.display.set_mode((800, 600))
pygame.display.set_caption("Hello PyGame")

# Main game loop
running = True
while running:
    for event in pygame.event.get():
        if event.type == pygame.QUIT:
            running = False

    # Fill the screen with a color
    screen.fill((0, 0, 255))

    # Update the display
    pygame.display.flip()

# Quit PyGame
pygame.quit()
```

In this example, we initialize PyGame, set up a display window, and enter a main game loop where we handle events (like closing the window) and update the screen. This is a simple foundation that you can build upon to create more complex games.

# Why Raspberry Pi for Game Development?

The Raspberry Pi is a small, affordable computer that is ideal for learning programming and electronics. It was originally developed to promote computer science education, but it has since become popular among hobbyists and makers due to its versatility and low cost. The Raspberry Pi's GPIO pins also allow you to connect external hardware components, making it perfect for building interactive projects.

**Key Benefits of Using Raspberry Pi for Game Development:**

- **Low Cost**: Raspberry Pi boards are inexpensive, making them accessible for beginners and students.
- **Versatile Platform**: You can use Raspberry Pi for a wide range of projects, from game development to robotics.
- **Community Support**: There is a large community of Raspberry Pi enthusiasts who share tutorials, projects, and resources.
- **Educational Value**: Working with Raspberry Pi helps you learn not only programming but also basic electronics and hardware interaction.

The combination of Python and Raspberry Pi allows you to explore both software and hardware aspects of game development. You can write games that use standard keyboard and mouse input or create unique controllers using buttons and sensors connected to the GPIO pins.

# Setting Up Your Development Environment

Before you start creating games, you need to set up your development environment. This includes installing Python and PyGame on your Raspberry Pi.

## Installing Python

Python comes pre-installed on most Raspberry Pi distributions (like Raspberry Pi OS), but you can check the version or update it if necessary:

```
python3 --version
```

To update Python:

```
sudo apt update
sudo apt install python3
```

## Installing PyGame

To install PyGame, use the following command:

```
pip3 install pygame
```

After the installation is complete, you can test if PyGame was installed correctly:

```
import pygame
print(pygame.ver)
```

This setup prepares you to start coding games with Python and PyGame on your Raspberry Pi.

In the next section, we will dive deeper into creating your first simple game using PyGame, understanding its framework and structure.

# Overview of Python and PyGame

Python is a versatile and widely used programming language that is well-suited for beginners and experienced developers alike. It has a simple and readable syntax, making it an ideal choice for learning programming and creating a wide variety of applications. In this section, we will explore Python's capabilities, why it is particularly effective for game development, and how the PyGame library can simplify and accelerate the process of building interactive games.

### Why Choose Python for Game Development?

Python has several features that make it an excellent language for game development:

1. **Simple and Readable Syntax**: Python's syntax is clean and easy to understand, making it a great language for beginners. You can focus on learning game development concepts without getting bogged down by complex syntax.
2. **Extensive Libraries and Modules**: Python's standard library and third-party modules provide pre-built functionality for a wide range of tasks. This includes game development, where libraries like PyGame make it easy to create 2D games.
3. **Cross-Platform Compatibility**: Python code can run on various operating systems, including Windows, macOS, and Linux. This is particularly useful when developing games for multiple platforms.
4. **Active Community Support**: Python has a large and active community that contributes to a vast collection of resources, tutorials, and forums. If you encounter any issues, you are likely to find a solution quickly online.
5. **Rapid Prototyping**: Python's interpretive nature allows for quick testing and iteration. This is crucial in game development, where testing game mechanics and making adjustments is a regular part of the process.

### Introduction to PyGame

PyGame is a Python library designed specifically for creating 2D games. It is built on top of the SDL (Simple DirectMedia Layer) library, which provides low-level access to audio, keyboard, mouse, and graphics hardware. PyGame simplifies many aspects of game development, allowing you to focus on the gameplay rather than the underlying complexities of rendering graphics and handling input.

**Key Features of PyGame:**

- **Simple API**: PyGame provides a straightforward API for handling graphics, sound, and input, making it accessible for beginners.
- **Hardware Acceleration**: PyGame can utilize hardware acceleration to render graphics efficiently, providing smooth gameplay even for complex scenes.
- **Cross-Platform**: Like Python, PyGame is cross-platform, allowing you to develop games that run on multiple operating systems without modification.
- **Rich Multimedia Capabilities**: PyGame supports a wide range of multimedia elements, including images, sounds, and music, enabling you to create immersive experiences.

## Setting Up PyGame

Before you can start using PyGame, you need to install it. On most systems, this can be done using the Python package manager, `pip`. Here's the command to install PyGame:

```
pip3 install pygame
```

Once the installation is complete, you can verify it by importing the PyGame module in a Python script:

```
import pygame

print("PyGame version:", pygame.ver)
```

If the version number is displayed without errors, PyGame has been successfully installed, and you are ready to start building games.

## PyGame Architecture

To understand how to build a game using PyGame, it's important to grasp its basic architecture. At the core of every PyGame program is the **game loop**, which runs continuously while the game is active. The game loop handles the following main tasks:

1. **Event Handling**: Capturing user input (keyboard, mouse, etc.).
2. **Game Logic**: Updating the game state based on user input or time-based changes.
3. **Rendering**: Drawing graphics to the screen based on the updated game state.

Here's a basic template for a PyGame program that demonstrates the structure of the game loop:

```python
import pygame

# Initialize PyGame
pygame.init()

# Set up the display
screen = pygame.display.set_mode((800, 600))
pygame.display.set_caption("Basic PyGame Structure")

# Define game variables
running = True
background_color = (0, 0, 0)   # Black

# Main game loop
while running:
    # Event handling
    for event in pygame.event.get():
        if event.type == pygame.QUIT:
            running = False

    # Game logic (if any)

    # Rendering
    screen.fill(background_color)
    pygame.display.flip()

# Quit PyGame
pygame.quit()
```

In this example:

- We initialize PyGame and set up a display window with dimensions 800x600 pixels.
- The main game loop starts and continues running until the user closes the window.
- In the loop, we handle the "QUIT" event (when the window is closed) and update the display by filling it with a background color.

This template forms the basis of all PyGame programs, and you can build upon it by adding game elements like graphics, sounds, and animations.

## Drawing Graphics with PyGame

One of the first things you'll want to do when creating a game is to draw shapes and images on the screen. PyGame provides several functions for rendering basic shapes like rectangles, circles, and lines. Here's an example of how to draw some simple shapes:

```
import pygame

pygame.init()
screen = pygame.display.set_mode((800, 600))
pygame.display.set_caption("Drawing Shapes in PyGame")

running = True
while running:
    for event in pygame.event.get():
        if event.type == pygame.QUIT:
            running = False

    # Fill the screen with a white background
    screen.fill((255, 255, 255))

    # Draw a red rectangle
    pygame.draw.rect(screen, (255, 0, 0), (150, 150, 200, 100))

    # Draw a blue circle
    pygame.draw.circle(screen, (0, 0, 255), (400, 300), 50)

    # Draw a green line
    pygame.draw.line(screen, (0, 255, 0), (100, 100), (700, 500), 5)

    pygame.display.flip()

pygame.quit()
```

In this code:

- We draw a red rectangle, a blue circle, and a green line.
- The `pygame.draw.rect()`, `pygame.draw.circle()`, and `pygame.draw.line()` functions are used to draw these shapes.

This is just a glimpse of what you can do with PyGame. By combining these basic drawing functions, you can create more complex graphics and game elements.

## Adding Images and Sprites

In most games, you will want to use custom images instead of basic shapes. PyGame allows you to load images and display them on the screen easily. Here's an example of how to load and display an image:

```python
import pygame

pygame.init()
screen = pygame.display.set_mode((800, 600))
pygame.display.set_caption("Displaying an Image")

# Load an image
player_image = pygame.image.load("player.png")

running = True
while running:
    for event in pygame.event.get():
        if event.type == pygame.QUIT:
            running = False

    # Fill the screen with a color
    screen.fill((0, 0, 0))

    # Display the image at coordinates (100, 100)
    screen.blit(player_image, (100, 100))

    pygame.display.flip()

pygame.quit()
```

In this example:

- We use `pygame.image.load()` to load an image file named "player.png".
- The `blit()` function is used to draw the image onto the screen at the specified coordinates.

Using images and sprites will help you create visually appealing games. As you progress, you can use sprite animation techniques to bring your characters to life.

## Conclusion

In this section, you learned about the basics of Python and why it is an excellent choice for game development. We also introduced PyGame, a powerful library that makes it easy to create 2D games. You explored the basic structure of a PyGame program, learned how to draw graphics, and saw how to display images on the screen.

In the next section, we will dive into creating your first complete game using PyGame, where you will apply these concepts to build a simple "Hello World" game. This will set the stage for more advanced projects as we move forward.

# Why Raspberry Pi for Game Development?

The Raspberry Pi is a unique and versatile platform that combines low cost, flexibility, and a powerful suite of features, making it an ideal choice for learning game development. It was originally designed to teach basic computer science, but its capabilities have expanded far beyond educational use. In this section, we will explore the reasons why Raspberry Pi is an excellent platform for game development, its hardware features, and how you can leverage its capabilities to build interactive and engaging games.

### 1. Affordable and Accessible

One of the most compelling reasons to use Raspberry Pi for game development is its affordability. The various models of Raspberry Pi, from the basic Raspberry Pi Zero to the more powerful Raspberry Pi 4, offer a range of performance levels at very accessible prices. This makes it possible for anyone, from students to hobbyists, to get started with game development without a significant investment.

**Key Benefits of Raspberry Pi's Affordability:**

- **Low Cost of Entry**: For less than the price of a typical video game, you can own a fully functional computer capable of creating and running your own games.
- **Educational Value**: Schools and educational institutions often use Raspberry Pi because it provides an inexpensive way for students to learn programming, electronics, and computer science concepts.
- **Experimentation Without Risk**: The low cost makes it less risky to experiment, modify hardware, and even damage components during prototyping and learning.

### 2. Compact and Portable

The compact size of the Raspberry Pi makes it perfect for portable game projects. Measuring just a few inches across, it can easily fit into handheld devices, custom game consoles, or wearable tech projects. This opens up a world of possibilities for creating unique gaming experiences that aren't tied to a desktop or laptop.

**Use Cases for Portability:**

- **Portable Game Consoles**: With a small screen and battery, you can create a custom handheld gaming device using a Raspberry Pi.

- **Embedded Game Projects**: The small size allows you to embed the Raspberry Pi in toys, arcade machines, or even retro gaming cabinets.
- **Game Demos on the Go**: Developers can easily carry a Raspberry Pi to showcase their games or prototypes at events and meetups.

## 3. Extensive GPIO Capabilities

One of the standout features of the Raspberry Pi is its GPIO (General Purpose Input/Output) pins. These pins allow the Raspberry Pi to interface with external hardware components like buttons, sensors, LEDs, and more. This capability is particularly useful for game development, where custom controllers and interactive elements can be added to enhance gameplay.

### Example: Connecting a Button for Game Input

With a simple push-button, you can create an additional input for your game. Here's how you might connect and use a button with Python:

1. **Wiring the Button**: Connect one side of the button to a GPIO pin (e.g., GPIO 17) and the other side to a ground pin (GND).
2. **Python Code**: Use the `RPi.GPIO` library to read the button input.

```python
import RPi.GPIO as GPIO
import time

# Set up GPIO
GPIO.setmode(GPIO.BCM)
button_pin = 17
GPIO.setup(button_pin, GPIO.IN, pull_up_down=GPIO.PUD_UP)

print("Press the button to see the action!")

try:
    while True:
        if GPIO.input(button_pin) == GPIO.LOW:
            print("Button pressed!")
            time.sleep(0.2)  # Debounce delay
except KeyboardInterrupt:
    pass
finally:
    GPIO.cleanup()
```

In this script:

- We set up the GPIO pin as an input and use a pull-up resistor configuration.
- The script continuously checks if the button is pressed and prints a message when it is detected.

This simple example demonstrates how you can use the GPIO pins to add custom hardware inputs to your games, making the Raspberry Pi a powerful platform for interactive projects.

## 4. Versatile Software Environment

The Raspberry Pi typically runs on Raspberry Pi OS, a Debian-based Linux distribution. This operating system provides a versatile environment that supports a wide range of programming languages and tools. Python, C++, JavaScript, and Scratch are just a few of the languages available, making it easy to find a development setup that suits your skill level and project requirements.

### Python as the Primary Language for Game Development:

Python is the preferred language for many Raspberry Pi projects due to its simplicity and readability. Combined with the PyGame library, it provides everything you need to start creating games quickly. The availability of extensive libraries and pre-built modules simplifies many tasks, allowing you to focus on game design and mechanics.

### Using Other Tools and Frameworks:

- **RetroPie**: This is a software package that turns your Raspberry Pi into a retro gaming console. It supports a wide range of classic gaming emulators and allows you to integrate your custom games seamlessly.
- **Godot Engine**: A powerful open-source game engine that runs well on the Raspberry Pi. It provides a visual editor and scripting language (GDScript) similar to Python, making it a great choice for more advanced game projects.
- **Scratch**: A visual programming language designed for beginners. It is a great tool for teaching younger audiences the basics of programming and game development.

## 5. Active Community and Abundant Resources

The Raspberry Pi has one of the most active and enthusiastic communities in the tech world. This community-driven support means that you can find countless tutorials, forums, and projects to help you get started and overcome challenges. Whether you need help with setting up your Raspberry Pi, troubleshooting code, or designing a custom controller, there are numerous resources available.

### Popular Community Resources:

- **Raspberry Pi Foundation Website**: Offers official documentation, tutorials, and project ideas.
- **Forums and Reddit**: Places like the Raspberry Pi subreddit and official forums are great for asking questions and getting advice from experienced users.

- **Online Courses and Books**: There are many free and paid courses that teach Raspberry Pi programming, electronics, and game development, often using Python and PyGame.

## 6. Unique Project Opportunities

The combination of software flexibility and hardware capability allows for unique and innovative projects that go beyond traditional game development. By integrating sensors, cameras, and other peripherals, you can create projects that offer unique gaming experiences.

**Examples of Unique Game Projects:**

- **Motion-Controlled Games**: Using an accelerometer or gyroscope connected to the GPIO pins, you can create motion-controlled games that respond to the player's physical movements.
- **Augmented Reality (AR) Games**: By connecting a camera module, you can create AR games that overlay graphics onto the real world using computer vision libraries like OpenCV.
- **Voice-Controlled Games**: Integrate a microphone and use Python's speech recognition libraries to create games controlled by voice commands.

## Conclusion

The Raspberry Pi is an exceptional platform for game development due to its affordability, portability, extensive GPIO capabilities, versatile software environment, and strong community support. It provides a unique opportunity to explore both software and hardware aspects of game creation, offering a hands-on learning experience that goes beyond coding alone.

Whether you are interested in building simple 2D games, creating custom game controllers, or designing complex interactive projects, the Raspberry Pi has the tools and resources to help you succeed. In the next section, we will guide you through setting up your development environment and begin creating your first game using Python and PyGame.

# Setting Up Your Development Environment

Before diving into game development with Python and Raspberry Pi, it's essential to set up a proper development environment. This will allow you to write, test, and debug your code efficiently. In this section, we will guide you through setting up Python, installing essential libraries like PyGame, configuring your Raspberry Pi, and using development tools that streamline the coding process.

## 1. Preparing Your Raspberry Pi

First, ensure you have the necessary hardware to get started. You will need:

- A Raspberry Pi (any model, but a Raspberry Pi 4 or newer is recommended for better performance).
- A microSD card (16GB or larger) with Raspberry Pi OS installed.
- A monitor, keyboard, and mouse for setup.
- An internet connection (via Ethernet or Wi-Fi).

If you haven't already installed Raspberry Pi OS, follow these steps:

1. **Download Raspberry Pi Imager**: Go to the official Raspberry Pi website and download the Raspberry Pi Imager tool.
2. **Install Raspberry Pi OS**: Use the Raspberry Pi Imager to flash the Raspberry Pi OS (64-bit) onto your microSD card. Select the "Raspberry Pi OS with Desktop" version for a full desktop experience.
3. **First Boot**: Insert the microSD card into your Raspberry Pi, connect it to your monitor, keyboard, and mouse, then power it on. Follow the on-screen instructions to complete the initial setup, including setting up Wi-Fi and creating a user account.

## 2. Installing Python

Python is usually pre-installed on Raspberry Pi OS, but it's a good idea to verify the installation and update it if necessary. Open a terminal and check the Python version:

```
python3 --version
```

```
Python 3.11.5
```

If Python is not installed or you want to update it, run the following commands:

```
sudo apt update
sudo apt install python3
```

Next, install `pip`, the Python package manager, which will help you install additional libraries:

```
sudo apt install python3-pip
```

Verify the installation of `pip`:

```
pip3 --version
```

## 3. Setting Up PyGame

PyGame is a critical library for 2D game development in Python. It provides modules for handling graphics, sound, and input, simplifying the process of building interactive games.

To install PyGame, use `pip`:

```
pip3 install pygame
```

Test the installation by running the following script:

```
import pygame

pygame.init()
print("PyGame version:", pygame.ver)
pygame.quit()
```

If no errors appear and the version is printed, PyGame has been installed successfully.

## 4. Choosing an Integrated Development Environment (IDE)

An Integrated Development Environment (IDE) is a software application that provides comprehensive tools for coding, including a text editor, debugger, and code suggestions. Here are some popular IDEs and text editors for Python development on Raspberry Pi:

- **Thonny**: A lightweight and beginner-friendly Python IDE pre-installed on Raspberry Pi OS. It features a simple interface and built-in debugging tools.
- **VS Code**: A more powerful IDE with extensive features for coding, debugging, and version control. You can install it on Raspberry Pi with the following command:

```
sudo apt install code
```

- **Geany**: A fast and lightweight text editor with IDE-like features. It's a good choice if you prefer a simpler interface.

For this book, we recommend starting with Thonny if you are a beginner. As you gain experience, you can switch to VS Code for more advanced features.

## 5. Configuring Your Raspberry Pi for Development

For an optimal development experience, it's helpful to configure your Raspberry Pi settings. Here are some recommended configurations:

1. **Enable SSH**: If you want to access your Raspberry Pi remotely, enable SSH. Go to the terminal and run:

```
sudo raspi-config
```

Navigate to `Interfacing Options` > `SSH` and enable it.

2. **Increase GPU Memory**: If you plan to create graphics-intensive games, increase the GPU memory allocation. In `raspi-config`, go to `Performance Options` > `GPU Memory` and set it to 128MB or higher.
3. **Enable VNC**: For remote desktop access, enable VNC in the `raspi-config` menu. This allows you to control your Raspberry Pi from another computer with a graphical interface.
4. **Update Your System**: Keep your system up to date to avoid compatibility issues:

```
sudo apt update
sudo apt full-upgrade
```

## 6. Creating a Virtual Environment

A virtual environment is an isolated Python environment that helps you manage dependencies for your projects without affecting the system-wide Python installation. It's a good practice to use virtual environments for game development projects.

To create a virtual environment, use the following commands:

```
sudo apt install python3-venv
python3 -m venv game-env
```

Activate the virtual environment:

```
source game-env/bin/activate
```

You will see the environment name in your terminal prompt. To deactivate it, simply run:

```
deactivate
```

## 7. Setting Up Version Control with Git

Version control is essential for tracking changes in your code and collaborating with others. Git is the most popular version control system, and it's easy to set up on Raspberry Pi.

Install Git:

```
sudo apt install git
```

Configure Git with your name and email:

```
git config --global user.name "Your Name"
git config --global user.email "your.email@example.com"
```

To create a new repository for your project, navigate to your project folder and initialize Git:

```
git init
```

You can now start tracking your files with Git, making commits as you progress in your game development journey.

## 8. Setting Up Game Project Structure

A well-organized project structure makes it easier to manage your game's assets, code, and resources. Here's a recommended folder layout for your game project:

```
my_game/
├── assets/
│   ├── images/
│   └── sounds/
├── src/
│   ├── main.py
│   └── game.py
├── README.md
└── requirements.txt
```

- `assets/` contains all your game assets like images and sounds.
- `src/` holds your Python source code files.

- `README.md` provides an overview of your project.
- `requirements.txt` lists the Python libraries your project depends on.

## 9. Creating a Basic Game Template

Now that your environment is set up, let's create a basic game template using PyGame. This will serve as a starting point for all your projects.

```
import pygame
import sys

# Initialize PyGame
pygame.init()

# Set up display
WIDTH, HEIGHT = 800, 600
screen = pygame.display.set_mode((WIDTH, HEIGHT))
pygame.display.set_caption("Basic Game Template")

# Define colors
WHITE = (255, 255, 255)
BLACK = (0, 0, 0)

# Game loop
while True:
    for event in pygame.event.get():
        if event.type == pygame.QUIT:
            pygame.quit()
            sys.exit()

    # Fill the screen
    screen.fill(WHITE)

    # Update the display
    pygame.display.flip()
```

This template includes:

- Initialization of PyGame.
- A display window of 800x600 pixels.
- An infinite game loop that checks for the quit event and updates the display.

You can expand this template by adding game elements, graphics, and logic as you develop your projects.

## Conclusion

Setting up a development environment on your Raspberry Pi is the first step toward building your own games. By installing Python, PyGame, and an IDE, configuring your system, and organizing your project structure, you have laid a solid foundation for game development. In the following chapters, we will build on this setup and guide you through creating your first game using Python and PyGame. Get ready to turn your ideas into interactive experiences!

# Chapter 2: Getting Started with Raspberry Pi and Python

## Introduction to Raspberry Pi

The Raspberry Pi is a versatile and affordable single-board computer that has become popular for a wide range of projects, including game development. In this section, we will dive into what makes the Raspberry Pi a fantastic platform for both beginner and advanced developers alike. We will explore its history, capabilities, and why it is a great choice for game development, especially when paired with Python.

### What is the Raspberry Pi?

The Raspberry Pi was created by the Raspberry Pi Foundation in 2012 with the goal of promoting computer science education. It is a credit-card-sized computer that provides the core components needed to run a full operating system, connect peripherals, and interact with the physical world through GPIO (General-Purpose Input/Output) pins. The low cost and flexibility of the Raspberry Pi make it ideal for DIY projects, hobbyist development, and educational purposes.

### Key Features of Raspberry Pi

The Raspberry Pi series has several models, each with unique specifications tailored to different needs. Here are some of the key features common to most Raspberry Pi models:

- **CPU and GPU**: The Raspberry Pi uses an ARM-based CPU and comes with a GPU (Graphics Processing Unit) capable of handling basic graphical tasks, making it suitable for game development.
- **Memory (RAM)**: Depending on the model, the Raspberry Pi can have different amounts of RAM, typically ranging from 1GB to 8GB.
- **Connectivity**: Most models include Wi-Fi, Bluetooth, USB ports, and Ethernet, providing ample options for networking and connecting peripherals.
- **Storage**: The Raspberry Pi uses a microSD card for storage, which acts as its main drive. The operating system and all your files are stored on this card.
- **GPIO Pins**: One of the standout features of the Raspberry Pi is its GPIO pins, which allow you to connect various sensors, buttons, and other hardware components.

### Different Models of Raspberry Pi

There are several versions of the Raspberry Pi available, each with different features. The most common models are:

- **Raspberry Pi 3 Model B**: One of the most popular models, known for its balance between price and performance. It includes Wi-Fi, Bluetooth, and a quad-core CPU.

- **Raspberry Pi 4 Model B**: The latest and most powerful version, featuring up to 8GB of RAM, dual HDMI ports, and USB 3.0 support.
- **Raspberry Pi Zero**: A smaller and cheaper version of the Raspberry Pi, suitable for projects with space constraints or low processing needs.

The choice of model depends on your project requirements, but for game development, the Raspberry Pi 3 or 4 models are recommended due to their better performance and graphics capabilities.

## Setting Up Your Raspberry Pi

Before you can start using your Raspberry Pi for game development, you need to set it up. Follow these steps to get started:

1. **Gather the Required Components**:
    - Raspberry Pi board (Model 3, 4, or Zero)
    - MicroSD card (16GB or larger, Class 10 recommended)
    - MicroSD card reader
    - Power supply (5V, 2.5A or higher)
    - HDMI cable and a display (monitor or TV)
    - USB keyboard and mouse
    - Optional: Ethernet cable or Wi-Fi access
2. **Install the Operating System**: The Raspberry Pi runs on an OS called **Raspberry Pi OS** (formerly known as Raspbian). To install it:
    - Download the **Raspberry Pi Imager** from the official Raspberry Pi website.
    - Insert your microSD card into the card reader and connect it to your computer.
    - Launch the Raspberry Pi Imager, select "Raspberry Pi OS," and choose the microSD card.
    - Click "Write" to install the OS onto the microSD card.
3. **Boot Up the Raspberry Pi**:
    - Insert the microSD card into the Raspberry Pi.
    - Connect the keyboard, mouse, and monitor.
    - Plug in the power supply. The Raspberry Pi will automatically boot up and display the setup screen.
4. **Configure Initial Settings**:
    - Follow the on-screen instructions to set up your language, timezone, and Wi-Fi connection.
    - Update the system by opening a terminal and running the following commands:

bash

```
sudo apt update
sudo apt upgrade -y
```

5.

## Exploring the Raspberry Pi Desktop

Once your Raspberry Pi has booted up and is configured, you will see the **Raspberry Pi Desktop**, which is similar to a standard Linux desktop environment. You can interact with it using the mouse and keyboard, launch applications, and access the terminal for command-line tasks.

Key applications include:

- **Terminal**: For running commands and scripts.
- **File Manager**: For browsing files and directories.
- **Python IDE (Thonny)**: A beginner-friendly Python development environment.
- **Web Browser**: For browsing the internet.

## Basic Linux Commands for Raspberry Pi

The Raspberry Pi OS is based on Debian Linux, so familiarity with basic Linux commands will help you navigate the system. Here are some essential commands to get you started:

**List files in a directory**:
bash

```
ls
```

-

**Change directory**:
bash

```
cd /path/to/directory
```

-

**Create a new directory**:
bash

```
mkdir my_project
```

-

**Edit a file using Nano text editor**:
bash

```
nano myfile.py
```

-

**Check the system's IP address**:
bash

```
hostname -I
```

- 

## Installing Python on Raspberry Pi

Python comes pre-installed on Raspberry Pi OS, but you may want to ensure you have the latest version. To check your Python version, open the terminal and type:

```
python3 --version
```

If you need to install or update Python, you can use the following command:

```
sudo apt install python3
```

To make Python development easier, you can install **pip**, the Python package installer, with:

```
sudo apt install python3-pip
```

## Using Python on the Raspberry Pi

The Raspberry Pi is an excellent platform for Python development. You can write Python code directly in the terminal or use the Thonny IDE for a graphical experience.

To start the Python interactive shell, type:

```
python3
```

You will see the Python prompt (`>>>`), where you can enter Python commands. For example:

```
print("Hello, Raspberry Pi!")
```

## Summary

The Raspberry Pi offers a powerful and flexible environment for game development. By setting up the hardware and software correctly, you have a platform ready to start building

Python-based games. With its GPIO pins, you can even extend your games to include custom controllers and external inputs. In the next sections, we will dive deeper into Python programming on the Raspberry Pi and explore how to use PyGame for creating interactive games.

# Installing Python on Raspberry Pi

Python is one of the most versatile and widely used programming languages, making it an excellent choice for Raspberry Pi projects, especially in game development. The Raspberry Pi OS comes pre-installed with Python, but ensuring you have the latest version and the right setup is crucial for smooth development. In this section, we will go through the process of installing, updating, and configuring Python on your Raspberry Pi, as well as setting up a virtual environment for your projects.

### Checking the Current Python Installation

To begin, let's verify whether Python is already installed on your Raspberry Pi and check its version. Open the terminal on your Raspberry Pi and type:

```
python3 --version
```

```
Python 3.11.4
```

If you see an output like the one above, Python is already installed. However, if you receive an error message or need a different version of Python, you may want to install or update it.

### Updating the System

Before installing or updating Python, it is good practice to update your system's package list to ensure you get the latest versions available. Run the following commands:

```
sudo apt update
sudo apt upgrade -y
```

The `update` command refreshes the list of available packages, while the `upgrade` command installs the latest versions of installed packages. The `-y` flag automatically confirms the installation of updates.

### Installing Python

If Python 3 is not installed or you want to install a specific version, you can do so using the `apt` package manager. For example, to install Python 3.11, use:

```
sudo apt install python3.11
```

This command installs Python 3.11 and any necessary dependencies. To verify the installation, check the version again:

```
python3.11 --version
```

```
Python 3.11.4
```

If you need to use this version as the default `python3` interpreter, update the alternatives:

```
sudo update-alternatives --install /usr/bin/python3 python3 /usr/bin/python3.11 1
```

## Installing pip: The Python Package Manager

`pip` is the package manager for Python, allowing you to easily install and manage additional Python packages. To install `pip`, use the following command:

```
sudo apt install python3-pip
```

Verify the installation by checking the version:

```
pip3 --version
```

The output should look like:

```
pip 23.2.1 from /usr/lib/python3/dist-packages/pip (python 3.11)
```

## Using pip to Install Python Packages

With `pip` installed, you can easily add Python packages required for your projects. For instance, to install `numpy`, a popular numerical computation library, use:

```
pip3 install numpy
```

You can also upgrade `pip` itself to the latest version:

```
pip3 install --upgrade pip
```

## Setting Up a Python Virtual Environment

Using a virtual environment is a best practice when working on Python projects, as it allows you to create an isolated environment for each project with its own dependencies. To create a virtual environment, first install the `venv` module if it is not already installed:

```
sudo apt install python3-venv
```

Navigate to your project directory and create a virtual environment:

```
mkdir my_game_project
cd my_game_project
python3 -m venv venv
```

This creates a virtual environment named `venv` inside your project directory. To activate it, use:

```
source venv/bin/activate
```

You should now see the prompt change, indicating that the virtual environment is active:

```
(venv) pi@raspberrypi:~/my_game_project $
```

When the virtual environment is active, any Python packages you install will only be available within this environment, preventing conflicts with system-wide packages.

To deactivate the virtual environment, simply run:

```
deactivate
```

## Installing Development Tools

For game development, you will often need additional tools and libraries. A common package that is useful is `build-essential`, which includes compilers and other essential tools for building software:

```
sudo apt install build-essential
```

You may also want to install `git` for version control:

```
sudo apt install git
```

## Installing PyGame

PyGame is a library for creating games in Python. It simplifies game development by providing modules for handling graphics, sound, and user input. To install PyGame, use:

```
pip3 install pygame
```

Verify the installation by checking the version:

```
python3 -m pygame --version
```

```
2.4.0
```

## Testing Your Python and PyGame Installation

Let's create a simple test script to ensure Python and PyGame are correctly installed. Create a new Python file named `test_pygame.py`:

```
nano test_pygame.py
```

Enter the following code:

```python
import pygame
import sys

pygame.init()

# Set up the display
screen = pygame.display.set_mode((640, 480))
pygame.display.set_caption("PyGame Test")

# Main loop
while True:
    for event in pygame.event.get():
        if event.type == pygame.QUIT:
            pygame.quit()
            sys.exit()

    screen.fill((0, 0, 255))
    pygame.display.flip()
```

Save the file and exit Nano by pressing CTRL + O, ENTER, and CTRL + X.

Run the script:

```
python3 test_pygame.py
```

A new window should open with a blue background. You can close the window by clicking the "X" button or pressing CTRL + C in the terminal.

## Setting Python 3 as the Default Python

To make Python 3 the default when you type `python` in the terminal, update the system's alternatives:

```
sudo update-alternatives --install /usr/bin/python python /usr/bin/python3 1
```

Check that the default is now Python 3:

```
python --version
```

Python 3.11.4

## Troubleshooting Common Issues

**Missing Dependencies**: If you encounter errors while installing packages, ensure you have the required dependencies. For example, you might need `libffi-dev` or `libssl-dev` for some packages:
bash

```
sudo apt install libffi-dev libssl-dev
```

1.
2. **Permission Issues**: If you receive a "Permission Denied" error while installing packages, try using `sudo` or ensure you are inside a virtual environment.

**PyGame Not Working**: If the PyGame window doesn't appear, ensure your Raspberry Pi has the necessary graphics drivers. Update your system and try installing PyGame again.
bash

```
sudo apt install libsdl2-dev
```

3.

## Summary

Installing and configuring Python on your Raspberry Pi is a critical step for game development. With the latest version of Python, `pip` for package management, and a virtual environment set up, you are ready to dive into building games. In the next section, we will explore the basics of Python programming to refresh your skills before moving on to more advanced topics in game development.

# Basic Python Programming Refresher

Python is known for its simplicity and readability, making it a popular choice for both beginners and experienced developers. In this section, we will cover the core concepts of Python programming, providing a solid foundation before we dive into more complex game development topics. Whether you are new to Python or need a refresher, this section will help you get comfortable with the essentials.

## Getting Started with Python

Python scripts typically use the `.py` extension and can be run directly from the terminal. To start a Python script, open the terminal and use:

```
python3 my_script.py
```

You can also open the interactive Python shell by simply typing:

```
python3
```

In the Python shell, you can enter commands line by line and see the output immediately.

## Variables and Data Types

Variables in Python are used to store data, and Python handles different data types automatically. Here are some common data types:

- **Integer (`int`)**: Whole numbers (e.g., `42`)
- **Float (`float`)**: Numbers with decimals (e.g., `3.14`)
- **String (`str`)**: Text (e.g., `"Hello, World!"`)
- **Boolean (`bool`)**: True or False values (e.g., `True`)

Example:

```
# Variables and data types
name = "Raspberry Pi"
version = 3.11
is_active = True

print(name, version, is_active)
```

Output:

```
Raspberry Pi 3.11 True
```

## Basic Arithmetic and Operators

Python supports basic arithmetic operations such as addition, subtraction, multiplication, and division:

```
a = 10
b = 3
```

```python
# Arithmetic operations
print("Addition:", a + b)
print("Subtraction:", a - b)
print("Multiplication:", a * b)
print("Division:", a / b)
print("Modulus:", a % b)
print("Exponent:", a ** b)
```

Output:

```
Addition: 13
Subtraction: 7
Multiplication: 30
Division: 3.3333333333333335
Modulus: 1
Exponent: 1000
```

## Strings and String Manipulation

Strings are sequences of characters enclosed in quotes. Python provides many ways to manipulate and format strings:

```python
greeting = "Hello, Raspberry Pi!"
print(greeting)

# String concatenation
name = "Python"
print(greeting + " Welcome to " + name + " programming.")

# String formatting
version = 3.11
print(f"Currently using Python version {version}")

# Slicing strings
print(greeting[0:5])   # Output: Hello
print(greeting[-3:])   # Output: Pi!
```

## Lists and Tuples

Lists and tuples are used to store collections of items. Lists are mutable (can be changed), while tuples are immutable (cannot be changed):

```python
# List
games = ["Tetris", "Pac-Man", "Space Invaders"]
print(games)
games.append("Donkey Kong")
print(games)

# Tuple
dimensions = (640, 480)
print(f"Width: {dimensions[0]}, Height: {dimensions[1]}")
```

Output:

```
['Tetris', 'Pac-Man', 'Space Invaders']
['Tetris', 'Pac-Man', 'Space Invaders', 'Donkey Kong']
Width: 640, Height: 480
```

## Dictionaries

Dictionaries are used to store data in key-value pairs:

```python
# Dictionary
game_data = {
    "title": "Breakout",
    "score": 0,
    "lives": 3
}

print(game_data)
print("Title:", game_data["title"])
game_data["score"] = 100
print("Updated Score:", game_data["score"])
```

Output:

```
{'title': 'Breakout', 'score': 0, 'lives': 3}
```

```
Title: Breakout
Updated Score: 100
```

## Conditional Statements

Python uses `if`, `elif`, and `else` to make decisions based on conditions:

```
score = 75

if score >= 90:
    print("Grade: A")
elif score >= 80:
    print("Grade: B")
elif score >= 70:
    print("Grade: C")
else:
    print("Grade: F")
```

Output:

```
Grade: C
```

## Loops

Python provides `for` and `while` loops for iteration:

```
# For loop
for i in range(5):
    print(f"Loop iteration: {i}")

# While loop
count = 0
while count < 3:
    print(f"Count is {count}")
    count += 1
```

Output:

```
Loop iteration: 0
Loop iteration: 1
Loop iteration: 2
Loop iteration: 3
Loop iteration: 4
Count is 0
Count is 1
Count is 2
```

## Functions

Functions are reusable blocks of code that perform a specific task:

```
def greet(name):
    return f"Hello, {name}!"

print(greet("Raspberry Pi"))
```

Output:

```
Hello, Raspberry Pi!
```

## Exception Handling

Python uses `try`, `except`, and `finally` for error handling:

```
try:
    result = 10 / 0
except ZeroDivisionError:
    print("Error: Division by zero is not allowed.")
finally:
    print("This code runs no matter what.")
```

Output:

```
Error: Division by zero is not allowed.
```

This code runs no matter what.

## File Handling

Python allows you to read from and write to files easily:

```python
# Writing to a file
with open("game_data.txt", "w") as file:
    file.write("Score: 100\nLives: 3")

# Reading from a file
with open("game_data.txt", "r") as file:
    content = file.read()
    print(content)
```

Output:

```
Score: 100
Lives: 3
```

## Importing Modules

Python's standard library includes many useful modules. You can also install third-party modules using `pip`:

```python
import math

radius = 5
area = math.pi * (radius ** 2)
print(f"Area of the circle: {area:.2f}")
```

Output:

```
Area of the circle: 78.54
```

## Using Command-Line Arguments

Python scripts can accept command-line arguments using the `sys` module:

```python
import sys

if len(sys.argv) > 1:
    print(f"Argument received: {sys.argv[1]}")
else:
    print("No arguments provided.")
```

Run this script with an argument:

```
python3 my_script.py Hello
```

Output:

```
Argument received: Hello
```

## Summary

In this section, we covered the basic concepts of Python programming, including variables, data types, control flow, functions, and file handling. These fundamentals will serve as the building blocks for creating more complex and interactive games on the Raspberry Pi. In the next section, we will explore how to leverage the GPIO pins of the Raspberry Pi for game controls, adding a physical dimension to your Python projects.

# Exploring GPIO Pins for Game Controls

The Raspberry Pi's GPIO (General-Purpose Input/Output) pins are one of its most exciting features, allowing you to interact with the physical world by connecting external components like buttons, LEDs, and sensors. In this section, we will explore the basics of GPIO, how to set up your Raspberry Pi for GPIO programming, and how to use these pins for game controls. We will also cover the Python `RPi.GPIO` library, which provides an interface to control the GPIO pins directly from Python scripts.

### What Are GPIO Pins?

The GPIO pins on the Raspberry Pi are a set of physical pins that allow the Raspberry Pi to interface with external hardware. They can be configured as input or output pins:

- **Input pins**: Used to read signals from external components like buttons and sensors.
- **Output pins**: Used to control components like LEDs, motors, and relays.

The Raspberry Pi typically has 40 GPIO pins, arranged in a specific layout:

- **Power pins**: Provide 3.3V or 5V power.
- **Ground (GND) pins**: Connect the circuit ground.
- **GPIO pins**: Configurable as input or output.

## Setting Up GPIO on Raspberry Pi

Before you can start using the GPIO pins, you need to configure your Raspberry Pi. Ensure you have the `RPi.GPIO` library installed, which is included by default in Raspberry Pi OS. You can verify or install it using:

```
sudo apt update
sudo apt install python3-rpi.gpio
```

You may also need to enable GPIO access in the Raspberry Pi configuration tool:

```
sudo raspi-config
```

Navigate to **Interface Options** and enable **GPIO**.

## Understanding the GPIO Pin Layout

The GPIO pins are numbered in two different ways:

1. **BCM (Broadcom) numbering**: Refers to the GPIO pin numbers as defined by the Broadcom chip.
2. **BOARD numbering**: Refers to the physical pin numbers on the Raspberry Pi board.

For example, physical pin 7 corresponds to GPIO 4 in BCM numbering. It is important to be consistent with the numbering scheme you choose.

## Basic GPIO Setup with Python

Let's create a simple Python script that configures a GPIO pin as output and turns it on and off. This example uses BCM numbering:

```
import RPi.GPIO as GPIO
import time

# Set the GPIO mode
GPIO.setmode(GPIO.BCM)
```

```python
# Set up the pin
LED_PIN = 17
GPIO.setup(LED_PIN, GPIO.OUT)

# Blink the LED
try:
    while True:
        GPIO.output(LED_PIN, GPIO.HIGH)
        print("LED ON")
        time.sleep(1)
        GPIO.output(LED_PIN, GPIO.LOW)
        print("LED OFF")
        time.sleep(1)
except KeyboardInterrupt:
    pass
finally:
    GPIO.cleanup()
```

Save the script as `blink.py` and run it using:

```
python3 blink.py
```

This script will blink an LED connected to GPIO 17.

## Using GPIO as Input: Reading Button Presses

In many games, user input is essential. You can use buttons connected to GPIO pins to capture player actions like jumping or shooting. Here's an example script that reads input from a button:

```python
import RPi.GPIO as GPIO
import time

BUTTON_PIN = 18

# Set up the GPIO mode and pin
GPIO.setmode(GPIO.BCM)
GPIO.setup(BUTTON_PIN, GPIO.IN, pull_up_down=GPIO.PUD_UP)

try:
```

```
    while True:
        button_state = GPIO.input(BUTTON_PIN)
        if button_state == GPIO.LOW:
            print("Button Pressed!")
        time.sleep(0.1)
except KeyboardInterrupt:
    pass
finally:
    GPIO.cleanup()
```

Connect a button to GPIO 18 and run the script:

```
python3 button_input.py
```

Press the button to see "Button Pressed!" printed on the screen.

## Debouncing Button Input

When reading input from a button, you may encounter **bouncing**, where a single press is registered multiple times due to mechanical noise. This can cause issues in games where precise input is needed. To solve this, we use **debouncing**.

```
import RPi.GPIO as GPIO
import time

BUTTON_PIN = 18

GPIO.setmode(GPIO.BCM)
GPIO.setup(BUTTON_PIN, GPIO.IN, pull_up_down=GPIO.PUD_UP)

def button_callback(channel):
    print("Button Pressed with Debouncing!")

GPIO.add_event_detect(BUTTON_PIN, GPIO.FALLING,
callback=button_callback, bouncetime=300)

try:
    while True:
        time.sleep(1)
except KeyboardInterrupt:
```

```python
        pass
finally:
    GPIO.cleanup()
```

The `bouncetime` parameter helps eliminate false triggers by ignoring input for a specified duration (in milliseconds).

## Building a Basic Game Controller

You can use multiple buttons connected to different GPIO pins to build a simple game controller. Let's create a script that reads input from two buttons: one for "jump" and one for "shoot."

```python
import RPi.GPIO as GPIO
import time

JUMP_PIN = 23
SHOOT_PIN = 24

GPIO.setmode(GPIO.BCM)
GPIO.setup(JUMP_PIN, GPIO.IN, pull_up_down=GPIO.PUD_UP)
GPIO.setup(SHOOT_PIN, GPIO.IN, pull_up_down=GPIO.PUD_UP)

def jump():
    print("Jump!")

def shoot():
    print("Shoot!")

try:
    while True:
        if GPIO.input(JUMP_PIN) == GPIO.LOW:
            jump()
        if GPIO.input(SHOOT_PIN) == GPIO.LOW:
            shoot()
        time.sleep(0.1)
except KeyboardInterrupt:
    pass
finally:
    GPIO.cleanup()
```

## Using GPIO with PyGame

Integrating GPIO input with PyGame allows you to control your game using physical buttons. Let's modify the basic PyGame loop to include GPIO input for player actions:

```python
import pygame
import RPi.GPIO as GPIO
import sys

# Initialize PyGame and GPIO
pygame.init()
GPIO.setmode(GPIO.BCM)

JUMP_PIN = 23
GPIO.setup(JUMP_PIN, GPIO.IN, pull_up_down=GPIO.PUD_UP)

# Set up the game window
screen = pygame.display.set_mode((640, 480))
pygame.display.set_caption("GPIO Game Control")

# Game loop
while True:
    for event in pygame.event.get():
        if event.type == pygame.QUIT:
            pygame.quit()
            sys.exit()

    if GPIO.input(JUMP_PIN) == GPIO.LOW:
        print("Player Jumps!")

    screen.fill((0, 0, 0))
    pygame.display.flip()
```

This setup allows you to use a button connected to the Raspberry Pi as a jump control in your PyGame project.

## Safety Tips for Working with GPIO

When working with GPIO pins, keep the following safety tips in mind:

1. **Never connect GPIO pins directly to power** without a resistor, as this can damage the Raspberry Pi.

2. **Use a pull-up or pull-down resistor** to ensure stable input signals.
3. **Always clean up GPIO settings** at the end of your script with `GPIO.cleanup()` to prevent unexpected behavior in future runs.

## Summary

In this section, we explored the basics of GPIO programming on the Raspberry Pi, learned how to read input from buttons, and integrated GPIO input with PyGame for game controls. GPIO adds an interactive, physical element to your projects, making it possible to create custom game controllers and enhance the gaming experience. In the next chapter, we will dive deeper into using PyGame for building your first interactive game on the Raspberry Pi.

# Chapter 3: Introduction to PyGame: Building Your First Game

## Installing and Setting Up PyGame

PyGame is an open-source Python library specifically designed for game development. It provides modules for handling graphics, sounds, and user input, allowing you to create games with ease. In this section, we'll cover how to install PyGame on your system and explore the basics needed to start building your first game.

### Why Use PyGame?

Before diving into installation, let's briefly discuss why PyGame is a popular choice for game development:

1. **Cross-Platform Compatibility**: PyGame works on multiple platforms, including Windows, macOS, and Linux (including Raspberry Pi).
2. **Comprehensive Library**: It offers modules for handling images, audio, and user input, providing everything you need for game development in one package.
3. **Beginner-Friendly**: PyGame is easy to learn and integrates well with Python, making it a great choice for new game developers.

### Setting Up Python and PyGame

#### Prerequisites

Before installing PyGame, ensure that Python is installed on your Raspberry Pi or system. You can verify this by running:

```
python --version
```

If Python is not installed, follow the steps in the previous chapter to install it.

#### Installing PyGame

You can install PyGame using `pip`, the Python package manager. Open your terminal and run the following command:

```
pip install pygame
```

This command downloads and installs the latest version of PyGame. You can verify the installation by running:

```
python -m pygame.examples.aliens
```

If a game window appears, your installation is successful!

### Troubleshooting Installation Issues

If you encounter any issues during installation, here are a few common fixes:

**Update `pip`**: Ensure `pip` is up to date with:
bash

```
pip install --upgrade pip
```

1.

**Install Dependencies**: On Linux, you may need to install additional dependencies:
bash

```
sudo apt-get install libsdl2-dev libsdl2-image-dev libsdl2-mixer-dev libsdl2-ttf-dev
```

2.
3. **Check Python Version**: PyGame requires Python 3.7 or higher. If you are using an older version, upgrade Python.

## Creating a New PyGame Project

With PyGame installed, let's set up a basic project structure. Create a new folder for your game project and navigate into it:

```
mkdir my_first_game
cd my_first_game
```

Inside this folder, create a new Python file named `main.py`:

```
touch main.py
```

## Writing Your First PyGame Script

Let's start by creating a simple PyGame window. Open `main.py` in your favorite text editor and write the following code:

```python
import pygame
import sys

# Initialize PyGame
pygame.init()

# Set up the game window
SCREEN_WIDTH = 800
SCREEN_HEIGHT = 600
screen = pygame.display.set_mode((SCREEN_WIDTH, SCREEN_HEIGHT))
pygame.display.set_caption("My First PyGame Window")

# Define colors
BLACK = (0, 0, 0)
WHITE = (255, 255, 255)

# Main game loop
while True:
    for event in pygame.event.get():
        if event.type == pygame.QUIT:
            pygame.quit()
            sys.exit()

    # Fill the screen with black
    screen.fill(BLACK)

    # Update the display
    pygame.display.flip()
```

**Code Breakdown**

- **Initializing PyGame**: `pygame.init()` initializes all PyGame modules.
- **Setting Up the Display**: `pygame.display.set_mode()` creates the game window with the specified dimensions.
- **Event Handling**: The loop checks for the `QUIT` event (clicking the window's close button) and exits the game if detected.
- **Updating the Screen**: `pygame.display.flip()` updates the entire screen with any changes made.

## Running the Game

To run your script, use the command:

```
python main.py
```

You should see a black game window appear. Although it's simple, this script is the foundation of every PyGame project.

## Adding a Background Color

Let's add a background color to the game window. Modify your `main.py` file as follows:

```python
import pygame
import sys

pygame.init()

SCREEN_WIDTH = 800
SCREEN_HEIGHT = 600
screen = pygame.display.set_mode((SCREEN_WIDTH, SCREEN_HEIGHT))
pygame.display.set_caption("Colored Background")

# Define colors
BLUE = (0, 0, 255)

while True:
    for event in pygame.event.get():
        if event.type == pygame.QUIT:
            pygame.quit()
            sys.exit()

    # Fill the screen with blue
    screen.fill(BLUE)
    pygame.display.flip()
```

This time, the window will display a blue background.

## Handling User Input

To make your game interactive, you need to handle user input. PyGame provides several ways to detect keyboard and mouse events. Here's an example of handling keyboard input:

```python
import pygame
import sys

pygame.init()

SCREEN_WIDTH = 800
SCREEN_HEIGHT = 600
screen = pygame.display.set_mode((SCREEN_WIDTH, SCREEN_HEIGHT))
pygame.display.set_caption("Keyboard Input")

WHITE = (255, 255, 255)
BLACK = (0, 0, 0)
color = WHITE

while True:
    for event in pygame.event.get():
        if event.type == pygame.QUIT:
            pygame.quit()
            sys.exit()
        elif event.type == pygame.KEYDOWN:
            if event.key == pygame.K_b:
                color = BLACK
            elif event.key == pygame.K_w:
                color = WHITE

    screen.fill(color)
    pygame.display.flip()
```

### Code Explanation

- **Keyboard Events**: The `KEYDOWN` event checks if a key is pressed. In this example, pressing 'B' changes the background to black, and pressing 'W' changes it to white.

## Creating a Moving Object

Let's add a simple square that moves based on user input. Update `main.py` as follows:

```python
import pygame
```

```python
import sys

pygame.init()

SCREEN_WIDTH = 800
SCREEN_HEIGHT = 600
screen = pygame.display.set_mode((SCREEN_WIDTH, SCREEN_HEIGHT))
pygame.display.set_caption("Moving Square")

WHITE = (255, 255, 255)
RED = (255, 0, 0)
square_pos = [SCREEN_WIDTH // 2, SCREEN_HEIGHT // 2]
square_size = 50
speed = 5

while True:
    for event in pygame.event.get():
        if event.type == pygame.QUIT:
            pygame.quit()
            sys.exit()

    keys = pygame.key.get_pressed()

    if keys[pygame.K_LEFT]:
        square_pos[0] -= speed
    if keys[pygame.K_RIGHT]:
        square_pos[0] += speed
    if keys[pygame.K_UP]:
        square_pos[1] -= speed
    if keys[pygame.K_DOWN]:
        square_pos[1] += speed

    screen.fill(WHITE)
    pygame.draw.rect(screen, RED, (*square_pos, square_size, square_size))
    pygame.display.flip()
```

**Key Concepts**

- **Movement**: The position of the square is updated based on arrow key input.
- **Rendering**: `pygame.draw.rect()` is used to draw the square on the screen.

## Summary

In this section, you learned how to set up PyGame, create a basic game window, handle user input, and render a moving object. This foundational knowledge will help you as we move on to creating more complex games in the next chapters.

# Understanding the PyGame Framework

The PyGame framework is the core toolset you'll use to develop games in Python. It provides the essential components for building a game, including handling graphics, audio, user input, and events. In this section, we'll explore the structure of a typical PyGame program, the main components of the framework, and how to build a solid foundation for your games.

### Basic Structure of a PyGame Program

A typical PyGame program follows a standard structure:

1. **Initialization**: Set up PyGame and any resources needed.
2. **Game Loop**: The main loop where the game logic is processed.
3. **Event Handling**: Responding to user input and system events.
4. **Game Logic**: Updating the game state.
5. **Rendering**: Drawing the game elements on the screen.
6. **Cleanup**: Exiting the game gracefully.

Here is a simple template for a PyGame program:

```
import pygame
import sys

# Initialization
pygame.init()
SCREEN_WIDTH, SCREEN_HEIGHT = 800, 600
screen = pygame.display.set_mode((SCREEN_WIDTH, SCREEN_HEIGHT))
pygame.display.set_caption("Basic PyGame Template")

# Main Game Loop
while True:
    # Event Handling
    for event in pygame.event.get():
        if event.type == pygame.QUIT:
            pygame.quit()
            sys.exit()
```

```
    # Game Logic
    screen.fill((0, 0, 0))

    # Rendering
    pygame.display.flip()
```

## Understanding the Game Loop

The **game loop** is the heart of every PyGame application. It runs continuously, allowing the game to update the screen and respond to user input. The game loop typically consists of the following parts:

1. **Event Handling**: Detects and responds to user input (e.g., keyboard presses, mouse clicks).
2. **Updating Game State**: Changes the state of the game based on input or other factors (e.g., moving a player character).
3. **Rendering**: Draws the updated game state on the screen.

The loop runs until the user decides to quit the game.

## Event Handling

PyGame's event system is used to capture user input, such as keyboard presses, mouse clicks, or window actions. PyGame stores these events in an event queue that you can process in the game loop.

Here's an example of handling some basic events:

```
import pygame
import sys

pygame.init()
screen = pygame.display.set_mode((800, 600))

while True:
    for event in pygame.event.get():
        if event.type == pygame.QUIT:
            pygame.quit()
            sys.exit()
        elif event.type == pygame.KEYDOWN:
            if event.key == pygame.K_ESCAPE:
                pygame.quit()
                sys.exit()
```

```
            elif event.key == pygame.K_SPACE:
                print("Spacebar pressed!")
        elif event.type == pygame.MOUSEBUTTONDOWN:
            print(f"Mouse clicked at {event.pos}")

    screen.fill((0, 0, 0))
    pygame.display.flip()
```

### Explanation

- **QUIT Event**: Detects when the user closes the game window.
- **KEYDOWN Event**: Captures key presses, such as the ESC key or spacebar.
- **MOUSEBUTTONDOWN Event**: Detects mouse clicks and prints the click position.

## Game Clock and Frame Rate

A key part of the game loop is controlling the frame rate, which is how many times the game updates per second. PyGame uses a `Clock` object to manage this. A common frame rate for games is 60 frames per second (FPS).

Here's how to set up a frame rate in your game:

```
import pygame
import sys

pygame.init()
screen = pygame.display.set_mode((800, 600))
clock = pygame.time.Clock()

while True:
    for event in pygame.event.get():
        if event.type == pygame.QUIT:
            pygame.quit()
            sys.exit()

    screen.fill((0, 0, 0))
    pygame.display.flip()

    # Limit the frame rate to 60 FPS
    clock.tick(60)
```

### Explanation

- **Clock Object**: `pygame.time.Clock()` creates a clock object to control the frame rate.
- **tick() Method**: `clock.tick(60)` ensures the game updates at most 60 times per second.

## Using Sprites for Game Objects

Sprites are an essential concept in game development. They represent game objects like players, enemies, or obstacles. PyGame provides a `Sprite` class to help manage these objects efficiently.

Here's an example of creating a simple sprite:

```
import pygame
import sys

class Player(pygame.sprite.Sprite):
    def __init__(self):
        super().__init__()
        self.image = pygame.Surface((50, 50))
        self.image.fill((0, 255, 0))
        self.rect = self.image.get_rect(center=(400, 300))

    def update(self):
        keys = pygame.key.get_pressed()
        if keys[pygame.K_LEFT]:
            self.rect.x -= 5
        if keys[pygame.K_RIGHT]:
            self.rect.x += 5
        if keys[pygame.K_UP]:
            self.rect.y -= 5
        if keys[pygame.K_DOWN]:
            self.rect.y += 5

pygame.init()
screen = pygame.display.set_mode((800, 600))
clock = pygame.time.Clock()
player = Player()
all_sprites = pygame.sprite.Group(player)

while True:
    for event in pygame.event.get():
```

```
        if event.type == pygame.QUIT:
            pygame.quit()
            sys.exit()

    all_sprites.update()

    screen.fill((0, 0, 0))
    all_sprites.draw(screen)
    pygame.display.flip()
    clock.tick(60)
```

**Explanation**

- **Player Class**: Inherits from `pygame.sprite.Sprite` and defines a simple player character.
- **update() Method**: Updates the player's position based on keyboard input.
- **Sprite Group**: `pygame.sprite.Group` manages multiple sprites and handles their updates and drawing.

## Handling Collisions

Collision detection is crucial in most games. PyGame offers several methods for checking collisions between sprites.

Here's an example of simple collision detection:

```
import pygame
import sys

class Block(pygame.sprite.Sprite):
    def __init__(self, x, y):
        super().__init__()
        self.image = pygame.Surface((50, 50))
        self.image.fill((255, 0, 0))
        self.rect = self.image.get_rect(topleft=(x, y))

pygame.init()
screen = pygame.display.set_mode((800, 600))
clock = pygame.time.Clock()

player = Player()
block = Block(400, 300)
```

```python
all_sprites = pygame.sprite.Group(player, block)

while True:
    for event in pygame.event.get():
        if event.type == pygame.QUIT:
            pygame.quit()
            sys.exit()

    all_sprites.update()

    # Check for collision
    if pygame.sprite.collide_rect(player, block):
        print("Collision detected!")

    screen.fill((0, 0, 0))
    all_sprites.draw(screen)
    pygame.display.flip()
    clock.tick(60)
```

**Explanation**

- **collide_rect()**: Checks if the rectangles of two sprites overlap, indicating a collision.

## Conclusion

The PyGame framework provides a powerful, flexible set of tools for building games. Understanding the structure of a PyGame program and mastering the game loop, event handling, sprites, and collision detection will give you the foundation you need to start building your own games.

In the next section, we'll apply these concepts to create a simple game and dive deeper into PyGame's features.

# Creating a Simple "Hello World" Game

In this section, we will build a basic "Hello World" game using PyGame. This project will introduce you to the core concepts of game development: initializing a game window, handling events, rendering text, and creating simple animations. Although simple, this project is an important step in understanding how PyGame works.

### Setting Up the Project

Start by creating a new folder for this project and a Python file named `hello_world.py`:

```
mkdir hello_world_game
cd hello_world_game
touch hello_world.py
```

In this project, we will cover the following concepts:

1. Setting up the game window
2. Displaying text on the screen
3. Handling user input
4. Adding simple animations

## Importing PyGame and Initializing the Game

Let's begin by importing PyGame and setting up the basic game window:

```
import pygame
import sys

# Initialize PyGame
pygame.init()

# Screen dimensions and settings
SCREEN_WIDTH, SCREEN_HEIGHT = 800, 600
screen = pygame.display.set_mode((SCREEN_WIDTH, SCREEN_HEIGHT))
pygame.display.set_caption("Hello World Game")

# Define colors
BLACK = (0, 0, 0)
WHITE = (255, 255, 255)

# Game clock
clock = pygame.time.Clock()
```

### Explanation

- `pygame.init()`: Initializes all PyGame modules.
- `pygame.display.set_mode()`: Sets the size of the game window.
- `pygame.display.set_caption()`: Sets the title of the window.
- `clock`: Controls the frame rate of the game.

## Rendering Text with PyGame

One of the simplest ways to display content in a game is by rendering text. PyGame's `Font` module allows us to create text objects and draw them on the screen.

Add the following code to define a font and render a "Hello, World!" message:

```python
# Define font and text
font = pygame.font.Font(None, 74)
text = font.render("Hello, World!", True, WHITE)
text_rect = text.get_rect(center=(SCREEN_WIDTH // 2, SCREEN_HEIGHT // 2))
```

**Explanation**

- `pygame.font.Font()`: Creates a font object. `None` uses the default font.
- `font.render()`: Renders the text with the specified color (WHITE).
- `get_rect()`: Retrieves the rectangular area of the text for positioning.

## Main Game Loop

Now that we have the text ready, let's create the main game loop. This loop will handle events, update the game state, and draw content on the screen:

```python
while True:
    for event in pygame.event.get():
        if event.type == pygame.QUIT:
            pygame.quit()
            sys.exit()

    # Fill the screen with black
    screen.fill(BLACK)

    # Draw the text on the screen
    screen.blit(text, text_rect)

    # Update the display
    pygame.display.flip()

    # Limit the frame rate to 60 FPS
    clock.tick(60)
```

**Explanation**

- `screen.fill(BLACK)`: Clears the screen by filling it with a black color.
- `blit()`: Draws the text surface on the screen at the specified rectangle (`text_rect`).
- `pygame.display.flip()`: Updates the entire screen with any changes.

## Adding User Interaction

Let's make the game interactive by responding to key presses. We'll update the game to change the text color when certain keys are pressed:

```
color = WHITE

while True:
    for event in pygame.event.get():
        if event.type == pygame.QUIT:
            pygame.quit()
            sys.exit()
        elif event.type == pygame.KEYDOWN:
            if event.key == pygame.K_r:
                color = (255, 0, 0)   # Red
            elif event.key == pygame.K_q:
                color = (0, 255, 0)   # Green
            elif event.key == pygame.K_b:
                color = (0, 0, 255)   # Blue
            elif event.key == pygame.K_w:
                color = WHITE

    # Update the text color
    text = font.render("Hello, World!", True, color)

    screen.fill(BLACK)
    screen.blit(text, text_rect)
    pygame.display.flip()
    clock.tick(60)
```

### Explanation

- **Key Events**: `pygame.KEYDOWN` detects when a key is pressed. Depending on the key, the text color changes.
- **Text Rendering**: The text is re-rendered with the new color whenever a key is pressed.

## Adding Simple Animation

To make the game more dynamic, let's add a simple animation by moving the text across the screen. We will update the text's position in each frame.

Add the following variables to control the animation:

```
text_speed = [2, 2]

while True:
    for event in pygame.event.get():
        if event.type == pygame.QUIT:
            pygame.quit()
            sys.exit()

    # Move the text
    text_rect.x += text_speed[0]
    text_rect.y += text_speed[1]

    # Bounce the text off the edges
    if text_rect.left <= 0 or text_rect.right >= SCREEN_WIDTH:
        text_speed[0] = -text_speed[0]
    if text_rect.top <= 0 or text_rect.bottom >= SCREEN_HEIGHT:
        text_speed[1] = -text_speed[1]

    screen.fill(BLACK)
    screen.blit(text, text_rect)
    pygame.display.flip()
    clock.tick(60)
```

**Explanation**

- **Text Movement**: The x and y positions of `text_rect` are updated each frame.
- **Collision Detection**: The text bounces off the edges of the screen by reversing its speed when it hits a boundary.

## Handling Mouse Events

In addition to keyboard input, PyGame also supports mouse events. We can detect when the user clicks on the text and change its color.

Modify the game loop to include the following:

```
while True:
    for event in pygame.event.get():
        if event.type == pygame.QUIT:
            pygame.quit()
            sys.exit()
        elif event.type == pygame.MOUSEBUTTONDOWN:
            if text_rect.collidepoint(event.pos):
                color = (255, 255, 0)  # Yellow
                text = font.render("You clicked me!", True, color)

    screen.fill(BLACK)
    screen.blit(text, text_rect)
    pygame.display.flip()
    clock.tick(60)
```

#### Explanation

- **MOUSEBUTTONDOWN Event**: Detects when the mouse button is clicked.
- **collidepoint() Method**: Checks if the click position is inside the `text_rect`.

### Summary and Next Steps

In this simple "Hello World" game, we covered:

- Setting up the PyGame window and main loop
- Rendering text and handling basic user input
- Creating simple animations and responding to mouse clicks

This project serves as an introduction to the PyGame framework and provides the basic skills needed to build more complex games. In the next chapter, we will explore how to add graphics, sound, and more interactive elements to enhance your games.

## Game Loop: The Heart of Every Game

The game loop is the core of any video game and forms the foundation of how the game updates and interacts with players. It's responsible for processing user input, updating the game state, and rendering the graphics. In this section, we'll dive deep into the mechanics of the game loop, explore different types of loops, and look at best practices for creating efficient game loops in PyGame.

### What is a Game Loop?

A game loop is a cycle that repeats continuously while the game is running. It typically consists of three main parts:

1. **Event Handling**: Captures and processes user input (e.g., keyboard presses, mouse clicks).
2. **Game Logic Update**: Updates the game state based on user input and other factors (e.g., moving characters, checking collisions).
3. **Rendering**: Draws the updated game state on the screen.

The loop runs until the player decides to quit the game, at which point the loop ends, and the game exits.

## Anatomy of a Basic Game Loop

Here's a simple example of a game loop in PyGame:

```python
import pygame
import sys

# Initialize PyGame
pygame.init()

# Screen setup
SCREEN_WIDTH, SCREEN_HEIGHT = 800, 600
screen = pygame.display.set_mode((SCREEN_WIDTH, SCREEN_HEIGHT))
pygame.display.set_caption("Basic Game Loop")

# Clock to control the frame rate
clock = pygame.time.Clock()

# Main game loop
while True:
    # Event Handling
    for event in pygame.event.get():
        if event.type == pygame.QUIT:
            pygame.quit()
            sys.exit()

    # Game Logic Update
    # (Game state changes would go here)

    # Rendering
    screen.fill((0, 0, 0))   # Clear the screen with black
    pygame.display.flip()    # Update the display

    # Frame rate control
```

```
    clock.tick(60)    # Limit the loop to 60 frames per second
```

**Explanation**

- **Event Handling**: Processes all user inputs and system events.
- **Game Logic Update**: Updates the game state (e.g., moving objects, checking for collisions).
- **Rendering**: Draws everything on the screen and refreshes the display.
- **Frame Rate Control**: Uses `clock.tick(60)` to cap the frame rate at 60 FPS.

## Managing Time in the Game Loop

Time management is crucial in a game loop to ensure smooth animations and consistent gameplay across different systems. PyGame provides a `Clock` object to help manage time and frame rate.

**Delta Time**

Delta time (`dt`) represents the time elapsed between each frame. It's used to make game updates independent of the frame rate, which is essential for consistency on different devices.

Here's an example using delta time:

```
import pygame
import sys

pygame.init()
screen = pygame.display.set_mode((800, 600))
clock = pygame.time.Clock()

# Position and speed of a moving object
x_pos = 0
speed = 300   # Pixels per second

while True:
    dt = clock.tick(60) / 1000   # Convert milliseconds to seconds

    for event in pygame.event.get():
        if event.type == pygame.QUIT:
            pygame.quit()
            sys.exit()
```

```python
# Update position based on delta time
x_pos += speed * dt
if x_pos > 800:    # Reset position when it goes off screen
    x_pos = 0

screen.fill((0, 0, 0))
pygame.draw.rect(screen, (255, 0, 0), (x_pos, 300, 50, 50))
pygame.display.flip()
```

**Explanation**

- **Delta Time Calculation**: `clock.tick(60)` returns the time in milliseconds since the last call. Dividing by 1000 converts it to seconds.
- **Frame-Independent Movement**: The object's position is updated based on its speed and delta time, making it consistent regardless of the frame rate.

## Handling Input in the Game Loop

Efficient input handling is key to responsive gameplay. PyGame offers several ways to capture user input:

### Using the Event Queue

The event queue captures discrete user inputs (e.g., key presses, mouse clicks). Here's an example of handling keyboard events:

```python
while True:
    for event in pygame.event.get():
        if event.type == pygame.KEYDOWN:
            if event.key == pygame.K_ESCAPE:
                pygame.quit()
                sys.exit()
            elif event.key == pygame.K_LEFT:
                print("Left arrow key pressed")

    screen.fill((0, 0, 0))
    pygame.display.flip()
    clock.tick(60)
```

**Using `pygame.key.get_pressed()`**

For continuous input detection, such as holding down a key, use `pygame.key.get_pressed()`:

```
keys = pygame.key.get_pressed()
if keys[pygame.K_UP]:
    print("Up arrow key held down")
```

## Different Types of Game Loops

Depending on the complexity of your game, you might use different types of game loops. Let's look at some common variations.

### Fixed-Time Step Loop

A fixed-time step loop ensures that the game updates at a consistent interval, regardless of the frame rate. This is often used in games with precise physics calculations.

```
time_step = 1 / 60   # 60 updates per second
accumulator = 0.0

while True:
    dt = clock.tick(120) / 1000   # Allow high frame rate
    accumulator += dt

    while accumulator >= time_step:
        # Update game logic with a fixed time step
        update(time_step)
        accumulator -= time_step

    render()
```

### Variable-Time Step Loop

This loop updates the game state based on the time elapsed since the last frame. It's simpler but can lead to inconsistent physics if the frame rate drops.

```
while True:
    dt = clock.tick() / 1000
    update(dt)
    render()
```

## Optimizing the Game Loop

To create smooth and efficient gameplay, you should consider optimizing your game loop:

1. **Limit the Frame Rate**: Use `clock.tick()` to cap the FPS and prevent the loop from running too fast.
2. **Efficient Event Handling**: Only process relevant events to reduce overhead.
3. **Minimize Rendering Calls**: Only update parts of the screen that have changed.
4. **Use Double Buffering**: PyGame's `pygame.display.flip()` uses double buffering by default, which helps reduce screen tearing.

## Example: Putting It All Together

Let's combine everything we've learned into a complete game loop example:

```python
import pygame
import sys

pygame.init()
screen = pygame.display.set_mode((800, 600))
pygame.display.set_caption("Full Game Loop Example")
clock = pygame.time.Clock()

# Game state variables
x, y = 400, 300
speed = 200
color = (255, 255, 255)

while True:
    dt = clock.tick(60) / 1000

    for event in pygame.event.get():
        if event.type == pygame.QUIT:
            pygame.quit()
            sys.exit()
        elif event.type == pygame.KEYDOWN:
            if event.key == pygame.K_c:
                color = (0, 255, 0)

    # Movement using delta time
    keys = pygame.key.get_pressed()
    if keys[pygame.K_LEFT]:
        x -= speed * dt
```

```
if keys[pygame.K_RIGHT]:
    x += speed * dt
if keys[pygame.K_UP]:
    y -= speed * dt
if keys[pygame.K_DOWN]:
    y += speed * dt

# Keep the rectangle within screen bounds
x = max(0, min(x, 750))
y = max(0, min(y, 550))

# Render
screen.fill((0, 0, 0))
pygame.draw.rect(screen, color, (x, y, 50, 50))
pygame.display.flip()
```

## Summary

In this section, we explored the game loop, the central structure of every game. We discussed how to:

- Set up a basic game loop in PyGame
- Manage time and frame rate using the `Clock` object
- Handle user input effectively
- Optimize the loop for better performance

Understanding the game loop is fundamental to mastering game development with PyGame. With this knowledge, you're well-prepared to build interactive and engaging games. In the next chapter, we'll expand on this by adding graphics, sound, and animation to our projects.

# Chapter 4: Game Elements: Graphics, Sound, and Animation

## Working with Graphics in PyGame

Creating visually appealing graphics is a key aspect of game development. In PyGame, we can handle graphics using surfaces, images, and colors. This section covers the essentials of working with graphics, including how to load images, draw shapes, and apply transformations like scaling and rotating.

### 1. Introduction to Surfaces

In PyGame, every graphical element is represented as a "Surface" object. The game window itself is a Surface, and all images and drawings are rendered onto surfaces before being displayed.

To create a Surface in PyGame:

```
import pygame

# Initialize PyGame
pygame.init()

# Create a display surface (game window)
screen = pygame.display.set_mode((800, 600))

# Set a title for the window
pygame.display.set_caption("Graphics in PyGame")

# Create a new surface
my_surface = pygame.Surface((200, 150))

# Fill the surface with a color (RGB: Red, Green, Blue)
my_surface.fill((255, 0, 0))

# Main loop
running = True
while running:
    for event in pygame.event.get():
```

```
        if event.type == pygame.QUIT:
            running = False

    # Draw the surface onto the screen at position (100, 100)
    screen.blit(my_surface, (100, 100))

    # Update the display
    pygame.display.flip()

pygame.quit()
```

In this example:

- `screen` is the main display surface.
- `my_surface` is a smaller, red rectangle surface that we draw onto the main screen using `blit()`.

## 2. Drawing Basic Shapes

PyGame provides functions to draw simple shapes like rectangles, circles, lines, and polygons. These shapes are useful for creating game elements like platforms, bullets, or boundaries.

### Drawing a Rectangle

```
# Draw a blue rectangle (x, y, width, height)
pygame.draw.rect(screen, (0, 0, 255), (50, 50, 200, 100))
```

### Drawing a Circle

```
# Draw a green circle (surface, color, center, radius)
pygame.draw.circle(screen, (0, 255, 0), (400, 300), 50)
```

### Drawing a Line

```
# Draw a white line (surface, color, start_pos, end_pos, width)
pygame.draw.line(screen, (255, 255, 255), (0, 0), (800, 600), 5)
```

## 3. Loading and Displaying Images

Using custom images in your game can make it visually more interesting. PyGame allows you to load and display images easily using the `pygame.image.load()` function.

```
# Load an image file
player_image = pygame.image.load("player.png")

# Scale the image (optional)
player_image = pygame.transform.scale(player_image, (50, 50))

# Display the image at a specific position
screen.blit(player_image, (200, 200))
```

Ensure that your image file ("player.png") is in the same directory as your script, or provide the full path.

## 4. Image Transformations

PyGame includes functions for common image transformations, such as scaling, rotating, and flipping.

### Scaling an Image

```
# Scale the image to a new size
scaled_image = pygame.transform.scale(player_image, (100, 100))
```

### Rotating an Image

```
# Rotate the image by 45 degrees
rotated_image = pygame.transform.rotate(player_image, 45)
```

### Flipping an Image

```
# Flip the image horizontally
flipped_image = pygame.transform.flip(player_image, True, False)
```

## 5. Using Transparency and Alpha Channels

Transparency is essential for creating sprites with non-rectangular shapes. In PyGame, you can handle transparency using an "alpha channel" or by setting a specific color to be transparent.

## Setting a Transparent Color

```
# Set the color white (255, 255, 255) as transparent
player_image.set_colorkey((255, 255, 255))
```

## Using Alpha for Opacity

```
# Set the alpha level (0: fully transparent, 255: fully opaque)
player_image.set_alpha(128)
```

## 6. Creating a Background

A background image can make your game look more professional. To set a background image:

```
# Load the background image
background = pygame.image.load("background.png")

# In the main loop, draw the background first
screen.blit(background, (0, 0))
```

## 7. Handling Display Updates

In PyGame, the display doesn't update automatically. You need to call `pygame.display.flip()` or `pygame.display.update()` to refresh the screen.

- `pygame.display.flip()` updates the entire display.
- `pygame.display.update()` can update specific areas, making it more efficient in some cases.

## 8. Creating a Simple Animation

Animations in PyGame are achieved by updating the position of an image or shape in each frame of the game loop.

```
# Simple animation example
x_pos = 0

# Main loop
while running:
```

```
    for event in pygame.event.get():
        if event.type == pygame.QUIT:
            running = False

    # Clear the screen
    screen.fill((0, 0, 0))

    # Update the x position
    x_pos += 5
    if x_pos > 800:
        x_pos = 0

    # Draw the moving rectangle
    pygame.draw.rect(screen, (255, 0, 0), (x_pos, 300, 50, 50))

    # Update the display
    pygame.display.flip()
```

This code animates a red rectangle moving from left to right across the screen.

## 9. Tips for Optimizing Graphics Performance

- **Use Surfaces Wisely:** Creating many surfaces can be resource-intensive. Reuse surfaces where possible.
- **Limit Image Scaling:** Avoid scaling images frequently in the game loop. Pre-scale them before the loop if possible.
- **Use Double Buffering:** Enable double buffering in `pygame.display.set_mode()` to reduce flickering.
- **Clear the Screen Efficiently:** Instead of redrawing the entire screen, update only the parts that have changed.

```
# Enable double buffering
screen = pygame.display.set_mode((800, 600), pygame.DOUBLEBUF)
```

By following these tips, you can improve the performance of your game, especially on devices with limited hardware like the Raspberry Pi.

## Summary

In this section, we explored the basics of working with graphics in PyGame, including surfaces, drawing shapes, loading images, transformations, transparency, and basic animation techniques. With these tools, you can start building more visually complex and interactive games.

Next, we'll dive into adding sound effects and music, which will bring another layer of immersion to your game.

## Adding Sound Effects and Music

Sound effects and music play a crucial role in enhancing the player's experience by adding auditory feedback, atmosphere, and emotional cues. In PyGame, the `pygame.mixer` module provides functionalities for playing and managing sound effects and music files. In this section, we will explore how to use the `mixer` module to integrate audio into your game.

### 1. Initializing the Mixer

Before using any audio features, you need to initialize the `pygame.mixer` module. This is typically done alongside the main `pygame.init()` call.

```
import pygame

# Initialize PyGame and the mixer module
pygame.init()
pygame.mixer.init()

# Set up the display
screen = pygame.display.set_mode((800, 600))
pygame.display.set_caption("Sound Effects and Music in PyGame")
```

In this example, `pygame.mixer.init()` initializes the mixer, allowing you to load and play sound files. You can configure the mixer with specific settings like frequency, size, and channels if needed, but the default settings usually work well.

### 2. Loading Sound Effects

Sound effects are short audio clips like button clicks, explosions, or jump sounds. PyGame uses the Sound object to handle these. To load a sound effect, use the `pygame.mixer.Sound()` function.

```
# Load a sound effect
jump_sound = pygame.mixer.Sound("jump.wav")
```

# Chapter 4: Game Elements: Graphics, Sound, and Animation

In this example, `"jump.wav"` should be a short audio file (WAV format). PyGame also supports other formats like MP3 and OGG, but WAV is the most reliable for sound effects.

**Playing a Sound Effect**

```
# Play the sound effect
jump_sound.play()
```

You can adjust the volume of the sound effect using the `set_volume()` method:

```
# Set the volume (0.0 to 1.0)
jump_sound.set_volume(0.5)
```

## 3. Using Music in PyGame

Music files are typically longer audio tracks used as background music. Unlike sound effects, which use the `Sound` object, music is played using the `pygame.mixer.music` module.

**Loading and Playing Music**

```
# Load a music file
pygame.mixer.music.load("background.mp3")

# Play the music (loop=-1 makes it loop indefinitely)
pygame.mixer.music.play(loops=-1)
```

In this code:

- `load()` prepares the music file for playback.
- `play()` starts playing the music. The `loops` parameter controls how many times the music repeats. `-1` means it will loop indefinitely.

**Pausing, Stopping, and Resuming Music**

```
# Pause the music
pygame.mixer.music.pause()

# Resume the music
pygame.mixer.music.unpause()

# Stop the music
```

```
pygame.mixer.music.stop()
```

You can also set the volume for the music:

```
pygame.mixer.music.set_volume(0.7)
```

## 4. Handling Audio Events

You might want to play specific sounds based on game events like collisions, user inputs, or level changes. Using PyGame's event handling system, you can trigger sound effects when certain conditions are met.

```
# Example of playing a sound when the player jumps
running = True
player_jumping = False

while running:
    for event in pygame.event.get():
        if event.type == pygame.QUIT:
            running = False
        elif event.type == pygame.KEYDOWN:
            if event.key == pygame.K_SPACE:
                jump_sound.play()
                player_jumping = True

    # Update the game logic
    if player_jumping:
        print("Player is jumping!")
        player_jumping = False

    # Refresh the display
    pygame.display.flip()

pygame.quit()
```

In this example:

- The `jump_sound` effect plays when the spacebar is pressed.
- The event loop listens for user inputs and triggers the corresponding sound effect.

## 5. Mixing Multiple Sounds

PyGame allows you to play multiple sound effects simultaneously while music is playing in the background. This creates a rich audio experience.

```
# Load multiple sound effects
shoot_sound = pygame.mixer.Sound("shoot.wav")
explosion_sound = pygame.mixer.Sound("explosion.wav")

# Play them simultaneously
shoot_sound.play()
explosion_sound.play()
```

This feature is useful in games with complex audio requirements, such as when multiple actions are happening at once.

## 6. Adding Audio Feedback to User Actions

Audio feedback can significantly enhance the user experience by providing immediate responses to actions like button clicks or collisions.

```
# Example: Button click sound
button_click_sound = pygame.mixer.Sound("click.wav")

def check_button_click(mouse_pos, button_rect):
    if button_rect.collidepoint(mouse_pos):
        button_click_sound.play()
        print("Button clicked!")

# Main loop
button_rect = pygame.Rect(100, 100, 200, 50)

while running:
    for event in pygame.event.get():
        if event.type == pygame.QUIT:
            running = False
        elif event.type == pygame.MOUSEBUTTONDOWN:
            check_button_click(event.pos, button_rect)

    pygame.display.flip()
```

In this example, a sound effect plays whenever the user clicks a button on the screen.

## 7. Fading In and Out

Fading music in and out can create smoother transitions between tracks or sound effects. PyGame provides the `fadein()` and `fadeout()` methods for this purpose.

```
# Fade in the music over 2 seconds
pygame.mixer.music.play(fade_ms=2000)

# Fade out the music over 3 seconds
pygame.mixer.music.fadeout(3000)
```

Fading is useful when switching between background tracks or when the game transitions to a different scene.

## 8. Handling Audio Playback Errors

Audio playback might fail if the file format is unsupported or the file is missing. It is good practice to handle these errors gracefully.

```
try:
    jump_sound = pygame.mixer.Sound("jump.wav")
    jump_sound.play()
except pygame.error as e:
    print(f"Error playing sound: {e}")
```

In this code, the program catches any errors related to audio playback and prints an error message.

## 9. Optimizing Audio Performance

To ensure smooth audio playback, especially on devices like Raspberry Pi, consider the following tips:

- **Preload Sounds:** Load all sound effects at the start of the game to minimize delays during gameplay.
- **Use Appropriate Formats:** WAV files are best for short sound effects, while OGG or MP3 files work well for music.
- **Reduce Audio File Size:** Compress audio files if necessary to reduce memory usage.
- **Control Volume Levels:** Set balanced volume levels to avoid distortion when multiple sounds play together.

## Summary

In this section, we covered the basics of adding sound effects and music to your game using the `pygame.mixer` module. We explored how to load and play sounds, control playback, handle audio events, and optimize audio performance. With these techniques, you can create a more immersive gaming experience that appeals to players' senses and enhances gameplay.

In the next section, we will dive into animation techniques, combining graphics and sound to bring your game to life.

# Basic Animation Techniques

Animation is a key element in game development, bringing characters and objects to life by creating movement and visual effects. In PyGame, animations are typically achieved by updating the position or appearance of game elements frame by frame. This section explores various techniques for creating basic animations, including frame-based animations, sprite animations, and handling smooth transitions.

## 1. Understanding the Game Loop and Frame Rate

Before diving into animation techniques, it's important to understand the game loop and frame rate. The game loop is the central part of any game, where updates and rendering occur repeatedly. The frame rate, measured in frames per second (FPS), determines how fast the game loop runs.

A typical game loop structure looks like this:

```
import pygame

# Initialize PyGame
pygame.init()

# Set up the display
screen = pygame.display.set_mode((800, 600))
clock = pygame.time.Clock()

# Set the desired frame rate
FPS = 60

# Main game loop
running = True
while running:
    for event in pygame.event.get():
```

```
        if event.type == pygame.QUIT:
            running = False

    # Update game state

    # Render graphics
    screen.fill((0, 0, 0))  # Clear the screen

    # Refresh the display
    pygame.display.flip()

    # Control the frame rate
    clock.tick(FPS)

pygame.quit()
```

The `clock.tick(FPS)` function ensures that the game runs at a consistent frame rate, making animations smooth and predictable.

## 2. Frame-Based Animation

Frame-based animation involves changing the position of an object slightly in each frame to create the illusion of movement. Let's create a simple example of a ball bouncing across the screen.

```
# Ball animation example
ball_x = 100
ball_y = 100
ball_speed_x = 5
ball_speed_y = 3

while running:
    for event in pygame.event.get():
        if event.type == pygame.QUIT:
            running = False

    # Update ball position
    ball_x += ball_speed_x
    ball_y += ball_speed_y

    # Check for collisions with screen edges
```

```python
    if ball_x <= 0 or ball_x >= 800:
        ball_speed_x = -ball_speed_x
    if ball_y <= 0 or ball_y >= 600:
        ball_speed_y = -ball_speed_y

    # Clear the screen
    screen.fill((0, 0, 0))

    # Draw the ball
    pygame.draw.circle(screen, (255, 0, 0), (ball_x, ball_y), 20)

    # Update the display
    pygame.display.flip()
    clock.tick(FPS)
```

In this example:

- The ball's position is updated in each frame based on its speed.
- The ball bounces off the edges of the screen when it reaches the boundaries.

## 3. Sprite-Based Animation

Sprites are individual images or frames used to represent characters or objects in a game. Sprite-based animation involves displaying different frames of a sprite in sequence to create the illusion of movement.

### Loading a Sprite Sheet

A sprite sheet is a single image file containing multiple frames of a character or object. PyGame allows you to extract individual frames from the sprite sheet using the `subsurface()` method.

```python
# Load the sprite sheet
sprite_sheet = pygame.image.load("character_sprites.png")

# Define the dimensions of each frame
frame_width = 64
frame_height = 64

# Extract individual frames
frame_1 = sprite_sheet.subsurface((0, 0, frame_width, frame_height))
frame_2 = sprite_sheet.subsurface((64, 0, frame_width, frame_height))
```

```
frame_3 = sprite_sheet.subsurface((128, 0, frame_width,
frame_height))

# Store frames in a list
frames = [frame_1, frame_2, frame_3]

# Animation variables
current_frame = 0
animation_speed = 0.1   # Adjust speed of animation
frame_counter = 0
```

**Displaying the Animated Sprite**

```
while running:
    for event in pygame.event.get():
        if event.type == pygame.QUIT:
            running = False

    # Update the current frame
    frame_counter += animation_speed
    if frame_counter >= len(frames):
        frame_counter = 0
    current_frame = int(frame_counter)

    # Clear the screen
    screen.fill((0, 0, 0))

    # Draw the current frame
    screen.blit(frames[current_frame], (300, 300))

    # Update the display
    pygame.display.flip()
    clock.tick(FPS)
```

This example cycles through three frames of the character sprite to create an animation. The `frame_counter` is used to control the speed of the animation.

## 4. Smooth Movement and Interpolation

Smooth movement is essential for creating realistic animations. Interpolation is a technique that helps in transitioning an object's position gradually, making animations appear fluid.

## Linear Interpolation (Lerp)

Linear interpolation calculates a point between two positions based on a percentage value. It can be used to move an object smoothly from one point to another.

```
def lerp(start, end, t):
    return start + (end - start) * t

# Start and end positions
start_x = 100
end_x = 700
t = 0  # Interpolation factor (0.0 to 1.0)

while running:
    for event in pygame.event.get():
        if event.type == pygame.QUIT:
            running = False

    # Update the interpolation factor
    t += 0.01
    if t > 1.0:
        t = 0

    # Calculate the current position using interpolation
    current_x = lerp(start_x, end_x, t)

    # Clear the screen
    screen.fill((0, 0, 0))

    # Draw the moving object
    pygame.draw.circle(screen, (0, 255, 0), (int(current_x), 300), 20)

    # Update the display
    pygame.display.flip()
    clock.tick(FPS)
```

In this code:

- The `lerp()` function calculates a position between `start_x` and `end_x` based on the interpolation factor `t`.

- The object moves smoothly between the start and end positions.

## 5. Easing Functions for Natural Animations

Easing functions provide more natural-looking animations by accelerating or decelerating the movement. Common easing functions include "ease-in," "ease-out," and "ease-in-out."

**Ease-In Animation**

```python
import math

def ease_in(t):
    return t * t

t = 0

while running:
    for event in pygame.event.get():
        if event.type == pygame.QUIT:
            running = False

    # Update the interpolation factor
    t += 0.01
    if t > 1.0:
        t = 0

    # Apply the ease-in function
    current_x = lerp(start_x, end_x, ease_in(t))

    # Clear the screen
    screen.fill((0, 0, 0))

    # Draw the easing animation
    pygame.draw.circle(screen, (255, 255, 0), (int(current_x), 300), 20)

    # Update the display
    pygame.display.flip()
    clock.tick(FPS)
```

In this example, the `ease_in()` function accelerates the object's movement at the beginning, creating a more dynamic effect.

## 6. Using Animated Sprites for Characters

Animated sprites are commonly used for player characters, enemies, and other dynamic elements in games. To manage animations effectively, create a class for the animated sprite.

```python
class AnimatedSprite(pygame.sprite.Sprite):
    def __init__(self, frames, pos):
        super().__init__()
        self.frames = frames
        self.current_frame = 0
        self.image = self.frames[self.current_frame]
        self.rect = self.image.get_rect(center=pos)

    def update(self):
        self.current_frame += 0.2
        if self.current_frame >= len(self.frames):
            self.current_frame = 0
        self.image = self.frames[int(self.current_frame)]

# Initialize the animated sprite
animated_sprite = AnimatedSprite(frames, (400, 300))
all_sprites = pygame.sprite.Group(animated_sprite)

while running:
    for event in pygame.event.get():
        if event.type == pygame.QUIT:
            running = False

    # Update and draw all sprites
    all_sprites.update()
    screen.fill((0, 0, 0))
    all_sprites.draw(screen)

    pygame.display.flip()
    clock.tick(FPS)
```

This class handles updating the current frame and drawing the animated sprite on the screen.

## Summary

In this section, we covered various animation techniques in PyGame, including frame-based animation, sprite-based animation, smooth movement with interpolation, easing functions, and animated sprites. By mastering these techniques, you can create dynamic and engaging visuals for your games, enhancing the overall player experience.

In the next section, we will explore handling user input and events, allowing players to interact with your animated game world.

# Handling User Input and Events

User input and events are at the core of any interactive game. In PyGame, user actions such as keyboard presses, mouse movements, and joystick inputs are handled through events. This section covers how to detect and respond to various types of user input, allowing you to make your game interactive and engaging.

### 1. Introduction to Event Handling

PyGame uses an event queue to manage user input. Every time an input action occurs, such as a key press or mouse click, an event is added to the queue. You can access these events using `pygame.event.get()`.

```
import pygame

# Initialize PyGame
pygame.init()

# Set up the display
screen = pygame.display.set_mode((800, 600))
pygame.display.set_caption("User Input and Events")

# Main game loop
running = True
while running:
    for event in pygame.event.get():
        if event.type == pygame.QUIT:
            running = False

    # Clear the screen
    screen.fill((0, 0, 0))

    # Refresh the display
    pygame.display.flip()
```

```
pygame.quit()
```

In this basic example:

- `pygame.event.get()` retrieves all events from the event queue.
- The `pygame.QUIT` event is triggered when the user closes the game window.

## 2. Handling Keyboard Input

Keyboard input is one of the most common methods for player control. PyGame allows you to detect both individual key presses and continuous key states.

### Detecting Key Press Events

```
while running:
    for event in pygame.event.get():
        if event.type == pygame.QUIT:
            running = False
        elif event.type == pygame.KEYDOWN:
            if event.key == pygame.K_LEFT:
                print("Left arrow key pressed!")
            elif event.key == pygame.K_RIGHT:
                print("Right arrow key pressed!")
```

In this example:

- `pygame.KEYDOWN` is triggered when a key is pressed.
- `event.key` contains the specific key that was pressed (e.g., `pygame.K_LEFT` for the left arrow key).

### Checking Continuous Key States

For smoother player controls, you often need to check the current state of keys rather than relying on individual key press events.

```
keys = pygame.key.get_pressed()
if keys[pygame.K_UP]:
    print("Up arrow key is held down!")
```

This method is useful for handling continuous movement, such as holding down a key to move a character.

## 3. Handling Mouse Input

Mouse input can be used for actions like clicking buttons, dragging objects, or aiming in a shooting game. PyGame provides functions for detecting mouse position, clicks, and movement.

**Detecting Mouse Clicks**

```
while running:
    for event in pygame.event.get():
        if event.type == pygame.QUIT:
            running = False
        elif event.type == pygame.MOUSEBUTTONDOWN:
            if event.button == 1:   # Left mouse button
                print("Left mouse button clicked!")
            elif event.button == 3:   # Right mouse button
                print("Right mouse button clicked!")
```

In this example:

- `pygame.MOUSEBUTTONDOWN` is triggered when a mouse button is pressed.
- `event.button` specifies which mouse button was clicked (1 for left, 2 for middle, 3 for right).

**Getting Mouse Position**

You can get the current position of the mouse using `pygame.mouse.get_pos()`.

```
mouse_x, mouse_y = pygame.mouse.get_pos()
print(f"Mouse position: ({mouse_x}, {mouse_y})")
```

This function returns the x and y coordinates of the mouse relative to the game window.

## 4. Creating Clickable Buttons

Let's create a simple clickable button using mouse input.

```
button_rect = pygame.Rect(300, 250, 200, 100)

while running:
    for event in pygame.event.get():
        if event.type == pygame.QUIT:
```

```
            running = False
        elif event.type == pygame.MOUSEBUTTONDOWN:
            if button_rect.collidepoint(event.pos):
                print("Button clicked!")

    # Draw the button
    screen.fill((0, 0, 0))
    pygame.draw.rect(screen, (0, 128, 255), button_rect)
    pygame.display.flip()
```

In this example:

- `collidepoint()` checks if the mouse click occurred within the button's rectangular area.
- The button changes color or triggers an action when clicked.

## 5. Handling Joystick and Gamepad Input

PyGame supports joystick and gamepad input, which is often used in console-style games. You need to initialize the joystick module and access the joystick device.

**Initializing the Joystick**

```
pygame.joystick.init()
joystick = pygame.joystick.Joystick(0)
joystick.init()
print(f"Joystick name: {joystick.get_name()}")
```

This code initializes the first connected joystick and prints its name.

**Reading Joystick Input**

You can read joystick axes, buttons, and hats (D-pad) using the following functions:

```
while running:
    for event in pygame.event.get():
        if event.type == pygame.QUIT:
            running = False

    # Get joystick axis values
    x_axis = joystick.get_axis(0)
    y_axis = joystick.get_axis(1)
```

```
    print(f"Joystick axes: x={x_axis}, y={y_axis}")

    # Check joystick button press
    if joystick.get_button(0):
        print("Button 0 pressed!")

    # Check D-pad (hat) input
    hat_x, hat_y = joystick.get_hat(0)
    print(f"D-pad position: x={hat_x}, y={hat_y}")
```

In this example:

- `get_axis()` returns the value of the specified axis (from -1.0 to 1.0).
- `get_button()` checks if a specific button is pressed.
- `get_hat()` returns the position of the D-pad.

## 6. Customizing User Input for Gameplay

Let's implement a basic player movement system using keyboard input.

```
player_x = 400
player_y = 300
player_speed = 5

while running:
    keys = pygame.key.get_pressed()
    if keys[pygame.K_w]:
        player_y -= player_speed
    if keys[pygame.K_s]:
        player_y += player_speed
    if keys[pygame.K_a]:
        player_x -= player_speed
    if keys[pygame.K_d]:
        player_x += player_speed

    # Clear the screen
    screen.fill((0, 0, 0))

    # Draw the player character
    pygame.draw.circle(screen, (255, 0, 0), (player_x, player_y),
20)
```

```
        pygame.display.flip()
        clock.tick(FPS)
```

In this example:

- The player moves up, down, left, or right using the W, A, S, and D keys.
- The `pygame.key.get_pressed()` function checks the state of multiple keys simultaneously, providing responsive controls.

## 7. Handling Complex Input Sequences

You can detect complex input sequences like "double-tap" or "combo moves" by tracking the time and order of key presses.

```
import time

last_tap = 0
double_tap_threshold = 0.3    # Time in seconds

while running:
    for event in pygame.event.get():
        if event.type == pygame.QUIT:
            running = False
        elif event.type == pygame.KEYDOWN:
            if event.key == pygame.K_SPACE:
                current_time = time.time()
                if current_time - last_tap < double_tap_threshold:
                    print("Double-tap detected!")
                last_tap = current_time
```

In this code:

- A double-tap is detected if the spacebar is pressed twice within a short period.
- The `time.time()` function is used to measure the elapsed time between presses.

## Summary

In this section, we explored how to handle user input and events in PyGame, covering keyboard input, mouse input, joystick controls, and creating interactive elements like clickable buttons. By mastering event handling, you can build responsive and interactive games that engage the player effectively.

In the next chapter, we will delve into designing and implementing a complete game, combining all the elements we have learned so far.

# Chapter 5: Building a Classic Arcade Game: Breakout

## Game Design Overview: Breakout

The game Breakout is a classic arcade game that was originally developed by Atari in the 1970s. It features a simple yet engaging gameplay loop where the player controls a paddle at the bottom of the screen, aiming to bounce a ball upwards to break a wall of bricks. As the ball collides with the bricks, they disappear, and the player earns points. The game ends when the player loses all their lives, which happens if the ball falls below the paddle.

### Key Game Elements

Breakout consists of several core game elements:

1. **Paddle**: The player controls a horizontal paddle at the bottom of the screen. It moves left and right, controlled by the arrow keys.
2. **Ball**: The ball bounces around the screen, interacting with the paddle, walls, and bricks.
3. **Bricks**: The wall of bricks is the main target. Each brick disappears when hit by the ball.
4. **Score and Lives**: The player earns points for each brick broken. The game tracks the player's score and the remaining lives.

### Game Mechanics

The gameplay mechanics are straightforward but require careful implementation:

- **Ball Physics**: The ball moves continuously, bouncing off the walls and the paddle. The angle of the bounce depends on the point of collision on the paddle.
- **Collision Detection**: Detecting collisions between the ball and other game elements (paddle, bricks, walls) is crucial for the game logic.
- **Game Over Condition**: The game ends when the ball falls below the paddle, and the player has no remaining lives.

### Tools and Framework

We will use **PyGame** to build Breakout due to its simplicity and effectiveness in handling 2D graphics and user input. The game will be developed on **Raspberry Pi**, making it a great project for showcasing the capabilities of both Python and the Raspberry Pi platform.

### Planning the Code Structure

Before we start coding, it is helpful to outline the structure of our game code:

1. **Initialize PyGame**: Set up the game window, define colors, and load assets.
2. **Create Game Objects**: Define classes for the paddle, ball, and bricks.
3. **Handle Game Loop**: Manage the main game loop, including updates and rendering.
4. **Implement Collision Logic**: Write the code for detecting and handling collisions.
5. **Display Score and Lives**: Add a simple HUD to show the player's current score and remaining lives.
6. **End Game Logic**: Define conditions for winning or losing the game.

## Setting Up the Game

Let's dive into the code. Start by setting up your development environment with Python and PyGame installed. You can install PyGame using:

```
pip install pygame
```

Now, create a new Python file called `breakout.py` and start by importing the necessary libraries:

```python
import pygame
import random
import sys
```

Next, initialize PyGame and define some global variables:

```python
# Initialize PyGame
pygame.init()

# Screen settings
SCREEN_WIDTH = 800
SCREEN_HEIGHT = 600
FPS = 60

# Colors
BLACK = (0, 0, 0)
WHITE = (255, 255, 255)
RED = (255, 0, 0)
GREEN = (0, 255, 0)
BLUE = (0, 0, 255)

# Paddle settings
```

```
PADDLE_WIDTH = 100
PADDLE_HEIGHT = 10
PADDLE_SPEED = 10

# Ball settings
BALL_RADIUS = 10
BALL_SPEED_X = 5
BALL_SPEED_Y = -5

# Brick settings
BRICK_ROWS = 5
BRICK_COLUMNS = 10
BRICK_WIDTH = 75
BRICK_HEIGHT = 20
BRICK_PADDING = 5

# Initialize the screen
screen = pygame.display.set_mode((SCREEN_WIDTH, SCREEN_HEIGHT))
pygame.display.set_caption("Breakout Game")
clock = pygame.time.Clock()
```

## Creating the Paddle Class

The paddle is controlled by the player, so we need to handle user input to move it left and right:

```
class Paddle:
    def __init__(self):
        self.rect = pygame.Rect(
            (SCREEN_WIDTH - PADDLE_WIDTH) // 2,
            SCREEN_HEIGHT - PADDLE_HEIGHT - 30,
            PADDLE_WIDTH,
            PADDLE_HEIGHT
        )

    def move(self, dx):
        self.rect.x += dx
        # Keep the paddle within the screen bounds
        if self.rect.left < 0:
            self.rect.left = 0
        if self.rect.right > SCREEN_WIDTH:
```

## Creating the Ball Class

The ball needs to move and bounce off the walls, paddle, and bricks:

```python
            self.rect.right = SCREEN_WIDTH

    def draw(self):
        pygame.draw.rect(screen, WHITE, self.rect)
```

## Creating the Ball Class

The ball needs to move and bounce off the walls, paddle, and bricks:

```python
class Ball:
    def __init__(self):
        self.rect = pygame.Rect(
            (SCREEN_WIDTH - BALL_RADIUS) // 2,
            SCREEN_HEIGHT // 2,
            BALL_RADIUS * 2,
            BALL_RADIUS * 2
        )
        self.speed_x = BALL_SPEED_X
        self.speed_y = BALL_SPEED_Y

    def move(self):
        self.rect.x += self.speed_x
        self.rect.y += self.speed_y

        # Bounce off the left and right walls
        if self.rect.left <= 0 or self.rect.right >= SCREEN_WIDTH:
            self.speed_x = -self.speed_x

        # Bounce off the top wall
        if self.rect.top <= 0:
            self.speed_y = -self.speed_y

    def draw(self):
        pygame.draw.ellipse(screen, RED, self.rect)
```

## Creating the Bricks

We will use a list to store multiple brick objects:

```python
class Brick:
```

```
    def __init__(self, x, y):
        self.rect = pygame.Rect(x, y, BRICK_WIDTH, BRICK_HEIGHT)

    def draw(self):
        pygame.draw.rect(screen, BLUE, self.rect)

# Create a grid of bricks
bricks = []
for row in range(BRICK_ROWS):
    for col in range(BRICK_COLUMNS):
        x = col * (BRICK_WIDTH + BRICK_PADDING)
        y = row * (BRICK_HEIGHT + BRICK_PADDING)
        bricks.append(Brick(x, y))
```

## Main Game Loop

The main game loop handles user input, updates game objects, and renders the screen:

```
def main():
    paddle = Paddle()
    ball = Ball()
    running = True

    while running:
        screen.fill(BLACK)

        # Event handling
        for event in pygame.event.get():
            if event.type == pygame.QUIT:
                pygame.quit()
                sys.exit()

        keys = pygame.key.get_pressed()
        if keys[pygame.K_LEFT]:
            paddle.move(-PADDLE_SPEED)
        if keys[pygame.K_RIGHT]:
            paddle.move(PADDLE_SPEED)

        # Move the ball
        ball.move()
```

```
        # Check for collisions
        if ball.rect.colliderect(paddle.rect):
            ball.speed_y = -ball.speed_y

        # Draw game elements
        paddle.draw()
        ball.draw()
        for brick in bricks:
            brick.draw()

        pygame.display.flip()
        clock.tick(FPS)

if __name__ == "__main__":
    main()
```

## Conclusion

This section covered the initial setup and the basic structure of the Breakout game. We implemented the paddle, ball, and brick classes, and created a main game loop to handle updates and rendering. In the next section, we will add more features such as collision detection with bricks, scoring, and game-over conditions.

With this foundation, you have a simple but functional version of Breakout that you can build upon and customize.

## Setting Up the Game Screen and Paddle

To begin building our Breakout game, we need to first set up a well-defined game screen and implement the paddle, which is the primary control element for the player. This section will guide you through designing the game window, defining the visual elements, and creating the player-controlled paddle.

### Defining the Game Window

The game window is the area where all the game action will take place. We will use PyGame's `display` module to create the screen. The typical resolution for a classic arcade game like Breakout is around **800x600 pixels**, which gives enough room for the paddle, ball, and bricks while keeping the game visually manageable.

Let's start by setting up the basic structure of our game and initializing the screen:

```
import pygame
```

```python
import sys

# Initialize PyGame
pygame.init()

# Screen dimensions
SCREEN_WIDTH = 800
SCREEN_HEIGHT = 600

# Colors
BLACK = (0, 0, 0)
WHITE = (255, 255, 255)

# Create the screen object
screen = pygame.display.set_mode((SCREEN_WIDTH, SCREEN_HEIGHT))
pygame.display.set_caption("Breakout Game")

# Main game loop
def main():
    running = True
    while running:
        for event in pygame.event.get():
            if event.type == pygame.QUIT:
                pygame.quit()
                sys.exit()

            # Fill the background with black
            screen.fill(BLACK)

            # Update the display
            pygame.display.flip()

# Start the game
if __name__ == "__main__":
    main()
```

In the code above, we initialize PyGame and create a game window. The main loop handles events, such as quitting the game, and continuously updates the screen. This forms the basic structure upon which we will build the rest of the game.

## Designing the Paddle

The paddle is the player's tool for controlling the ball. It moves horizontally at the bottom of the screen and bounces the ball back into play. We will implement the paddle as a PyGame `Rect` object because it provides convenient methods for collision detection and movement.

Let's define the `Paddle` class:

```
class Paddle:
    def __init__(self):
        # Define the paddle's size and initial position
        self.width = 100
        self.height = 10
        self.color = WHITE
        self.speed = 10
        self.rect = pygame.Rect(
            (SCREEN_WIDTH - self.width) // 2,
            SCREEN_HEIGHT - self.height - 30,
            self.width,
            self.height
        )

    def move(self, direction):
        # Move the paddle left or right based on user input
        if direction == "left":
            self.rect.x -= self.speed
        elif direction == "right":
            self.rect.x += self.speed

        # Prevent the paddle from going off the screen
        if self.rect.left < 0:
            self.rect.left = 0
        if self.rect.right > SCREEN_WIDTH:
            self.rect.right = SCREEN_WIDTH

    def draw(self, surface):
        pygame.draw.rect(surface, self.color, self.rect)
```

In this class, we:

- Define the paddle's size and initial position.
- Implement movement controls with boundary checks to prevent the paddle from going off-screen.
- Use the `draw()` method to render the paddle on the game surface.

## Handling User Input

The player will control the paddle using the arrow keys. We can capture keyboard input in our main game loop and update the paddle's position accordingly.

Add the following input handling to the main game loop:

```python
def main():
    paddle = Paddle()
    running = True

    while running:
        for event in pygame.event.get():
            if event.type == pygame.QUIT:
                pygame.quit()
                sys.exit()

        # Get the state of all keys
        keys = pygame.key.get_pressed()
        if keys[pygame.K_LEFT]:
            paddle.move("left")
        if keys[pygame.K_RIGHT]:
            paddle.move("right")

        # Fill the background
        screen.fill(BLACK)

        # Draw the paddle
        paddle.draw(screen)

        # Update the display
        pygame.display.flip()
```

This code snippet captures user input using `pygame.key.get_pressed()`, which returns the current state of all keyboard keys. If the left or right arrow keys are pressed, the paddle's position is updated accordingly.

## Fine-Tuning the Paddle Movement

We can make the game feel more responsive by adjusting the paddle's speed based on the frame rate. Instead of moving the paddle by a fixed number of pixels, we can use a speed factor that considers the time elapsed between frames. This will ensure consistent movement regardless of the frame rate.

```python
class Paddle:
    def __init__(self):
        self.width = 100
        self.height = 10
        self.color = WHITE
        self.speed = 300  # Pixels per second
        self.rect = pygame.Rect(
            (SCREEN_WIDTH - self.width) // 2,
            SCREEN_HEIGHT - self.height - 30,
            self.width,
            self.height
        )

    def move(self, direction, dt):
        if direction == "left":
            self.rect.x -= self.speed * dt
        elif direction == "right":
            self.rect.x += self.speed * dt

        if self.rect.left < 0:
            self.rect.left = 0
        if self.rect.right > SCREEN_WIDTH:
            self.rect.right = SCREEN_WIDTH
```

In this updated version of the `Paddle` class, the `move()` method now takes `dt` (delta time) as an argument. This represents the time elapsed since the last frame, which allows us to adjust the paddle's movement speed dynamically.

## Implementing Frame Rate Control

To maintain smooth gameplay, we need to control the frame rate using PyGame's `Clock` object. This will also allow us to pass the `dt` value to the paddle for consistent movement.

```python
def main():
    paddle = Paddle()
    clock = pygame.time.Clock()
    running = True
```

# Chapter 5: Building a Classic Arcade Game: Breakout

```
while running:
    dt = clock.tick(60) / 1000  # Get delta time in seconds

    for event in pygame.event.get():
        if event.type == pygame.QUIT:
            pygame.quit()
            sys.exit()

    keys = pygame.key.get_pressed()
    if keys[pygame.K_LEFT]:
        paddle.move("left", dt)
    if keys[pygame.K_RIGHT]:
        paddle.move("right", dt)

    screen.fill(BLACK)
    paddle.draw(screen)
    pygame.display.flip()
```

With `clock.tick(60)`, we limit the frame rate to 60 FPS. This keeps the game running smoothly and provides a consistent `dt` value for time-based calculations.

## Testing the Paddle

Run the current code to test the paddle movement. You should see a responsive paddle that moves left and right across the bottom of the screen. Try adjusting the paddle's speed and size to fit your preferences.

## Customizing the Paddle

To make the game more engaging, consider experimenting with the paddle's properties:

1. **Size**: Change the width of the paddle to make the game easier or more challenging.
2. **Speed**: Increase the speed for a faster-paced game.
3. **Color**: Choose different colors for a visually distinct paddle.

Here is an example of customizing the paddle:

```
paddle = Paddle()
paddle.width = 150          # Wider paddle
paddle.color = (0, 255, 0)  # Green color
```

## Conclusion

In this section, we set up the game screen and implemented a responsive paddle that the player can control using keyboard input. The paddle is a crucial part of the Breakout game, and ensuring smooth movement is key to providing a good user experience.

In the next section, we will move on to creating the ball and implementing its movement, including collision detection with the paddle and the screen boundaries. This will lay the foundation for the core gameplay mechanics of Breakout.

# Adding Bricks and Collision Detection

In this section, we will build the main playing field by adding a wall of bricks, which are the primary targets in Breakout. The ball will collide with these bricks, removing them from the screen and increasing the player's score. We will also implement collision detection to ensure that the ball interacts properly with the bricks, paddle, and screen boundaries.

### Designing the Brick Structure

The bricks in Breakout are arranged in a grid pattern at the top of the screen. We will create a `Brick` class to represent each brick and use a list to store all the bricks. This list will be dynamically generated based on the number of rows and columns we want in the game.

Let's define some constants for the brick layout:

```
# Brick settings
BRICK_ROWS = 5
BRICK_COLUMNS = 10
BRICK_WIDTH = 75
BRICK_HEIGHT = 20
BRICK_PADDING = 5
BRICK_OFFSET_TOP = 50
BRICK_OFFSET_LEFT = 35
```

These constants define the number of rows and columns of bricks, their dimensions, and padding between them. The `BRICK_OFFSET_TOP` and `BRICK_OFFSET_LEFT` determine the starting position of the brick wall.

### Creating the Brick Class

Now, let's define the `Brick` class. Each brick will be a rectangle with a specific position and color.

```
class Brick:
    def __init__(self, x, y):
```

```
        self.rect = pygame.Rect(x, y, BRICK_WIDTH, BRICK_HEIGHT)
        self.color = (random.randint(50, 255), random.randint(50,
255), random.randint(50, 255))
        self.active = True

    def draw(self, surface):
        if self.active:
            pygame.draw.rect(surface, self.color, self.rect)

    def hit(self):
        self.active = False
```

In the `Brick` class:

- `rect`: Represents the brick's position and size.
- `color`: Each brick is given a random color for visual variety.
- `active`: Tracks whether the brick is still present on the screen.
- `hit()`: Marks the brick as inactive when the ball collides with it.

## Generating the Brick Wall

We will create a grid of bricks using a nested loop and store them in a list called `bricks`.

```
bricks = []

def create_bricks():
    for row in range(BRICK_ROWS):
        for col in range(BRICK_COLUMNS):
            x = BRICK_OFFSET_LEFT + col * (BRICK_WIDTH + BRICK_PADDING)
            y = BRICK_OFFSET_TOP + row * (BRICK_HEIGHT + BRICK_PADDING)
            bricks.append(Brick(x, y))
```

The `create_bricks()` function initializes the brick grid by calculating the position of each brick based on its row and column index.

## Drawing the Bricks

To render the bricks on the screen, we iterate through the list of bricks and call the `draw()` method for each active brick.

Add the following code to your main game loop:

```
for brick in bricks:
    brick.draw(screen)
```

This simple loop ensures that all bricks are drawn on the screen, creating the classic Breakout layout.

## Implementing Ball Movement

The ball is a critical game element that interacts with the paddle, bricks, and screen boundaries. Let's define a `Ball` class that handles its movement and collision detection.

```
class Ball:
    def __init__(self):
        self.rect = pygame.Rect(
            (SCREEN_WIDTH - BALL_RADIUS) // 2,
            SCREEN_HEIGHT // 2,
            BALL_RADIUS * 2,
            BALL_RADIUS * 2
        )
        self.color = (255, 255, 255)
        self.speed_x = BALL_SPEED_X
        self.speed_y = BALL_SPEED_Y

    def move(self):
        self.rect.x += self.speed_x
        self.rect.y += self.speed_y

        # Bounce off the left and right walls
        if self.rect.left <= 0 or self.rect.right >= SCREEN_WIDTH:
            self.speed_x = -self.speed_x

        # Bounce off the top wall
        if self.rect.top <= 0:
            self.speed_y = -self.speed_y

    def draw(self, surface):
        pygame.draw.ellipse(surface, self.color, self.rect)
```

The `Ball` class includes basic movement and boundary collision detection. The ball bounces off the left, right, and top edges of the screen.

## Detecting Collisions with Bricks

To make the game interactive, we need to detect when the ball collides with a brick. We can use PyGame's built-in `colliderect()` method to check for collisions between the ball and each brick.

Add the following code to the main game loop to handle brick collisions:

```python
for brick in bricks:
    if brick.active and ball.rect.colliderect(brick.rect):
        ball.speed_y = -ball.speed_y
        brick.hit()
        score += 10
```

In this code snippet:

- We check if the brick is active and if the ball's rectangle collides with the brick's rectangle.
- If a collision is detected, the ball's vertical speed is reversed (simulating a bounce).
- The brick is marked as inactive, and the player's score is increased.

## Implementing a Scoring System

We will use a simple variable to keep track of the player's score. Add the following line to initialize the score at the beginning of your game:

```python
score = 0
```

To display the score on the screen, we can use PyGame's font rendering capabilities:

```python
font = pygame.font.Font(None, 36)

def draw_score():
    score_text = font.render(f"Score: {score}", True, WHITE)
    screen.blit(score_text, (10, 10))
```

Call `draw_score()` in the main game loop to render the current score at the top-left corner of the screen:

```
draw_score()
```

## Handling Game Over

The game ends when the ball falls below the paddle. We can implement a simple game-over condition by checking the ball's position:

```
if ball.rect.top > SCREEN_HEIGHT:
    running = False
```

When the ball moves beyond the bottom of the screen, we set `running` to `False`, ending the game loop. You can extend this logic to include multiple lives or a restart option.

## Enhancing Collision Detection

To improve the realism of the ball's bounce, we can adjust the bounce angle based on the collision point. For example, if the ball hits the edge of the paddle, it should bounce at a steeper angle. We can modify the ball's speed based on the point of collision:

```
if ball.rect.colliderect(paddle.rect):
    offset = (ball.rect.centerx - paddle.rect.centerx) / (paddle.width // 2)
    ball.speed_x = BALL_SPEED_X * offset
    ball.speed_y = -abs(ball.speed_y)
```

This code adjusts the horizontal speed (`speed_x`) of the ball based on the distance from the center of the paddle. The ball will bounce off at different angles depending on where it hits the paddle.

## Testing and Debugging

Run the game and test the interactions between the ball and the bricks. If you notice any issues with collision detection, try adjusting the speed or dimensions of the ball. Debugging tips:

1. **Slow Down the Ball**: Decrease `BALL_SPEED_X` and `BALL_SPEED_Y` to observe collisions in slow motion.
2. **Print Statements**: Add print statements inside the collision detection logic to check if the collisions are being detected correctly.
3. **Enable Debug Mode**: Render additional information like the ball's position or speed to help diagnose issues.

## Conclusion

In this section, we created a grid of bricks, implemented the ball's movement, and added collision detection. We also introduced a scoring system to provide feedback to the player. With these elements in place, we have a fully functional game loop where the player can bounce the ball off the paddle and break bricks.

In the next section, we will add more advanced features like power-ups, animations, and a game-over screen to enhance the gameplay experience.

# Scoring System and Game Over Conditions

In this section, we will implement a scoring system to reward the player for breaking bricks and add game-over conditions to define when the game ends. A well-designed scoring system increases player engagement, while clear game-over conditions help create a satisfying gameplay loop. We will also introduce basic UI elements to display the score, lives, and game-over messages.

## Designing the Scoring System

In Breakout, the player earns points for each brick they destroy. We can define a simple scoring system where:

- Each brick broken awards **10 points**.
- Special bricks (if we choose to add them later) can award **20 points** or more.

To track the score, we need to declare a global `score` variable at the start of our program:

```
score = 0
```

We can then update the score whenever a brick is hit:

```
if brick.active and ball.rect.colliderect(brick.rect):
    ball.speed_y = -ball.speed_y
    brick.hit()
    score += 10
```

## Displaying the Score on the Screen

To provide real-time feedback to the player, we will display the score in the top-left corner of the game window. PyGame offers a straightforward way to render text using the Font module.

```
# Initialize the font
pygame.font.init()
font = pygame.font.Font(None, 36)

def draw_score():
    score_text = font.render(f"Score: {score}", True, (255, 255, 255))
    screen.blit(score_text, (10, 10))
```

The `draw_score()` function creates a text surface displaying the current score and blits it onto the screen at coordinates `(10, 10)`.

## Implementing Lives

To make the game more challenging and engaging, we will introduce a lives system. The player will start with **3 lives**, and they lose a life each time the ball falls below the paddle. When all lives are lost, the game ends.

Define a `lives` variable at the start of your program:

```
lives = 3
```

Whenever the ball falls below the screen, we decrement the number of lives:

```
if ball.rect.top > SCREEN_HEIGHT:
    lives -= 1
    reset_ball()
```

In the `reset_ball()` function, we will reposition the ball to its starting position and reset its speed:

```
def reset_ball():
    ball.rect.x = (SCREEN_WIDTH - BALL_RADIUS) // 2
    ball.rect.y = SCREEN_HEIGHT // 2
    ball.speed_x = BALL_SPEED_X
    ball.speed_y = BALL_SPEED_Y
```

This ensures that the game continues smoothly after losing a life.

## Displaying Lives

We can display the remaining lives in the top-right corner of the screen, similar to the score display:

```python
def draw_lives():
    lives_text = font.render(f"Lives: {lives}", True, (255, 255, 255))
    screen.blit(lives_text, (SCREEN_WIDTH - 100, 10))
```

Call `draw_lives()` in the main game loop to render the current number of lives.

## Handling Game Over

When the player runs out of lives, the game should end with a clear "Game Over" message. We can implement a simple game-over condition by checking the number of lives left:

```python
if lives <= 0:
    game_over()
```

The `game_over()` function will display a message and wait for the player to quit or restart:

```python
def game_over():
    screen.fill((0, 0, 0))
    game_over_text = font.render("Game Over", True, (255, 0, 0))
    restart_text = font.render("Press R to Restart or Q to Quit", True, (255, 255, 255))

    screen.blit(game_over_text, ((SCREEN_WIDTH - game_over_text.get_width()) // 2, SCREEN_HEIGHT // 2 - 50))
    screen.blit(restart_text, ((SCREEN_WIDTH - restart_text.get_width()) // 2, SCREEN_HEIGHT // 2 + 10))

    pygame.display.flip()

    waiting = True
    while waiting:
        for event in pygame.event.get():
            if event.type == pygame.QUIT:
                pygame.quit()
```

```
                sys.exit()
            elif event.type == pygame.KEYDOWN:
                if event.key == pygame.K_r:
                    restart_game()
                elif event.key == pygame.K_q:
                    pygame.quit()
                    sys.exit()
```

## Restarting the Game

The player should have the option to restart the game without closing the application. We can implement a simple `restart_game()` function to reset the game state:

```
def restart_game():
    global score, lives, bricks
    score = 0
    lives = 3
    create_bricks()
    reset_ball()
```

In this function, we reset the `score` and `lives` variables, recreate the bricks, and reposition the ball.

## Adding a High Score System

To add a sense of progression, we can implement a high score system that records the player's best score. This high score can be displayed during gameplay and saved between sessions using a text file.

Initialize the `high_score` variable at the start of the program:

```
try:
    with open("high_score.txt", "r") as file:
        high_score = int(file.read())
except FileNotFoundError:
    high_score = 0
```

Update the high score whenever the player achieves a new best score:

```python
if score > high_score:
    high_score = score
    with open("high_score.txt", "w") as file:
        file.write(str(high_score))
```

Display the high score on the screen:

```python
def draw_high_score():
    high_score_text = font.render(f"High Score: {high_score}", True, (255, 255, 0))
    screen.blit(high_score_text, (SCREEN_WIDTH // 2 - 100, 10))
```

Call `draw_high_score()` in the main game loop.

## Adding Game Over Sound Effects

To enhance the game experience, we can play a sound effect when the game ends. Load the sound effect at the beginning of your program:

```python
game_over_sound = pygame.mixer.Sound("game_over.wav")
```

Play the sound effect in the `game_over()` function:

```python
game_over_sound.play()
```

Ensure that the sound file is in the same directory as your script, or provide the correct path.

## Enhancing the Game Over Screen

To make the game-over screen more engaging, we can add an animation or visual effect. For example, we can fade the screen to black gradually:

```python
def fade_out():
    fade_surface = pygame.Surface((SCREEN_WIDTH, SCREEN_HEIGHT))
    fade_surface.fill((0, 0, 0))

    for alpha in range(0, 300, 5):
        fade_surface.set_alpha(alpha)
```

```
screen.blit(fade_surface, (0, 0))
pygame.display.flip()
pygame.time.delay(30)
```

Call `fade_out()` before displaying the game-over message.

## Testing the Scoring and Game Over System

To test your implementation, play the game and observe the following:

1. **Score Updates**: Ensure that the score increases correctly when bricks are hit.
2. **Lives Decrement**: Check that the player loses a life when the ball falls below the paddle.
3. **Game Over Behavior**: Verify that the game ends when all lives are lost and that the game-over screen displays correctly.
4. **High Score Persistence**: Restart the game and confirm that the high score is saved and displayed.

## Conclusion

In this section, we implemented a scoring system, lives counter, and game-over conditions. We also added a high score feature for increased player motivation and introduced basic UI elements for a more polished game experience. These features complete the core gameplay loop of Breakout, making it a fun and engaging game.

In the next chapter, we will explore ways to enhance the game further by adding power-ups, more complex animations, and visual effects to create a dynamic and visually appealing game.

# Chapter 6: Implementing Game Physics and Enhancements

## Understanding Game Physics and Mechanics

Game physics is a crucial aspect of any game that aims to provide a realistic experience. It deals with the implementation of movement, collision detection, gravity, and other physical behaviors in a virtual environment. In this section, we will explore how to introduce physics into our game using PyGame and Python. We will also discuss important physics concepts like velocity, acceleration, friction, and collision response. This knowledge will help you make your game feel more dynamic and engaging.

### Physics Basics in Game Development

Before diving into the implementation, let's cover some fundamental physics concepts:

- **Velocity**: This is the rate of change of an object's position. In games, velocity is usually represented as a vector with x and y components, determining movement along horizontal and vertical axes.
- **Acceleration**: This is the rate of change of velocity. It can be used to simulate gravity, speed boosts, or other gradual changes in speed.
- **Gravity**: Gravity is a force that pulls objects towards the ground. In most 2D games, gravity affects only the vertical movement (y-axis).
- **Friction**: Friction is a force that opposes the motion of an object. It can be used to slow down objects gradually.
- **Collision Detection**: This is the process of detecting when two objects in a game intersect or come into contact.
- **Collision Response**: After a collision is detected, the response dictates how the objects behave. For example, a ball might bounce off a wall, or a player might stop when hitting a barrier.

### Implementing Basic Physics in PyGame

Let's start by implementing a simple physics engine in PyGame that includes velocity, gravity, and collision detection. We will use a basic game loop and a simple object (like a ball) to demonstrate these concepts.

```
import pygame
import sys

# Initialize PyGame
pygame.init()
```

```python
# Constants
WIDTH, HEIGHT = 800, 600
BALL_RADIUS = 20
GRAVITY = 0.5
FRICTION = 0.99
BALL_COLOR = (0, 0, 255)
BG_COLOR = (255, 255, 255)

# Set up the display
screen = pygame.display.set_mode((WIDTH, HEIGHT))
pygame.display.set_caption("Physics Simulation")

# Ball properties
ball_pos = [WIDTH // 2, HEIGHT // 2]
ball_velocity = [0, 0]

clock = pygame.time.Clock()

while True:
    for event in pygame.event.get():
        if event.type == pygame.QUIT:
            pygame.quit()
            sys.exit()

    # Apply gravity
    ball_velocity[1] += GRAVITY

    # Update ball position
    ball_pos[0] += ball_velocity[0]
    ball_pos[1] += ball_velocity[1]

    # Collision detection with the screen boundaries
    if ball_pos[1] + BALL_RADIUS > HEIGHT:
        ball_pos[1] = HEIGHT - BALL_RADIUS
        ball_velocity[1] = -ball_velocity[1] * FRICTION

    if ball_pos[0] - BALL_RADIUS < 0 or ball_pos[0] + BALL_RADIUS > WIDTH:
        ball_velocity[0] = -ball_velocity[0] * FRICTION
```

```python
    # Clear the screen
    screen.fill(BG_COLOR)

    # Draw the ball
    pygame.draw.circle(screen, BALL_COLOR, (int(ball_pos[0]), int(ball_pos[1])), BALL_RADIUS)

    # Update the display
    pygame.display.flip()
    clock.tick(60)
```

## Explanation of the Code

- **Gravity**: We add a constant value to the vertical velocity (`ball_velocity[1]`) on each frame to simulate gravity.
- **Velocity Update**: The ball's position is updated based on its velocity.
- **Collision Detection**: We check if the ball hits the ground (bottom of the screen). If it does, we reverse its vertical velocity (making it bounce).
- **Friction**: We apply a friction factor to reduce the velocity after a bounce, making the ball lose energy gradually.

## Adding User Input for Movement

Now, let's add user input to control the ball's movement using arrow keys. This will introduce a way to modify the ball's velocity directly.

```python
for event in pygame.event.get():
    if event.type == pygame.QUIT:
        pygame.quit()
        sys.exit()

# Handle user input
keys = pygame.key.get_pressed()
if keys[pygame.K_LEFT]:
    ball_velocity[0] -= 0.5
if keys[pygame.K_RIGHT]:
    ball_velocity[0] += 0.5
if keys[pygame.K_UP]:
    ball_velocity[1] -= 0.5

# Apply gravity
ball_velocity[1] += GRAVITY
```

## Enhancing Physics with Acceleration and Drag

To make the game physics more realistic, we can introduce acceleration and drag. Drag is a force that slows down an object over time, simulating air resistance.

```
# Constants for drag and acceleration
ACCELERATION = 0.2
DRAG = 0.98

# Apply drag to velocity
ball_velocity[0] *= DRAG
ball_velocity[1] *= DRAG

# User input for acceleration
if keys[pygame.K_LEFT]:
    ball_velocity[0] -= ACCELERATION
if keys[pygame.K_RIGHT]:
    ball_velocity[0] += ACCELERATION
```

## Introducing Advanced Collision Response

In most games, simple collision response (like reversing velocity) is not enough. We can implement more complex physics using restitution and impulse. Restitution is a measure of how "bouncy" an object is.

```
RESTITUTION = 0.8  # Bounciness factor

if ball_pos[1] + BALL_RADIUS > HEIGHT:
    ball_pos[1] = HEIGHT - BALL_RADIUS
    ball_velocity[1] = -ball_velocity[1] * RESTITUTION

if ball_pos[0] - BALL_RADIUS < 0 or ball_pos[0] + BALL_RADIUS > WIDTH:
    ball_velocity[0] = -ball_velocity[0] * RESTITUTION
```

## Implementing Complex Physics: Simulating a Platform

Let's add a simple platform to the game and implement collision detection with the platform. This will introduce basic platform mechanics.

```python
# Platform properties
platform_rect = pygame.Rect(300, 500, 200, 20)

# Draw the platform
pygame.draw.rect(screen, (0, 128, 0), platform_rect)

# Collision detection with the platform
if platform_rect.collidepoint(ball_pos[0], ball_pos[1] +
BALL_RADIUS):
    ball_pos[1] = platform_rect.top - BALL_RADIUS
    ball_velocity[1] = -ball_velocity[1] * RESTITUTION
```

## Tips for Improving Game Physics

- **Adjust Constants**: Tweaking gravity, friction, drag, and restitution can significantly change the feel of your game. Experiment with these values.
- **Use Vectors**: PyGame has a `Vector2` class that makes it easier to handle 2D movement and physics calculations.
- **Optimize Collision Detection**: For games with many objects, use spatial partitioning techniques like grids or quadtrees to improve performance.

By implementing these physics principles and techniques, you can enhance the realism and enjoyment of your game. In the next section, we'll explore how to add power-ups and further refine the gameplay experience.

# Adding Physics to the Ball Movement

Physics plays a central role in creating an immersive gaming experience. In this section, we will expand on the previous concepts and dive deeper into implementing physics-based ball movement. We will incorporate velocity, acceleration, drag, gravity, and collision response to make the ball behave in a realistic manner.

## Overview of Enhanced Ball Physics

We want our ball to feel dynamic, with responsive movement influenced by forces and the environment. To achieve this, we will:

1. **Define the physics properties** for the ball, such as mass, velocity, acceleration, drag, and gravity.
2. **Implement a physics engine** that updates the ball's position based on these properties.
3. **Handle collisions and responses** for realistic bouncing and rolling effects.
4. **Introduce damping** to simulate energy loss due to air resistance or friction.

## Setting Up the Physics Engine

We'll start by creating a Python class for our ball, encapsulating its properties and physics behaviors. This approach makes the code modular and easier to maintain.

```python
import pygame
import sys
import math

# Initialize PyGame
pygame.init()

# Constants
WIDTH, HEIGHT = 800, 600
BALL_RADIUS = 15
BALL_COLOR = (0, 0, 255)
BG_COLOR = (255, 255, 255)
GRAVITY = 9.8
DRAG_COEFFICIENT = 0.01
DAMPING = 0.99
TIME_STEP = 0.016  # Assuming 60 FPS

# Set up the display
screen = pygame.display.set_mode((WIDTH, HEIGHT))
pygame.display.set_caption("Enhanced Ball Physics")

class Ball:
    def __init__(self, x, y, mass=1.0):
        self.pos = pygame.Vector2(x, y)
        self.velocity = pygame.Vector2(0, 0)
        self.acceleration = pygame.Vector2(0, 0)
        self.mass = mass

    def apply_force(self, force):
        # Newton's Second Law: F = m * a -> a = F / m
        self.acceleration += force / self.mass

    def update(self):
        # Apply gravity
        gravity_force = pygame.Vector2(0, GRAVITY * self.mass)
        self.apply_force(gravity_force)
```

```python
        # Apply drag (air resistance)
        drag = self.velocity * -DRAG_COEFFICIENT
        self.apply_force(drag)

        # Update velocity and position
        self.velocity += self.acceleration * TIME_STEP
        self.pos += self.velocity * TIME_STEP

        # Reset acceleration
        self.acceleration = pygame.Vector2(0, 0)

        # Apply damping to simulate energy loss
        self.velocity *= DAMPING

    def draw(self, surface):
        pygame.draw.circle(surface, BALL_COLOR, (int(self.pos.x), int(self.pos.y)), BALL_RADIUS)

ball = Ball(WIDTH // 2, HEIGHT // 2)
clock = pygame.time.Clock()
```

## Understanding the Ball Class

- **Position, Velocity, and Acceleration**: These are represented using PyGame's Vector2 class, which simplifies 2D vector calculations.
- **apply_force() Method**: This method adds a force to the ball, updating its acceleration based on Newton's second law (F = m * a).
- **update() Method**: This updates the ball's velocity and position each frame. It also applies gravity, drag, and damping.

## Handling Collisions with the Ground

We need to ensure that the ball interacts with the ground realistically, bouncing back when it hits the bottom of the screen. Let's extend the update() method to handle this.

```python
def check_collision(ball):
    # Collision with the ground
    if ball.pos.y + BALL_RADIUS > HEIGHT:
        ball.pos.y = HEIGHT - BALL_RADIUS
        ball.velocity.y = -ball.velocity.y  # Reverse velocity
```

```
            ball.velocity *= DAMPING  # Apply damping on collision

while True:
    for event in pygame.event.get():
        if event.type == pygame.QUIT:
            pygame.quit()
            sys.exit()

    # Update ball physics
    ball.update()
    check_collision(ball)

    # Clear the screen
    screen.fill(BG_COLOR)

    # Draw the ball
    ball.draw(screen)

    # Update the display
    pygame.display.flip()
    clock.tick(60)
```

## Improving Collision Response with Restitution

To make the ball bounce more naturally, we introduce a **restitution coefficient**, which determines how bouncy the ball is. A higher restitution results in a more elastic collision.

```
RESTITUTION = 0.8  # Bounciness factor

def check_collision(ball):
    if ball.pos.y + BALL_RADIUS > HEIGHT:
        ball.pos.y = HEIGHT - BALL_RADIUS
        ball.velocity.y = -ball.velocity.y * RESTITUTION
        ball.velocity *= DAMPING
```

## Simulating Rolling Friction

In addition to damping, we can simulate **rolling friction** when the ball moves horizontally. Rolling friction reduces the ball's horizontal velocity over time, making it come to a stop naturally.

# Chapter 6: Implementing Game Physics and Enhancements

```python
ROLLING_FRICTION = 0.02

def apply_rolling_friction(ball):
    if abs(ball.velocity.x) > 0.1:  # Only apply if there is noticeable movement
        friction_force = pygame.Vector2(-ball.velocity.x, 0) * ROLLING_FRICTION
        ball.apply_force(friction_force)

# Include in the game loop
apply_rolling_friction(ball)
```

## Adding User Control and Interaction

Let's add user controls to allow the player to apply forces to the ball using the arrow keys.

```python
for event in pygame.event.get():
    if event.type == pygame.QUIT:
        pygame.quit()
        sys.exit()

# User input for controlling the ball
keys = pygame.key.get_pressed()
if keys[pygame.K_LEFT]:
    ball.apply_force(pygame.Vector2(-50, 0))
if keys[pygame.K_RIGHT]:
    ball.apply_force(pygame.Vector2(50, 0))
if keys[pygame.K_UP]:
    ball.apply_force(pygame.Vector2(0, -150))
```

## Advanced Physics: Simulating Angular Motion

To take our physics simulation a step further, we can simulate angular motion. This will make the ball spin when it rolls or bounces.

```python
class Ball:
    def __init__(self, x, y, mass=1.0):
        self.pos = pygame.Vector2(x, y)
        self.velocity = pygame.Vector2(0, 0)
```

```
        self.acceleration = pygame.Vector2(0, 0)
        self.mass = mass
        self.angular_velocity = 0
        self.angle = 0

    def update(self):
        # Apply angular motion
        self.angle += self.angular_velocity * TIME_STEP
        self.velocity *= DAMPING

    def draw(self, surface):
        # Draw the ball with rotation
        rotated_ball = pygame.transform.rotate(ball_surface, self.angle)
        rect = rotated_ball.get_rect(center=(int(self.pos.x), int(self.pos.y)))
        surface.blit(rotated_ball, rect)
```

## Final Thoughts on Enhanced Ball Physics

By incorporating forces, collision responses, and angular motion, we have created a physics-based ball movement system that feels realistic and responsive. You can experiment with different values for gravity, drag, damping, and restitution to achieve various effects. Physics simulations are powerful tools that, when used effectively, can greatly enhance the user experience and make your game more engaging.

In the next section, we will explore how to add power-ups to enhance the gameplay experience further, utilizing the physics engine we have built here.

# Enhancing Gameplay with Power-Ups

Power-ups are a popular game mechanic used to enhance the gameplay experience. They provide temporary or permanent bonuses, encouraging players to engage more actively and strategize their actions. In this section, we will discuss how to implement various types of power-ups in our game and integrate them seamlessly with the physics engine we developed earlier. We will cover different types of power-ups, their effects, and best practices for creating a balanced gameplay experience.

### Types of Power-Ups

Power-ups can be broadly categorized into the following types:

1. **Speed Boosts**: Increases the player's speed for a limited time.
2. **Invincibility**: Makes the player immune to collisions or damage.

3. **Gravity Reduction**: Temporarily reduces the effect of gravity, allowing the player to jump higher.
4. **Size Alteration**: Changes the size of the ball, affecting its movement and collision properties.
5. **Score Multipliers**: Increases the points scored during a specific time period.

Each power-up type offers unique advantages, and the key is to balance these effects so that the game remains challenging yet rewarding.

## Designing the Power-Up System

To implement power-ups, we need a flexible system that can manage different power-up types, durations, and effects. We will use an object-oriented approach by creating a `PowerUp` class and integrating it into the game loop.

```python
import random

class PowerUp:
    def __init__(self, x, y, power_type, duration=5):
        self.pos = pygame.Vector2(x, y)
        self.power_type = power_type
        self.duration = duration
        self.active = False
        self.timer = 0
        self.color = (255, 0, 0) if power_type == "speed" else (0, 255, 0)

    def activate(self, ball):
        self.active = True
        self.timer = self.duration

        if self.power_type == "speed":
            ball.velocity *= 1.5
        elif self.power_type == "invincibility":
            ball.invincible = True
        elif self.power_type == "gravity":
            ball.gravity_effect *= 0.5
        elif self.power_type == "size":
            ball.radius *= 1.5
        elif self.power_type == "multiplier":
            ball.score_multiplier = 2

    def deactivate(self, ball):
```

```
            self.active = False

            if self.power_type == "speed":
                ball.velocity /= 1.5
            elif self.power_type == "invincibility":
                ball.invincible = False
            elif self.power_type == "gravity":
                ball.gravity_effect = 1.0
            elif self.power_type == "size":
                ball.radius /= 1.5
            elif self.power_type == "multiplier":
                ball.score_multiplier = 1

    def update(self, ball):
        if self.active:
            self.timer -= 1
            if self.timer <= 0:
                self.deactivate(ball)

    def draw(self, surface):
        pygame.draw.circle(surface, self.color, (int(self.pos.x), int(self.pos.y)), 10)
```

## Integrating Power-Ups into the Game Loop

To include power-ups in our game, we need to generate them randomly on the screen and check for collisions with the ball. When a collision is detected, the power-up should activate and provide its effect.

```
power_ups = []
POWER_UP_TYPES = ["speed", "invincibility", "gravity", "size", "multiplier"]

def spawn_power_up():
    x = random.randint(50, WIDTH - 50)
    y = random.randint(50, HEIGHT - 50)
    power_type = random.choice(POWER_UP_TYPES)
    power_up = PowerUp(x, y, power_type)
    power_ups.append(power_up)

def check_power_up_collision(ball):
```

```
for power_up in power_ups:
    if ball.pos.distance_to(power_up.pos) < ball.radius + 10:
        power_up.activate(ball)
        power_ups.remove(power_up)
        break
```

## Adding Visual Feedback

Visual feedback is crucial for informing the player about active power-ups. We can use colors, text, or particle effects to indicate when a power-up is in effect.

```
font = pygame.font.Font(None, 36)

def draw_active_power_up(ball, surface):
    if ball.invincible:
        text = font.render("Invincibility Active", True, (255, 255, 0))
        surface.blit(text, (10, 10))
    elif ball.gravity_effect < 1.0:
        text = font.render("Low Gravity Active", True, (0, 255, 255))
        surface.blit(text, (10, 10))
    elif ball.score_multiplier > 1:
        text = font.render("Score Multiplier Active", True, (255, 0, 255))
        surface.blit(text, (10, 10))
```

## Managing Power-Up Duration

Each power-up effect should only last for a limited duration. We manage this using a timer that decreases each frame. When the timer reaches zero, the effect is deactivated.

```
def update_power_ups(ball):
    for power_up in power_ups:
        power_up.update(ball)

    # Remove expired power-ups from the active list
    power_ups[:] = [p for p in power_ups if p.active]
```

## Balancing Power-Ups

Balancing is an essential part of designing power-ups. Here are some tips:

1. **Limit Frequency**: Don't spawn too many power-ups; this can make the game too easy.
2. **Adjust Duration**: The duration of the effects should be short enough to provide a temporary advantage but not long enough to break the game.
3. **Combine Effects Carefully**: Be cautious when allowing multiple power-ups to be active at once, as certain combinations might make the player overpowered.
4. **Provide Clear Indications**: Make sure the player can easily recognize when a power-up is active and what effect it has.

## Example Game Loop with Power-Ups

```
while True:
    for event in pygame.event.get():
        if event.type == pygame.QUIT:
            pygame.quit()
            sys.exit()

    # Spawn a power-up periodically
    if random.random() < 0.01:
        spawn_power_up()

    # Update ball physics and check for collisions
    ball.update()
    check_power_up_collision(ball)
    update_power_ups(ball)

    # Clear the screen
    screen.fill(BG_COLOR)

    # Draw ball and power-ups
    ball.draw(screen)
    for power_up in power_ups:
        power_up.draw(screen)

    # Draw active power-up status
    draw_active_power_up(ball, screen)

    # Update the display
    pygame.display.flip()
```

```
clock.tick(60)
```

## Testing and Debugging Power-Ups

Testing power-ups can be challenging because they are often triggered randomly. Here are some strategies for effective testing:

1. **Manual Activation**: Allow the player to activate specific power-ups using keyboard shortcuts for testing.
2. **Debug Logging**: Print messages to the console when power-ups are activated and deactivated.
3. **Adjust Parameters**: Temporarily increase the spawn rate and duration of power-ups during testing.

```
# Debug key bindings for testing
if keys[pygame.K_1]:
    power_up = PowerUp(ball.pos.x, ball.pos.y, "speed")
    power_up.activate(ball)
if keys[pygame.K_2]:
    power_up = PowerUp(ball.pos.x, ball.pos.y, "invincibility")
    power_up.activate(ball)
```

## Conclusion

Incorporating power-ups into your game can significantly enhance the player's experience by adding excitement and variety. By using a modular design for the `PowerUp` class and carefully integrating it into the game loop, you can easily expand this system to include new types of power-ups and effects. In the next section, we will discuss techniques for improving the user experience with smooth animations and visual effects, building on the dynamic gameplay introduced here.

# Improving User Experience with Smooth Animations

Creating a polished user experience is key to keeping players engaged. Smooth animations, responsive feedback, and visually appealing transitions make the game feel more professional and enjoyable. In this section, we will discuss various techniques for implementing smooth animations and improving the overall fluidity of your game using PyGame.

## Understanding Animation Basics

Animation in games involves displaying a series of images or frames in rapid succession to create the illusion of motion. In PyGame, we can animate objects by updating their properties (such as position, size, or rotation) in each frame of the game loop. Here are some key concepts:

- **Frame Rate (FPS)**: The number of frames displayed per second. Higher FPS results in smoother animations but requires more processing power.
- **Interpolation**: A technique used to create smooth transitions between two values, often used for moving objects or fading effects.
- **Easing Functions**: Mathematical functions that control the speed of an animation, allowing for effects like acceleration, deceleration, and elastic movements.

## Setting Up a Basic Animation Framework

To manage animations effectively, we can create an `Animator` class. This class will handle interpolation and provide utility functions for common animation effects.

```python
class Animator:
    def __init__(self):
        self.animations = []

    def add_animation(self, target, attribute, start_value, end_value, duration, easing=lambda x: x):
        animation = {
            "target": target,
            "attribute": attribute,
            "start_value": start_value,
            "end_value": end_value,
            "duration": duration,
            "elapsed": 0,
            "easing": easing
        }
        self.animations.append(animation)

    def update(self, dt):
        for animation in self.animations[:]:
            animation["elapsed"] += dt
            progress = min(animation["elapsed"] / animation["duration"], 1)
            eased_progress = animation["easing"](progress)
            current_value = (1 - eased_progress) * animation["start_value"] + eased_progress * animation["end_value"]
            setattr(animation["target"], animation["attribute"], current_value)
```

```
            if progress >= 1:
                self.animations.remove(animation)

animator = Animator()
```

## Easing Functions for Smoother Transitions

Easing functions define how an animation progresses over time. Instead of moving linearly from start to end, easing functions can create more natural motion by accelerating or decelerating the animation.

```
def ease_in_out_quad(t):
    if t < 0.5:
        return 2 * t * t
    return -1 + (4 - 2 * t) * t

def ease_out_bounce(t):
    if t < 0.3636:
        return 7.5625 * t * t
    elif t < 0.7272:
        t -= 0.5454
        return 7.5625 * t * t + 0.75
    elif t < 0.9090:
        t -= 0.8181
        return 7.5625 * t * t + 0.9375
    t -= 0.9545
    return 7.5625 * t * t + 0.984375
```

These functions can be used to create animations that feel dynamic and responsive. For example, `ease_in_out_quad` can be used for smooth transitions, while `ease_out_bounce` adds a playful bouncing effect.

## Implementing a Fade-In Animation

A common effect in games is a fade-in animation for objects, where the object gradually becomes visible. We can use the `Animator` class to implement this.

```
class GameObject:
    def __init__(self, x, y, radius):
        self.pos = pygame.Vector2(x, y)
```

```
            self.radius = radius
            self.opacity = 0

    def draw(self, surface):
            color = (0, 0, 255, int(self.opacity))
            s = pygame.Surface((self.radius * 2, self.radius * 2), pygame.SRCALPHA)
            pygame.draw.circle(s, color, (self.radius, self.radius), self.radius)
            surface.blit(s, (self.pos.x - self.radius, self.pos.y - self.radius))

ball = GameObject(WIDTH // 2, HEIGHT // 2, 20)
animator.add_animation(ball, "opacity", 0, 255, 2, ease_in_out_quad)
```

In the game loop, we update the `Animator` and draw the ball:

```
dt = clock.tick(60) / 1000   # Delta time in seconds
animator.update(dt)
ball.draw(screen)
```

## Creating Smooth Movement with Interpolation

Instead of abruptly changing an object's position, we can use interpolation to move it smoothly.

```
target_pos = pygame.Vector2(600, 300)

def move_towards(ball, target, speed, dt):
    direction = (target - ball.pos).normalize()
    ball.pos += direction * speed * dt

# In the game loop
move_towards(ball, target_pos, 200, dt)
```

## Implementing Sprite Animations

Sprite animations involve cycling through a series of images. This is useful for character animations, explosions, or any object that needs a sequence of frames.

```python
class SpriteAnimation:
    def __init__(self, frames, frame_duration):
        self.frames = frames
        self.frame_duration = frame_duration
        self.current_frame = 0
        self.elapsed = 0

    def update(self, dt):
        self.elapsed += dt
        if self.elapsed >= self.frame_duration:
            self.current_frame = (self.current_frame + 1) % len(self.frames)
            self.elapsed = 0

    def draw(self, surface, pos):
        surface.blit(self.frames[self.current_frame], pos)
```

## Adding Particle Effects

Particle effects add a layer of visual polish, making actions like collisions or power-ups more impactful. We can create a basic particle system that spawns small, short-lived particles.

```python
class Particle:
    def __init__(self, x, y, velocity, color, lifespan):
        self.pos = pygame.Vector2(x, y)
        self.velocity = velocity
        self.color = color
        self.lifespan = lifespan

    def update(self, dt):
        self.pos += self.velocity * dt
        self.lifespan -= dt

    def draw(self, surface):
        if self.lifespan > 0:
            pygame.draw.circle(surface, self.color, (int(self.pos.x), int(self.pos.y)), 3)

particles = []
```

```
def spawn_particles(x, y):
    for _ in range(20):
        velocity = pygame.Vector2(random.uniform(-1, 1), random.uniform(-1, 1)) * 100
        color = (255, random.randint(150, 255), 0)
        lifespan = random.uniform(0.5, 1.0)
        particles.append(Particle(x, y, velocity, color, lifespan))

# In the game loop
for particle in particles[:]:
    particle.update(dt)
    if particle.lifespan <= 0:
        particles.remove(particle)
    else:
        particle.draw(screen)
```

## Best Practices for Smooth Animations

1. **Use Delta Time**: Always multiply movements and animations by delta time (dt) to ensure consistent speed across different frame rates.
2. **Avoid Abrupt Changes**: Use easing functions and interpolation to make transitions smooth and natural.
3. **Limit Animation Duration**: Short animations feel more responsive, but avoid making them too short as they might seem jarring.
4. **Optimize Performance**: Keep the number of active animations and particles reasonable to maintain performance.

## Conclusion

Smooth animations and responsive feedback are critical components of a polished game experience. By using interpolation, easing functions, sprite animations, and particle effects, you can significantly enhance the visual appeal and fluidity of your game. In the next chapter, we will focus on integrating custom game controls using Raspberry Pi's GPIO pins to further enrich player interaction.

# Chapter 7: Using Raspberry Pi's GPIO for Custom Game Controls

## Introduction to GPIO Programming

The Raspberry Pi's GPIO (General-Purpose Input/Output) pins provide an incredible opportunity to interface your Python games with hardware components like buttons, LEDs, and sensors. This opens up a new realm of interactivity, allowing you to create physical controls for your games, from simple push-button input to more complex joystick controls.

### What Are GPIO Pins?

GPIO pins are versatile connectors found on the Raspberry Pi that can be programmed to read inputs (like button presses) and send outputs (like turning on an LED). These pins are physically located on the board and are often labeled with numbers corresponding to their Broadcom (BCM) pin number or physical board layout.

### Key Points:

- **Inputs**: Can detect external signals, such as a button press or sensor output.
- **Outputs**: Can control devices like LEDs or motors by sending electrical signals.

The standard Raspberry Pi model typically has 40 GPIO pins, with several reserved for power (3.3V, 5V) and ground (GND). The rest can be programmed as input or output.

### Setting Up the Development Environment

To use GPIO pins with Python, you need the `RPi.GPIO` library, which allows Python scripts to interface with the hardware components.

Install it using the following command:

```
sudo apt update
sudo apt install python3-rpi.gpio
```

Alternatively, you can install it using `pip`:

```
pip3 install RPi.GPIO
```

Now, import the library in your Python script:

```
import RPi.GPIO as GPIO
import time
```

## Configuring GPIO in Python

There are a few standard practices for configuring the GPIO pins in Python:

1. **Set the GPIO mode**: This determines whether you use the BCM numbering or the physical pin layout.
2. **Setup the pins**: Define which pins are inputs and which are outputs.
3. **Clean up**: Reset the pins when you're done to prevent issues.

```
GPIO.setmode(GPIO.BCM)     # Use BCM numbering
GPIO.setwarnings(False)    # Disable warnings
```

## Example: Controlling an LED with a Button

Let's build a simple circuit using an LED and a button. When the button is pressed, the LED will turn on.

### Components:

- Raspberry Pi
- 1 LED
- 1 Push button
- 1 220-ohm resistor
- Breadboard
- Jumper wires

### Circuit Setup:

1. Connect the longer leg of the LED (anode) to GPIO pin 18 through the resistor.
2. Connect the shorter leg (cathode) to the ground (GND).
3. Connect one side of the button to GPIO pin 17.
4. Connect the other side of the button to the ground (GND).

### Python Code:

```
import RPi.GPIO as GPIO
import time

# Set up the GPIO mode
GPIO.setmode(GPIO.BCM)
```

```python
# Define the pin numbers
LED_PIN = 18
BUTTON_PIN = 17

# Set up the pins
GPIO.setup(LED_PIN, GPIO.OUT)
GPIO.setup(BUTTON_PIN, GPIO.IN, pull_up_down=GPIO.PUD_UP)

try:
    while True:
        button_state = GPIO.input(BUTTON_PIN)
        if button_state == GPIO.LOW:
            GPIO.output(LED_PIN, GPIO.HIGH)   # Turn on LED
            print("Button Pressed: LED ON")
        else:
            GPIO.output(LED_PIN, GPIO.LOW)    # Turn off LED
            print("Button Released: LED OFF")
        time.sleep(0.1)
except KeyboardInterrupt:
    print("Exiting program")

finally:
    GPIO.cleanup()   # Reset GPIO settings
```

**Explanation:**

- **GPIO.setup()**: Configures the pins as input or output.
- **pull_up_down=GPIO.PUD_UP**: Enables the internal pull-up resistor, preventing the button from floating when not pressed.
- **GPIO.input()**: Reads the state of the input pin (HIGH or LOW).
- **GPIO.output()**: Sets the state of the output pin (HIGH or LOW).
- **GPIO.cleanup()**: Cleans up the GPIO state when the program ends.

## Using Event Detection

Polling the button state continuously can be inefficient. Instead, you can use **event detection**, where the program waits for an event (button press) and reacts accordingly.

**Example:**

```python
import RPi.GPIO as GPIO
import time
```

```python
# Set up the GPIO mode
GPIO.setmode(GPIO.BCM)

# Define the pin numbers
LED_PIN = 18
BUTTON_PIN = 17

# Set up the pins
GPIO.setup(LED_PIN, GPIO.OUT)
GPIO.setup(BUTTON_PIN, GPIO.IN, pull_up_down=GPIO.PUD_UP)

# Define a callback function
def button_callback(channel):
    print("Button was pressed!")
    GPIO.output(LED_PIN, not GPIO.input(LED_PIN))

# Set up event detection
GPIO.add_event_detect(BUTTON_PIN, GPIO.FALLING,
callback=button_callback, bouncetime=200)

try:
    print("Press the button to toggle the LED.")
    while True:
        time.sleep(1)
except KeyboardInterrupt:
    print("Exiting program")

finally:
    GPIO.cleanup()
```

**Explanation:**

- **GPIO.add_event_detect()**: Sets up an event listener for the specified pin.
- **callback=button_callback**: Specifies the function to call when the event is detected.
- **bouncetime**: Debounces the input to prevent multiple detections from a single press.

## Expanding the Example: Creating a Simple Game Controller

You can extend this basic setup to create a simple game controller using multiple buttons. For instance, you might have:

- A button for **left movement**.

# Chapter 7: Using Raspberry Pi's GPIO for Custom Game Controls

- A button for **right movement**.
- A button for **jump**.

**Circuit Setup:**

1. Connect three buttons to GPIO pins 17, 22, and 27.
2. Connect the other sides of the buttons to ground (GND).

**Python Code:**

```python
import RPi.GPIO as GPIO
import time

# Set up the GPIO mode
GPIO.setmode(GPIO.BCM)

# Define the pin numbers
LEFT_BUTTON = 17
RIGHT_BUTTON = 22
JUMP_BUTTON = 27

# Set up the pins
GPIO.setup(LEFT_BUTTON, GPIO.IN, pull_up_down=GPIO.PUD_UP)
GPIO.setup(RIGHT_BUTTON, GPIO.IN, pull_up_down=GPIO.PUD_UP)
GPIO.setup(JUMP_BUTTON, GPIO.IN, pull_up_down=GPIO.PUD_UP)

try:
    print("Game controller is ready.")
    while True:
        if GPIO.input(LEFT_BUTTON) == GPIO.LOW:
            print("Left button pressed")
        if GPIO.input(RIGHT_BUTTON) == GPIO.LOW:
            print("Right button pressed")
        if GPIO.input(JUMP_BUTTON) == GPIO.LOW:
            print("Jump button pressed")
        time.sleep(0.1)
except KeyboardInterrupt:
    print("Exiting program")

finally:
    GPIO.cleanup()
```

## Summary

In this section, you've learned:

- The basics of Raspberry Pi's GPIO pins.
- How to set up and program GPIO input and output in Python.
- How to create a simple circuit to control an LED with a button.
- How to use event detection for more efficient input handling.
- How to build a simple game controller using multiple buttons.

This foundational knowledge enables you to create custom physical game controls, making your Raspberry Pi game development projects more interactive and engaging. The next step is to integrate these controls with PyGame, allowing your hardware inputs to control the in-game actions directly.

# Connecting External Buttons and Joysticks

Interfacing external buttons and joysticks with the Raspberry Pi allows us to create custom game controllers for our projects. This section will walk you through connecting various input devices, configuring them in Python, and handling inputs to make your games more interactive.

### Understanding the Input Devices

Before diving into the setup, let's look at the components we'll be working with:

1. **Push Buttons**: Simple, momentary switches that complete a circuit when pressed.
2. **Analog Joysticks**: Provide two axes of movement (X and Y) and often include a button press when pushed down.
3. **Digital Joysticks**: Consist of multiple push buttons in different directions (up, down, left, right).

These components are typically used in game controllers to detect user inputs and translate them into actions in the game, such as moving a character or firing a weapon.

### Connecting Push Buttons to GPIO

We'll start with push buttons since they are straightforward and provide a good introduction to handling digital input.

#### Components Needed:

- Raspberry Pi
- Push button
- 10k ohm resistor (for pull-down configuration)
- Breadboard
- Jumper wires

## Chapter 7: Using Raspberry Pi's GPIO for Custom Game Controls

**Circuit Setup:**

1. Connect one terminal of the push button to GPIO pin 17.
2. Connect the other terminal to the ground (GND).
3. Place a 10k ohm pull-down resistor between the GPIO pin and ground. This ensures the pin reads LOW when the button is not pressed.

**Python Code:**

```python
import RPi.GPIO as GPIO
import time

# Set up the GPIO mode
GPIO.setmode(GPIO.BCM)

# Define the pin number
BUTTON_PIN = 17

# Set up the pin as input with pull-down resistor
GPIO.setup(BUTTON_PIN, GPIO.IN, pull_up_down=GPIO.PUD_DOWN)

try:
    print("Waiting for button press...")
    while True:
        if GPIO.input(BUTTON_PIN) == GPIO.HIGH:
            print("Button pressed!")
        time.sleep(0.1)
except KeyboardInterrupt:
    print("Exiting program")

finally:
    GPIO.cleanup()
```

**Explanation:**

- **GPIO.PUD_DOWN**: Configures an internal pull-down resistor, ensuring the pin is LOW when the button is not pressed.
- **GPIO.input()**: Reads the state of the pin (HIGH or LOW).
- The script continuously checks the button state and prints a message when it is pressed.

## Connecting a Digital Joystick

A digital joystick typically consists of five push buttons: up, down, left, right, and a central button (often labeled as "select"). Each button can be connected to a different GPIO pin.

**Components Needed:**

- Raspberry Pi
- Digital joystick module (or 5 push buttons)
- Breadboard
- Jumper wires

**Circuit Setup:**

1. Connect the **up** button to GPIO pin 17.
2. Connect the **down** button to GPIO pin 22.
3. Connect the **left** button to GPIO pin 23.
4. Connect the **right** button to GPIO pin 24.
5. Connect the **select** button to GPIO pin 27.
6. Connect the other terminals of all buttons to ground (GND).

**Python Code:**

```python
import RPi.GPIO as GPIO
import time

# Set up the GPIO mode
GPIO.setmode(GPIO.BCM)

# Define pin numbers for the joystick buttons
UP_PIN = 17
DOWN_PIN = 22
LEFT_PIN = 23
RIGHT_PIN = 24
SELECT_PIN = 27

# Set up the pins as input with pull-down resistors
GPIO.setup(UP_PIN, GPIO.IN, pull_up_down=GPIO.PUD_DOWN)
GPIO.setup(DOWN_PIN, GPIO.IN, pull_up_down=GPIO.PUD_DOWN)
GPIO.setup(LEFT_PIN, GPIO.IN, pull_up_down=GPIO.PUD_DOWN)
GPIO.setup(RIGHT_PIN, GPIO.IN, pull_up_down=GPIO.PUD_DOWN)
GPIO.setup(SELECT_PIN, GPIO.IN, pull_up_down=GPIO.PUD_DOWN)

try:
    print("Joystick is ready. Press any direction or select button.")
    while True:
```

```
        if GPIO.input(UP_PIN) == GPIO.HIGH:
            print("Up pressed")
        if GPIO.input(DOWN_PIN) == GPIO.HIGH:
            print("Down pressed")
        if GPIO.input(LEFT_PIN) == GPIO.HIGH:
            print("Left pressed")
        if GPIO.input(RIGHT_PIN) == GPIO.HIGH:
            print("Right pressed")
        if GPIO.input(SELECT_PIN) == GPIO.HIGH:
            print("Select pressed")
        time.sleep(0.1)
except KeyboardInterrupt:
    print("Exiting program")

finally:
    GPIO.cleanup()
```

**Explanation:**

- Each button state is checked in a loop.
- The corresponding message is printed when a button is pressed.
- The program ends gracefully with `GPIO.cleanup()` when interrupted.

## Connecting an Analog Joystick

An analog joystick provides two analog outputs (X and Y axes) and a digital button press. To read the analog values, you need an Analog-to-Digital Converter (ADC) like the MCP3008.

### Components Needed:

- Raspberry Pi
- Analog joystick
- MCP3008 ADC
- Breadboard
- Jumper wires

### Circuit Setup:

1. Connect the X-axis of the joystick to MCP3008 channel 0 (CH0).
2. Connect the Y-axis of the joystick to MCP3008 channel 1 (CH1).
3. Connect the button to GPIO pin 27.

### Python Code Using MCP3008:

```
import spidev
```

```python
import RPi.GPIO as GPIO
import time

# Set up the GPIO mode
GPIO.setmode(GPIO.BCM)

# Define the button pin
BUTTON_PIN = 27
GPIO.setup(BUTTON_PIN, GPIO.IN, pull_up_down=GPIO.PUD_DOWN)

# Set up SPI
spi = spidev.SpiDev()
spi.open(0, 0)
spi.max_speed_hz = 1350000

# Function to read from MCP3008
def read_channel(channel):
    adc = spi.xfer2([1, (8 + channel) << 4, 0])
    data = ((adc[1] & 3) << 8) + adc[2]
    return data

try:
    print("Analog joystick ready. Move the joystick or press the button.")
    while True:
        x_value = read_channel(0)
        y_value = read_channel(1)
        button_state = GPIO.input(BUTTON_PIN)

        print(f"X-axis: {x_value}, Y-axis: {y_value}")

        if button_state == GPIO.HIGH:
            print("Button pressed!")

        time.sleep(0.1)
except KeyboardInterrupt:
    print("Exiting program")

finally:
    spi.close()
    GPIO.cleanup()
```

**Explanation:**

- **spidev**: A Python module for interacting with SPI devices.
- **read_channel()**: Reads the analog value from the specified MCP3008 channel.
- The joystick's X and Y values are printed continuously, along with the button state.

## Summary

In this section, we covered:

- How to connect push buttons and digital joysticks to Raspberry Pi's GPIO.
- How to use pull-up and pull-down resistors to manage input states.
- How to handle digital input with Python using polling and event detection.
- How to connect an analog joystick using an MCP3008 ADC.

This foundational understanding enables you to create various custom controllers for your games, adding a layer of physical interactivity that enhances the gaming experience. In the next section, we will integrate these inputs with PyGame to control in-game elements directly.

# Building a Custom Game Controller

Creating a custom game controller with the Raspberry Pi takes your game development projects to the next level by allowing you to design physical inputs tailored to your games. In this section, we will walk through building a complete game controller using various input components such as buttons, joysticks, and potentiometers. We will also explore how to connect everything to the Raspberry Pi, write the Python code to handle input, and integrate the controller with your games.

## Planning Your Game Controller

Before starting the hardware setup, it's essential to plan the layout and functionality of your game controller. Here's a basic design to get started:

- **Directional Input**: Use a digital joystick or four push buttons for up, down, left, and right movements.
- **Action Buttons**: Include at least two action buttons for in-game actions like jump and shoot.
- **Analog Input**: Use a potentiometer or analog joystick for additional controls like speed adjustment or camera movement.

You can customize this layout based on your game's requirements. For example, if you're building a racing game, you might want a steering wheel and throttle input instead of a traditional joystick.

## Components Needed

- Raspberry Pi

- Digital joystick (4-directional)
- 2 Push buttons (action buttons)
- 1 Potentiometer (analog input)
- MCP3008 (Analog-to-Digital Converter for potentiometer input)
- Breadboard
- Jumper wires
- Enclosure (optional, for a finished controller look)

## Setting Up the Hardware

1. **Joystick Setup**:
   - Connect the joystick's up, down, left, and right terminals to GPIO pins 17, 22, 23, and 24 respectively.
   - Connect the common ground terminal of the joystick to the Raspberry Pi's GND.
2. **Push Buttons Setup**:
   - Connect one button to GPIO pin 27 and the other to GPIO pin 4.
   - Use pull-down resistors (10k ohm) to ensure the pins read LOW when the buttons are not pressed.
3. **Potentiometer Setup**:
   - Connect the middle terminal of the potentiometer to the MCP3008 channel 0 (CH0).
   - Connect the other two terminals to 3.3V and GND.
   - Connect the MCP3008 to the Raspberry Pi via SPI (MOSI, MISO, SCLK, and CS).

**MCP3008 Pin Connections:**

- **VDD** and **VREF**: 3.3V
- **AGND** and **DGND**: GND
- **CLK**: GPIO 11 (SCLK)
- **DOUT**: GPIO 9 (MISO)
- **DIN**: GPIO 10 (MOSI)
- **CS**: GPIO 8 (CE0)

## Python Code for the Game Controller

The following Python code demonstrates how to read inputs from all the connected components and print their states. This code will serve as the basis for integrating the custom controller with your game.

```python
import RPi.GPIO as GPIO
import spidev
import time

# Set up GPIO mode
```

# Chapter 7: Using Raspberry Pi's GPIO for Custom Game Controls

```python
GPIO.setmode(GPIO.BCM)

# Define GPIO pins
UP_PIN = 17
DOWN_PIN = 22
LEFT_PIN = 23
RIGHT_PIN = 24
BUTTON_A = 27
BUTTON_B = 4

# Set up input pins with pull-down resistors
GPIO.setup(UP_PIN, GPIO.IN, pull_up_down=GPIO.PUD_DOWN)
GPIO.setup(DOWN_PIN, GPIO.IN, pull_up_down=GPIO.PUD_DOWN)
GPIO.setup(LEFT_PIN, GPIO.IN, pull_up_down=GPIO.PUD_DOWN)
GPIO.setup(RIGHT_PIN, GPIO.IN, pull_up_down=GPIO.PUD_DOWN)
GPIO.setup(BUTTON_A, GPIO.IN, pull_up_down=GPIO.PUD_DOWN)
GPIO.setup(BUTTON_B, GPIO.IN, pull_up_down=GPIO.PUD_DOWN)

# Set up SPI for MCP3008
spi = spidev.SpiDev()
spi.open(0, 0)
spi.max_speed_hz = 1350000

# Function to read MCP3008 channel
def read_channel(channel):
    adc = spi.xfer2([1, (8 + channel) << 4, 0])
    data = ((adc[1] & 3) << 8) + adc[2]
    return data

try:
    print("Custom Game Controller is active.")
    while True:
        # Read digital inputs
        if GPIO.input(UP_PIN) == GPIO.HIGH:
            print("Up pressed")
        if GPIO.input(DOWN_PIN) == GPIO.HIGH:
            print("Down pressed")
        if GPIO.input(LEFT_PIN) == GPIO.HIGH:
            print("Left pressed")
        if GPIO.input(RIGHT_PIN) == GPIO.HIGH:
            print("Right pressed")
```

```
            if GPIO.input(BUTTON_A) == GPIO.HIGH:
                print("Button A pressed")
            if GPIO.input(BUTTON_B) == GPIO.HIGH:
                print("Button B pressed")

            # Read analog input
            potentiometer_value = read_channel(0)
            print(f"Potentiometer value: {potentiometer_value}")

            time.sleep(0.1)

except KeyboardInterrupt:
    print("Exiting program")

finally:
    spi.close()
    GPIO.cleanup()
```

**Explanation:**

- **Digital Inputs**: The joystick and buttons are read using `GPIO.input()`. Each pin is checked in a loop.
- **Analog Input**: The potentiometer value is read using the MCP3008 via SPI. The value ranges from 0 to 1023.
- **SPI Communication**: The `spidev` library is used for communication with the MCP3008 ADC.

## Building an Enclosure

To give your custom controller a finished look and make it easier to use, consider building an enclosure. You can use a project box or 3D-print a custom case. Drill holes for the joystick, buttons, and potentiometer, and secure them in place. Route the wires through the case and connect them to the Raspberry Pi.

## Integrating the Controller with PyGame

Now that your custom game controller is set up, it's time to integrate it with PyGame. We can use the inputs to control player movement and actions in a simple game.

**Example Game Code:**

```
import pygame
import RPi.GPIO as GPIO
import spidev
```

```python
# Initialize PyGame
pygame.init()

# Set up the game window
screen = pygame.display.set_mode((800, 600))
pygame.display.set_caption("Game with Custom Controller")

# Define colors
BLACK = (0, 0, 0)
WHITE = (255, 255, 255)

# Define player properties
player_x = 400
player_y = 300
player_speed = 5

# Set up GPIO and SPI (similar to previous code)
GPIO.setmode(GPIO.BCM)
UP_PIN = 17
DOWN_PIN = 22
LEFT_PIN = 23
RIGHT_PIN = 24
BUTTON_A = 27
BUTTON_B = 4
spi = spidev.SpiDev()
spi.open(0, 0)
spi.max_speed_hz = 1350000

def read_channel(channel):
    adc = spi.xfer2([1, (8 + channel) << 4, 0])
    return ((adc[1] & 3) << 8) + adc[2]

# Main game loop
running = True
while running:
    for event in pygame.event.get():
        if event.type == pygame.QUIT:
            running = False

    # Read controller input
```

```python
    if GPIO.input(UP_PIN) == GPIO.HIGH:
        player_y -= player_speed
    if GPIO.input(DOWN_PIN) == GPIO.HIGH:
        player_y += player_speed
    if GPIO.input(LEFT_PIN) == GPIO.HIGH:
        player_x -= player_speed
    if GPIO.input(RIGHT_PIN) == GPIO.HIGH:
        player_x += player_speed

    # Clear the screen
    screen.fill(BLACK)

    # Draw the player
    pygame.draw.rect(screen, WHITE, (player_x, player_y, 50, 50))

    # Update the display
    pygame.display.flip()

# Cleanup
spi.close()
GPIO.cleanup()
pygame.quit()
```

## Summary

In this section, you've learned:

- How to design and build a custom game controller using a variety of input components.
- How to connect the controller components to the Raspberry Pi's GPIO and read their states using Python.
- How to integrate the controller inputs with a PyGame-based game.

This custom game controller project offers a hands-on way to expand your game development skills and brings a physical, interactive element to your games. In the next section, we will explore how to integrate additional sensors and feedback mechanisms, such as vibration motors or LEDs, to further enhance your gaming experience.

## Integrating GPIO Input with PyGame

In this section, we will explore how to fully integrate the custom GPIO-based game controller into a Python game using PyGame. By doing this, we can leverage physical buttons, joysticks, and other hardware inputs to control elements of the game, creating a more immersive and interactive experience.

## Setting Up the Project

Before diving into the code, make sure you have the following prerequisites installed:

1. **PyGame**: Install PyGame using the following command:

```
pip3 install pygame
```

2. **RPi.GPIO**: This library should already be installed from previous sections. If not, install it using:

```
pip3 install RPi.GPIO
```

3. **Hardware Setup**: Ensure your custom game controller is connected as described in previous sections. The following setup will be assumed:
   - **Joystick**: GPIO pins 17 (up), 22 (down), 23 (left), 24 (right)
   - **Action Buttons**: GPIO pins 27 (button A) and 4 (button B)
   - **Potentiometer** (for analog input): Connected to MCP3008 channel 0 (CH0)

## Creating the Game Structure

We will create a simple game where the player controls a square that can move around the screen using the joystick and buttons. The potentiometer will be used to adjust the speed of the player.

### Game Code

```python
import pygame
import RPi.GPIO as GPIO
import spidev
import time

# Initialize PyGame
pygame.init()

# Set up the game window
SCREEN_WIDTH = 800
SCREEN_HEIGHT = 600
screen = pygame.display.set_mode((SCREEN_WIDTH, SCREEN_HEIGHT))
```

```python
pygame.display.set_caption("GPIO-Controlled Game")

# Define colors
BLACK = (0, 0, 0)
WHITE = (255, 255, 255)
RED = (255, 0, 0)

# Define player properties
player_x = SCREEN_WIDTH // 2
player_y = SCREEN_HEIGHT // 2
player_size = 50
player_speed = 5

# Set up GPIO
GPIO.setmode(GPIO.BCM)
UP_PIN = 17
DOWN_PIN = 22
LEFT_PIN = 23
RIGHT_PIN = 24
BUTTON_A = 27
BUTTON_B = 4

# Set up input pins with pull-down resistors
GPIO.setup(UP_PIN, GPIO.IN, pull_up_down=GPIO.PUD_DOWN)
GPIO.setup(DOWN_PIN, GPIO.IN, pull_up_down=GPIO.PUD_DOWN)
GPIO.setup(LEFT_PIN, GPIO.IN, pull_up_down=GPIO.PUD_DOWN)
GPIO.setup(RIGHT_PIN, GPIO.IN, pull_up_down=GPIO.PUD_DOWN)
GPIO.setup(BUTTON_A, GPIO.IN, pull_up_down=GPIO.PUD_DOWN)
GPIO.setup(BUTTON_B, GPIO.IN, pull_up_down=GPIO.PUD_DOWN)

# Set up SPI for MCP3008 (analog input)
spi = spidev.SpiDev()
spi.open(0, 0)
spi.max_speed_hz = 1350000

# Function to read MCP3008 channel
def read_channel(channel):
    adc = spi.xfer2([1, (8 + channel) << 4, 0])
    data = ((adc[1] & 3) << 8) + adc[2]
    return data
```

```python
# Main game loop
running = True
while running:
    for event in pygame.event.get():
        if event.type == pygame.QUIT:
            running = False

    # Read joystick input
    if GPIO.input(UP_PIN) == GPIO.HIGH:
        player_y -= player_speed
    if GPIO.input(DOWN_PIN) == GPIO.HIGH:
        player_y += player_speed
    if GPIO.input(LEFT_PIN) == GPIO.HIGH:
        player_x -= player_speed
    if GPIO.input(RIGHT_PIN) == GPIO.HIGH:
        player_x += player_speed

    # Read action button input
    if GPIO.input(BUTTON_A) == GPIO.HIGH:
        player_size += 5  # Increase player size
    if GPIO.input(BUTTON_B) == GPIO.HIGH:
        player_size = max(10, player_size - 5)  # Decrease player size

    # Read analog input (potentiometer)
    potentiometer_value = read_channel(0)
    player_speed = potentiometer_value // 100 + 1  # Adjust speed based on potentiometer value

    # Bound the player within the screen
    player_x = max(0, min(SCREEN_WIDTH - player_size, player_x))
    player_y = max(0, min(SCREEN_HEIGHT - player_size, player_y))

    # Clear the screen
    screen.fill(BLACK)

    # Draw the player
    pygame.draw.rect(screen, WHITE, (player_x, player_y, player_size, player_size))

    # Display player speed
```

```
        font = pygame.font.Font(None, 36)
        speed_text = font.render(f"Speed: {player_speed}", True, RED)
        screen.blit(speed_text, (10, 10))

        # Update the display
        pygame.display.flip()
        time.sleep(0.01)

# Cleanup
spi.close()
GPIO.cleanup()
pygame.quit()
```

**Explanation**

1. **Joystick Input**: The GPIO pins connected to the joystick are read using `GPIO.input()`. Based on the state of each pin, the player's position is updated.
2. **Button Actions**: The action buttons (A and B) modify the player's size when pressed.
3. **Analog Input for Speed Control**: The potentiometer value is read using the MCP3008 ADC and mapped to control the player's speed.
4. **Game Loop**: The game loop handles input, updates the player's position and speed, and redraws the screen at each frame.

## Handling Input Debouncing

When reading GPIO inputs, you may notice that pressing a button multiple times results in unintended behavior. This is caused by **bouncing**, where the physical contacts inside the button generate multiple signals. To address this, we can use software debouncing.

**Example with Debouncing**

```
GPIO.add_event_detect(BUTTON_A, GPIO.RISING, bouncetime=200)
GPIO.add_event_detect(BUTTON_B, GPIO.RISING, bouncetime=200)

def button_a_callback(channel):
    global player_size
    player_size += 5

def button_b_callback(channel):
    global player_size
    player_size = max(10, player_size - 5)
```

```
GPIO.add_event_callback(BUTTON_A, button_a_callback)
GPIO.add_event_callback(BUTTON_B, button_b_callback)
```

## Enhancing User Feedback

Adding feedback mechanisms like LEDs or vibration motors can improve the gaming experience. For example, you could connect an LED to indicate when a special action is performed or use a vibration motor to give haptic feedback when the player collides with an obstacle.

### LED Feedback Example

```
LED_PIN = 5
GPIO.setup(LED_PIN, GPIO.OUT)

if GPIO.input(BUTTON_A) == GPIO.HIGH:
    GPIO.output(LED_PIN, GPIO.HIGH)   # Turn on LED
else:
    GPIO.output(LED_PIN, GPIO.LOW)    # Turn off LED
```

## Integrating with a More Complex Game

This basic game can be extended to include additional mechanics, such as enemy movement, collision detection, and scoring. By integrating more advanced game logic and graphical elements, you can create a fully functional game controlled entirely by your custom hardware.

### Tips for Advanced Integration:

1. **Multiple Players**: Use additional GPIO pins to add inputs for a second player.
2. **Game States**: Implement game states (e.g., menu, playing, paused) to handle different phases of the game.
3. **Custom Controls**: Map specific in-game actions to the physical buttons on your controller based on the game genre.

## Summary

In this section, you have learned how to:

- Integrate GPIO input with PyGame to create a fully interactive game.
- Handle joystick, button, and analog inputs in a Python game.
- Address input issues like debouncing and provide feedback using LEDs.
- Extend your game with more complex mechanics and custom controls.

This hands-on approach brings together software and hardware, allowing you to build a unique gaming experience powered by your custom game controller. In the next chapter, we will explore multiplayer game design using the Raspberry Pi and networked game controllers.

# Chapter 8: Creating a Multiplayer Game with Raspberry Pi

## Game Design for Multiplayer Experiences

Designing a multiplayer game can be one of the most rewarding yet challenging aspects of game development. With Raspberry Pi, you have the flexibility to create both local multiplayer games (using the same device) and networked multiplayer games (connecting multiple devices). This section focuses on designing and implementing a simple local multiplayer game where two players can interact using connected input devices or GPIO controls.

### Introduction to Multiplayer Game Design

Multiplayer games involve multiple players engaging with the game environment and with each other. The key design considerations for multiplayer games include:

- **Player Input:** How players interact with the game and each other, including input devices and methods.
- **Game Mechanics:** The rules and mechanics governing how the game responds to multiple players.
- **Screen Layout:** How the game display is shared among players (e.g., split-screen, shared screen).
- **Synchronization:** Ensuring that game elements respond correctly to simultaneous inputs.
- **Network Considerations:** Handling latency, player synchronization, and data exchange for networked games.

For this project, we'll focus on a **local multiplayer game** where two players can use connected input devices, such as USB controllers or custom GPIO buttons, to control their in-game characters.

### Choosing the Right Game Type

When designing a multiplayer game, simplicity is key, especially when starting out. The game should be easy to understand, and players should be able to quickly engage without a steep learning curve. Consider the following popular genres for local multiplayer games:

1. **Racing Games:** Players compete to reach a finish line.
2. **Fighting Games:** Players battle against each other in a confined arena.
3. **Puzzle Games:** Players solve puzzles cooperatively or competitively.
4. **Arcade Games:** Classic arcade games like Pong or Snake adapted for multiplayer.

For this section, we'll create a simple **multiplayer Pong game**, a classic two-player game where each player controls a paddle to bounce a ball back and forth. This game is ideal for demonstrating basic multiplayer mechanics and input handling.

## Setting Up the Game Environment

Before coding, ensure that you have the following setup:

- A Raspberry Pi running Python and PyGame installed.
- Two input devices (e.g., USB controllers, keyboards, or custom GPIO buttons).
- A basic understanding of Python and PyGame.

If you haven't installed PyGame, you can do so using:

```
sudo apt-get update
sudo apt-get install python3-pygame
```

## Creating the Game Window

We'll start by setting up a basic game window using PyGame. This will be the canvas for our multiplayer Pong game.

```
import pygame

# Initialize PyGame
pygame.init()

# Set up the game window
WINDOW_WIDTH = 800
WINDOW_HEIGHT = 600
window = pygame.display.set_mode((WINDOW_WIDTH, WINDOW_HEIGHT))
pygame.display.set_caption("Multiplayer Pong")

# Define colors
BLACK = (0, 0, 0)
WHITE = (255, 255, 255)

# Set up the game clock
clock = pygame.time.Clock()
FPS = 60

# Main game loop
```

```python
running = True
while running:
    for event in pygame.event.get():
        if event.type == pygame.QUIT:
            running = False

    # Fill the window with black
    window.fill(BLACK)

    # Update the display
    pygame.display.flip()
    clock.tick(FPS)

pygame.quit()
```

This code creates a simple game window and handles the basic event loop. You can run it to see an empty black window titled "Multiplayer Pong."

## Implementing the Game Paddles

Next, we'll create two paddles for the players. Each paddle can be controlled using different input devices or keys on the keyboard.

```python
# Paddle properties
PADDLE_WIDTH = 10
PADDLE_HEIGHT = 100
PADDLE_SPEED = 5

# Paddle positions
left_paddle = pygame.Rect(50, (WINDOW_HEIGHT // 2) - (PADDLE_HEIGHT
// 2), PADDLE_WIDTH, PADDLE_HEIGHT)
right_paddle = pygame.Rect(WINDOW_WIDTH - 50 - PADDLE_WIDTH,
(WINDOW_HEIGHT // 2) - (PADDLE_HEIGHT // 2), PADDLE_WIDTH,
PADDLE_HEIGHT)

# Paddle controls (using keyboard keys for simplicity)
left_paddle_up = pygame.K_w
left_paddle_down = pygame.K_s
right_paddle_up = pygame.K_UP
right_paddle_down = pygame.K_DOWN
```

## Handling Player Input

We need to handle input for both players, allowing them to move their paddles up and down.

```
keys = pygame.key.get_pressed()

if keys[left_paddle_up]:
    left_paddle.y -= PADDLE_SPEED
if keys[left_paddle_down]:
    left_paddle.y += PADDLE_SPEED
if keys[right_paddle_up]:
    right_paddle.y -= PADDLE_SPEED
if keys[right_paddle_down]:
    right_paddle.y += PADDLE_SPEED

# Ensure paddles stay within the window bounds
left_paddle.y = max(0, min(WINDOW_HEIGHT - PADDLE_HEIGHT,
left_paddle.y))
right_paddle.y = max(0, min(WINDOW_HEIGHT - PADDLE_HEIGHT,
right_paddle.y))
```

## Adding the Ball

The ball is a central element of the game, bouncing between the paddles. We'll start with a simple ball implementation.

```
# Ball properties
BALL_SIZE = 20
ball = pygame.Rect(WINDOW_WIDTH // 2 - BALL_SIZE // 2, WINDOW_HEIGHT // 2 - BALL_SIZE // 2, BALL_SIZE, BALL_SIZE)
ball_speed_x = 4
ball_speed_y = 4
```

## Ball Movement and Collision Detection

To make the game interactive, the ball must move and bounce off the paddles and window edges.

```
# Update ball position
ball.x += ball_speed_x
```

```python
ball.y += ball_speed_y

# Bounce off top and bottom walls
if ball.top <= 0 or ball.bottom >= WINDOW_HEIGHT:
    ball_speed_y *= -1

# Bounce off paddles
if ball.colliderect(left_paddle) or ball.colliderect(right_paddle):
    ball_speed_x *= -1

# Reset the ball if it goes off the screen
if ball.left <= 0 or ball.right >= WINDOW_WIDTH:
    ball.x = WINDOW_WIDTH // 2 - BALL_SIZE // 2
    ball.y = WINDOW_HEIGHT // 2 - BALL_SIZE // 2
    ball_speed_x *= -1
```

## Drawing Game Elements

We can now draw the paddles, ball, and the center line of the game.

```python
# Draw paddles and ball
pygame.draw.rect(window, WHITE, left_paddle)
pygame.draw.rect(window, WHITE, right_paddle)
pygame.draw.ellipse(window, WHITE, ball)

# Draw center line
pygame.draw.aaline(window, WHITE, (WINDOW_WIDTH // 2, 0),
(WINDOW_WIDTH // 2, WINDOW_HEIGHT))
```

## Conclusion

This simple Pong game provides a foundation for creating more complex multiplayer experiences. You can expand this project by:

- Adding a scoring system.
- Implementing different power-ups.
- Creating variations of the game with different rules or mechanics.
- Integrating custom controllers using Raspberry Pi's GPIO pins.

Experimenting with different features and mechanics will help you gain a deeper understanding of multiplayer game development and Python programming on Raspberry Pi.

## Setting Up Networked Games with Python

Creating a networked multiplayer game allows players to connect over a local network or the internet, enabling a shared gaming experience on separate devices. In this section, we will cover the essentials of setting up a networked game using Python. We'll use Python's built-in socket library to establish communication between a server (hosting the game) and multiple clients (the players).

### Understanding Networking in Games

Networking in games is about facilitating communication between multiple devices. The two most common networking models are:

1. **Client-Server Model:** One device acts as the server, handling the game's logic and state. The clients connect to the server and send input data (e.g., player movements) to the server, which processes the data and sends updates back to the clients.
2. **Peer-to-Peer Model:** Each device is both a client and a server. This model is harder to implement due to synchronization issues but can be useful for specific game types.

In this section, we will use the **Client-Server Model**. One Raspberry Pi will act as the server, and other devices will connect as clients.

### Setting Up the Server

Let's start by writing a simple server script. This script will listen for incoming connections from clients and handle basic data exchange.

```
import socket

# Server configuration
SERVER_IP = "0.0.0.0"  # Listen on all network interfaces
SERVER_PORT = 5555
BUFFER_SIZE = 1024

# Create a TCP socket
server_socket = socket.socket(socket.AF_INET, socket.SOCK_STREAM)
server_socket.bind((SERVER_IP, SERVER_PORT))
server_socket.listen()

print(f"Server started on {SERVER_IP}:{SERVER_PORT}")

# Accept client connections
clients = []
```

```python
def handle_client(client_socket, client_address):
    print(f"Client connected: {client_address}")
    while True:
        try:
            data = client_socket.recv(BUFFER_SIZE)
            if not data:
                break
            print(f"Received from {client_address}: {data.decode()}")
            # Echo the data back to the client
            client_socket.send(data)
        except ConnectionError:
            break

    print(f"Client disconnected: {client_address}")
    client_socket.close()

# Main server loop
try:
    while True:
        client_socket, client_address = server_socket.accept()
        clients.append(client_socket)
        handle_client(client_socket, client_address)
except KeyboardInterrupt:
    print("Server shutting down.")
finally:
    server_socket.close()
```

**Explanation**

- **Socket Creation:** We create a TCP socket using `socket.AF_INET` for IPv4 addresses and `socket.SOCK_STREAM` for TCP.
- **Binding:** The server binds to a specific IP address and port.
- **Listening:** The server listens for incoming client connections.
- **Handling Clients:** When a client connects, the server accepts the connection and handles data exchange.

You can run this server script on your Raspberry Pi:

```
python3 server.py
```

## Setting Up the Client

The client script will connect to the server and allow the player to send and receive data.

```
import socket

# Server configuration
SERVER_IP = "192.168.1.10"  # Replace with your server's IP address
SERVER_PORT = 5555
BUFFER_SIZE = 1024

# Create a TCP socket
client_socket = socket.socket(socket.AF_INET, socket.SOCK_STREAM)
client_socket.connect((SERVER_IP, SERVER_PORT))

print("Connected to the server.")

try:
    while True:
        message = input("Enter a message to send: ")
        if message.lower() == "exit":
            break
        client_socket.send(message.encode())

        # Receive response from the server
        response = client_socket.recv(BUFFER_SIZE)
        print(f"Received from server: {response.decode()}")
except KeyboardInterrupt:
    print("Disconnected from the server.")
finally:
    client_socket.close()
```

### Explanation

- **Socket Creation:** The client creates a TCP socket and connects to the server's IP address and port.
- **Data Exchange:** The client sends a message to the server, which echoes the message back.
- **Graceful Exit:** The client can disconnect by typing "exit" or pressing Ctrl+C.

Run this client script on a different device:

```
python3 client.py
```

## Testing the Connection

With both the server and client scripts running, you can test the connection by sending messages from the client to the server. The server should echo back the messages. This simple exchange forms the basis of communication for a networked game.

## Handling Multiple Clients

In a real multiplayer game, the server needs to handle multiple clients simultaneously. We can use Python's `threading` module to manage multiple client connections.

### Updated Server Script with Threading

```python
import socket
import threading

SERVER_IP = "0.0.0.0"
SERVER_PORT = 5555
BUFFER_SIZE = 1024

server_socket = socket.socket(socket.AF_INET, socket.SOCK_STREAM)
server_socket.bind((SERVER_IP, SERVER_PORT))
server_socket.listen()

clients = []

def handle_client(client_socket, client_address):
    print(f"Client connected: {client_address}")
    while True:
        try:
            data = client_socket.recv(BUFFER_SIZE)
            if not data:
                break
            broadcast(data, client_socket)
        except ConnectionError:
            break

    print(f"Client disconnected: {client_address}")
```

```
        clients.remove(client_socket)
        client_socket.close()

def broadcast(message, sender_socket):
    for client in clients:
        if client != sender_socket:
            try:
                client.send(message)
            except ConnectionError:
                clients.remove(client)

print("Server is running...")

try:
    while True:
        client_socket, client_address = server_socket.accept()
        clients.append(client_socket)
        threading.Thread(target=handle_client, args=(client_socket, client_address)).start()
except KeyboardInterrupt:
    print("Server shutting down.")
finally:
    server_socket.close()
```

### Explanation

- **Threading:** Each client connection is handled in a separate thread, allowing the server to manage multiple clients simultaneously.
- **Broadcast Function:** The `broadcast` function sends a message to all connected clients except the sender.

## Building a Simple Networked Game

Now that we have a basic server and client setup, let's create a simple networked game where two players control paddles in a Pong game.

The server will manage the game state, while the clients will send input data (e.g., paddle movements).

### Game Server Code

```
# Additional game logic for server-side
game_state = {
```

```python
    "left_paddle": 250,
    "right_paddle": 250,
    "ball_x": 400,
    "ball_y": 300,
    "ball_dx": 4,
    "ball_dy": 4
}

def update_game_state():
    game_state["ball_x"] += game_state["ball_dx"]
    game_state["ball_y"] += game_state["ball_dy"]

    # Bounce ball off top and bottom walls
    if game_state["ball_y"] <= 0 or game_state["ball_y"] >= 600:
        game_state["ball_dy"] *= -1

    # Broadcast updated game state
    message = 
f"{game_state['left_paddle']},{game_state['right_paddle']},{game_state['ball_x']},{game_state['ball_y']}"
    broadcast(message.encode(), None)

# Update game loop on the server
while True:
    update_game_state()
    time.sleep(1 / 60)    # 60 FPS
```

### Client Input Handling

The client sends paddle movements to the server based on player input.

```
keys = pygame.key.get_pressed()
if keys[pygame.K_w]:
    client_socket.send(b"left_up")
elif keys[pygame.K_s]:
    client_socket.send(b"left_down")
elif keys[pygame.K_UP]:
    client_socket.send(b"right_up")
elif keys[pygame.K_DOWN]:
    client_socket.send(b"right_down")
```

## Conclusion

This section covered the fundamental aspects of setting up a networked multiplayer game using Python and sockets. By building on this foundation, you can create more complex and interactive multiplayer games, integrating features like chat, real-time synchronization, and custom game controllers. Experiment with different game designs and network configurations to enhance your multiplayer experience.

# Coding a Simple Local Multiplayer Game

Local multiplayer games are a great way to bring friends and family together for a shared gaming experience. In this section, we will create a simple local multiplayer game using Python and PyGame. The game will be similar to Pong but with enhancements and customization options. Each player will control a paddle, and the objective is to bounce the ball past the opponent's paddle to score points.

### Game Overview

Our game will feature the following components:

- **Game Window:** The main display where all game elements are rendered.
- **Player Paddles:** Two paddles controlled by the players using keyboard input or external controllers.
- **Ball:** A bouncing ball that players must hit with their paddles.
- **Scoring System:** A simple scoring system to track points for each player.
- **Win Condition:** The first player to reach a set score limit wins the game.

This section will guide you through building the entire game step by step.

### Setting Up the Game Window

We start by creating the game window and initializing PyGame. This window will be used to display the game elements.

```
import pygame
import sys

# Initialize PyGame
pygame.init()

# Constants
WINDOW_WIDTH = 800
WINDOW_HEIGHT = 600
FPS = 60
WHITE = (255, 255, 255)
```

```
BLACK = (0, 0, 0)

# Set up the game window
window = pygame.display.set_mode((WINDOW_WIDTH, WINDOW_HEIGHT))
pygame.display.set_caption("Local Multiplayer Pong")
clock = pygame.time.Clock()
```

**Explanation**

- **Initialization:** We initialize PyGame and set up the main game window.
- **Colors and FPS:** We define colors and the frames per second (FPS) for smooth gameplay.

## Creating the Game Elements

Next, we create the paddles and the ball. These are essential components for our Pong game.

```
# Paddle properties
PADDLE_WIDTH = 15
PADDLE_HEIGHT = 100
PADDLE_SPEED = 5

# Ball properties
BALL_SIZE = 20
ball_speed_x = 4
ball_speed_y = 4

# Paddle positions
left_paddle = pygame.Rect(50, (WINDOW_HEIGHT // 2) - (PADDLE_HEIGHT 
// 2), PADDLE_WIDTH, PADDLE_HEIGHT)
right_paddle = pygame.Rect(WINDOW_WIDTH - 50 - PADDLE_WIDTH, 
(WINDOW_HEIGHT // 2) - (PADDLE_HEIGHT // 2), PADDLE_WIDTH, 
PADDLE_HEIGHT)

# Ball position
ball = pygame.Rect(WINDOW_WIDTH // 2 - BALL_SIZE // 2, WINDOW_HEIGHT 
// 2 - BALL_SIZE // 2, BALL_SIZE, BALL_SIZE)
```

**Explanation**

- **Paddles:** We define two paddles, one for each player. They are positioned on the left and right sides of the screen.
- **Ball:** The ball starts in the center of the screen and moves diagonally.

## Handling Player Input

To control the paddles, we need to capture player input using the keyboard.

```
def handle_input():
    keys = pygame.key.get_pressed()

    # Left paddle controls (Player 1)
    if keys[pygame.K_w]:
        left_paddle.y -= PADDLE_SPEED
    if keys[pygame.K_s]:
        left_paddle.y += PADDLE_SPEED

    # Right paddle controls (Player 2)
    if keys[pygame.K_UP]:
        right_paddle.y -= PADDLE_SPEED
    if keys[pygame.K_DOWN]:
        right_paddle.y += PADDLE_SPEED

    # Ensure paddles stay within the screen bounds
    left_paddle.y = max(0, min(WINDOW_HEIGHT - PADDLE_HEIGHT, left_paddle.y))
    right_paddle.y = max(0, min(WINDOW_HEIGHT - PADDLE_HEIGHT, right_paddle.y))
```

#### Explanation

- **Keyboard Input:** We check for specific key presses (W, S for Player 1 and UP, DOWN for Player 2) to move the paddles.
- **Bounds Checking:** We ensure that the paddles do not move off the screen.

## Ball Movement and Collision Detection

The ball needs to move continuously and bounce off the paddles and screen edges.

```
def move_ball():
    global ball_speed_x, ball_speed_y
```

```python
    # Move the ball
    ball.x += ball_speed_x
    ball.y += ball_speed_y

    # Bounce off the top and bottom walls
    if ball.top <= 0 or ball.bottom >= WINDOW_HEIGHT:
        ball_speed_y *= -1

    # Bounce off the paddles
    if ball.colliderect(left_paddle) or
ball.colliderect(right_paddle):
        ball_speed_x *= -1

    # Reset ball position if it goes out of bounds
    if ball.left <= 0 or ball.right >= WINDOW_WIDTH:
        reset_ball()
```

### Explanation

- **Ball Movement:** The ball's position is updated based on its speed.
- **Collision Detection:** We check for collisions with the paddles and walls, reversing the ball's direction upon impact.
- **Out of Bounds:** If the ball goes off the left or right edge, it will be reset.

## Scoring System

We need a simple scoring system to keep track of the players' points.

```python
# Scoring
left_score = 0
right_score = 0
SCORE_LIMIT = 5
font = pygame.font.Font(None, 74)

def draw_score():
    left_text = font.render(str(left_score), True, WHITE)
    right_text = font.render(str(right_score), True, WHITE)
    window.blit(left_text, (WINDOW_WIDTH // 4, 20))
    window.blit(right_text, (3 * WINDOW_WIDTH // 4, 20))

def check_score():
    global left_score, right_score
```

```
        if ball.left <= 0:
            right_score += 1
            reset_ball()
        if ball.right >= WINDOW_WIDTH:
            left_score += 1
            reset_ball()
```

**Explanation**

- **Score Display:** The scores are displayed at the top of the screen.
- **Scoring Condition:** If the ball goes off one side, the opposing player scores a point.
- **Win Condition:** You can modify the code to declare a winner once a player reaches the `SCORE_LIMIT`.

## Resetting the Ball

We need a function to reset the ball after each point.

```
import random

def reset_ball():
    ball.x = WINDOW_WIDTH // 2 - BALL_SIZE // 2
    ball.y = WINDOW_HEIGHT // 2 - BALL_SIZE // 2
    ball_speed_x *= random.choice([-1, 1])
    ball_speed_y *= random.choice([-1, 1])
```

**Explanation**

- **Random Direction:** The ball's direction is randomized after each reset for added variety.

## Main Game Loop

The main loop ties all the game logic together and keeps the game running.

```
while True:
    for event in pygame.event.get():
        if event.type == pygame.QUIT:
            pygame.quit()
            sys.exit()
```

```python
    # Handle input and update game state
    handle_input()
    move_ball()
    check_score()

    # Draw everything
    window.fill(BLACK)
    pygame.draw.rect(window, WHITE, left_paddle)
    pygame.draw.rect(window, WHITE, right_paddle)
    pygame.draw.ellipse(window, WHITE, ball)
    pygame.draw.aaline(window, WHITE, (WINDOW_WIDTH // 2, 0),
(WINDOW_WIDTH // 2, WINDOW_HEIGHT))
    draw_score()

    # Update the display
    pygame.display.flip()
    clock.tick(FPS)
```

## Explanation

- **Event Handling:** We handle the quit event to allow the player to close the game window.
- **Game Logic:** We call the input, ball movement, and scoring functions in each frame.
- **Rendering:** We draw all game elements on the screen before updating the display.

## Enhancing the Game

You can enhance this basic Pong game by:

- **Adding Power-Ups:** Create special items that players can collect to gain advantages (e.g., speed boosts, larger paddles).
- **Custom Controls:** Integrate Raspberry Pi's GPIO pins to allow players to use physical buttons or joysticks for control.
- **Different Game Modes:** Implement variations like "Endless Mode" or "Time Attack."

## Conclusion

In this section, we built a complete local multiplayer game using Python and PyGame. This project is an excellent starting point for experimenting with game mechanics and learning more about game development. By expanding on this game, you can create more complex and engaging multiplayer experiences on the Raspberry Pi.

# Troubleshooting Common Network Issues

Developing a networked multiplayer game comes with its own set of challenges, particularly when dealing with connectivity and communication problems. In this section, we will explore some of the common issues you might face when building networked games using Python and Raspberry Pi. We will also provide practical solutions and debugging tips to help you resolve these issues.

## 1. Connectivity Issues

### Problem: Unable to Connect Client to Server

One of the most common issues is the failure of the client to establish a connection with the server. This can be caused by several factors:

- Incorrect server IP address or port.
- Firewall blocking the connection.
- Network configuration issues (e.g., different subnets).

### Solution

1. **Verify IP Address and Port:**

Ensure that the client is using the correct IP address of the server. You can find the server's IP address using the following command on the Raspberry Pi:

```
hostname -I
```

Make sure the port number matches the one used by the server script. For example, if your server listens on port 5555, the client must connect using the same port.

2. **Check Firewall Settings:**

Firewalls can block incoming and outgoing connections. On Raspberry Pi (Raspbian), you can use `ufw` (Uncomplicated Firewall) to manage firewall rules:

```
sudo ufw allow 5555/tcp
sudo ufw status
```

Ensure the firewall allows traffic on the specified port.

3. **Test Network Connectivity:**

Use the `ping` command to test connectivity between the client and server devices:

```
ping 192.168.1.10
```

If the ping fails, it indicates a network issue that needs to be resolved before the client can connect.

## 2. Socket Timeout Errors

### Problem: Socket Timeout or Connection Reset

Socket timeout errors often occur when the server or client is unable to send or receive data within a specified period. This can be due to slow network conditions or an unresponsive server.

### Solution

1. **Increase the Socket Timeout:**

By default, sockets have a short timeout period. You can increase this value in both the client and server scripts using the `settimeout` method:

```
client_socket.settimeout(10)   # 10 seconds timeout
```

This will give the connection more time to send or receive data before timing out.

2. **Handle Timeouts Gracefully:**

Use a `try-except` block to catch timeout errors and handle them appropriately:

```
try:
    data = client_socket.recv(1024)
except socket.timeout:
    print("Socket timeout occurred. Retrying...")
```

This prevents the script from crashing due to a timeout error and allows you to implement a retry mechanism.

## 3. Data Packet Loss

### Problem: Incomplete or Missing Data Packets

In networked games, especially over Wi-Fi, data packets can occasionally be lost or arrive out of order. This can result in missing or incorrect game state updates.

### Solution

1. **Implement Reliable Data Transmission:**

Consider using a reliable protocol like TCP, which ensures that all data packets are delivered in order. If you are already using TCP and still experiencing packet loss, you may need to implement a custom acknowledgment system.

For example, when the client sends a message, the server can respond with an acknowledgment:

```python
# Client sends data and waits for acknowledgment
client_socket.send(b"move_up")
ack = client_socket.recv(1024)
if ack.decode() != "ACK":
    print("Data not acknowledged. Resending...")
```

2. **Add Sequence Numbers to Packets:**

To handle out-of-order packets, you can include sequence numbers with each data packet. The client and server can then ignore any packets that arrive out of sequence.

```python
packet = f"{sequence_number}|move_up".encode()
client_socket.send(packet)
sequence_number += 1
```

The server can check the sequence number before processing the packet.

## 4. Lag and Latency Issues

### Problem: High Latency or Lag During Gameplay

Lag can severely impact the gameplay experience, making the game feel unresponsive. This issue is often caused by network delays or inefficient data processing.

### Solution

1. **Optimize Data Transmission:**

Reduce the amount of data being sent over the network. Instead of sending the entire game state, only send changes (e.g., player input or position updates).

For example:

```python
# Instead of sending the full game state:
```

```
# "left_paddle=150, right_paddle=250, ball_x=400, ball_y=300"
# Send only changes:
# "left_paddle_up"
```

2. **Implement Client-Side Prediction:**

To mitigate the effects of latency, use client-side prediction, where the client predicts the game state based on player input and updates its display accordingly. When the server response arrives, the client can correct any discrepancies.

Example of client-side prediction:

```
# Client predicts the new position of the paddle
left_paddle.y -= PADDLE_SPEED
# Update based on server response
server_response = client_socket.recv(1024).decode()
actual_position = int(server_response.split(",")[0])
left_paddle.y = actual_position
```

3. **Use a Fixed Tick Rate:**

Ensure that both the client and server run the game loop at a consistent tick rate (e.g., 60 FPS). This helps synchronize the game state and reduces jitter.

```
# On both client and server:
clock.tick(60)   # 60 frames per second
```

## 5. Debugging Network Code

### Problem: Difficulty Diagnosing Network Issues

Network code can be challenging to debug because issues often arise intermittently and may be affected by external factors like network traffic or device performance.

### Solution

1. **Use Logging:**

Add detailed logging to both the client and server scripts to track the flow of data and identify where problems occur. For example:

```
import logging
```

```
logging.basicConfig(level=logging.DEBUG, filename="network.log",
filemode="w")
logging.debug(f"Sent data: {data}")
logging.debug(f"Received data: {response}")
```

2. **Test with Network Tools:**

Use network analysis tools like `netcat` (nc) and `wireshark` to inspect network traffic and diagnose issues:

```
# Listen on port 5555 with netcat
nc -l 5555
```

This allows you to manually test the connection and view raw data being transmitted.

3. **Simulate Network Conditions:**

To test how your game handles different network conditions, use tools like `tc` on Linux to simulate latency or packet loss:

```
# Add 100ms latency
sudo tc qdisc add dev wlan0 root netem delay 100ms

# Add 10% packet loss
sudo tc qdisc add dev wlan0 root netem loss 10%
```

This can help you identify and fix issues before releasing your game.

## Conclusion

In this section, we explored various common network issues and provided solutions to help you troubleshoot and optimize your multiplayer game. By following these best practices and using the debugging techniques outlined here, you can create a smoother and more reliable gaming experience. Networking can be complex, but with persistence and careful testing, you can overcome these challenges and build robust multiplayer games on the Raspberry Pi.

# Troubleshooting Common Network Issues

Building networked multiplayer games can be a rewarding challenge, but it often comes with its own set of networking problems that can disrupt the gameplay experience. In this section, we will address the most common network issues you might face when developing multiplayer games on Raspberry Pi using Python. We will provide detailed explanations, practical solutions, and code examples to help you diagnose and fix these problems effectively.

## Network Connectivity Problems

### Problem: Client Cannot Connect to Server

One of the first issues you might encounter is the failure of the client to connect to the server. This can be due to a variety of reasons, including incorrect IP address, network misconfiguration, or firewall restrictions.

**Solution**

1. **Verify IP Address and Port Configuration:**

Ensure that the client is attempting to connect to the correct IP address and port. On the Raspberry Pi server, you can determine the IP address by running:

```
hostname -I
```

Ensure the client code uses the correct IP and port number:

```
SERVER_IP = "192.168.1.10"
SERVER_PORT = 5555
client_socket.connect((SERVER_IP, SERVER_PORT))
```

2. **Check Firewall and Network Settings:**

Firewalls can block incoming connections, preventing the client from connecting. On Raspberry Pi, you can check and modify firewall rules using `ufw`:

```
sudo ufw allow 5555/tcp
sudo ufw status
```

Ensure that the specified port is allowed through the firewall.

3. **Test Network Connection:**

Use the `ping` command to verify that the client can reach the server:

```
ping 192.168.1.10
```

If the ping test fails, there may be network configuration issues that need to be resolved before the client can connect.

## Socket Timeout Errors

### Problem: Socket Timeout During Data Transmission

Socket timeout errors occur when a client or server does not receive data within the expected time frame. This can happen due to network congestion, slow response times, or incorrect timeout settings.

### Solution

1. **Increase the Socket Timeout:**

Adjust the socket timeout value to allow more time for data transmission:

```
client_socket.settimeout(10)    # 10-second timeout
```

This modification gives the connection more time to complete before triggering a timeout error.

2. **Handle Timeout Errors Gracefully:**

Wrap the socket operations in a `try-except` block to manage timeout errors without crashing the application:

```
try:
    data = client_socket.recv(1024)
except socket.timeout:
    print("Socket timeout occurred. Retrying...")
```

Implementing a retry mechanism can help mitigate issues caused by temporary network delays.

## Packet Loss and Data Corruption

### Problem: Missing or Corrupted Data Packets

In networked games, packet loss can lead to missing updates, while data corruption can cause unexpected behavior. This is especially common on wireless networks with poor signal quality.

**Solution**

1. **Use a Reliable Transport Protocol:**

TCP is a reliable protocol that guarantees packet delivery and ordering. If you are experiencing packet loss issues with UDP, consider switching to TCP:

```python
server_socket = socket.socket(socket.AF_INET, socket.SOCK_STREAM)
server_socket.bind((SERVER_IP, SERVER_PORT))
server_socket.listen()
```

2. **Implement Error Detection:**

Include checksums or hash values with your data packets to detect corruption. For example, you can use Python's `hashlib` to compute a checksum:

```python
import hashlib

data = "player_move"
checksum = hashlib.md5(data.encode()).hexdigest()
packet = f"{data}|{checksum}"
```

On the receiving end, verify the checksum:

```python
received_data, received_checksum = packet.split("|")
if hashlib.md5(received_data.encode()).hexdigest() != received_checksum:
    print("Data corruption detected. Requesting retransmission.")
```

3. **Resend Lost Packets:**

If the client does not receive an expected packet, request a retransmission:

```python
client_socket.send(b"RESEND")
```

The server can respond by resending the last valid packet.

## High Latency and Lag

### Problem: High Latency Causing Laggy Gameplay

Latency refers to the delay between a player's input and the response they see on the screen. High latency can make a multiplayer game feel sluggish and unresponsive.

### Solution

1. **Optimize Data Transmission:**

Minimize the amount of data being sent over the network. Instead of sending the entire game state, only send changes or player inputs:

```
# Instead of sending full game state:
# "left_paddle=150, right_paddle=250, ball_x=400, ball_y=300"
# Send only changes:
# "player_move=left_paddle_up"
```

2. **Implement Client-Side Prediction:**

Client-side prediction can help reduce the perceived latency by updating the game state locally based on player input, without waiting for the server response:

```
# Predict new position locally
left_paddle.y -= PADDLE_SPEED

# Correct position based on server update
server_response = client_socket.recv(1024).decode()
left_paddle_position = int(server_response.split(",")[0])
left_paddle.y = left_paddle_position
```

3. **Use Lag Compensation:**

Incorporate a simple lag compensation mechanism where the server accounts for the latency when processing player inputs. Record the timestamp of each input and adjust the game state accordingly.

```
input_time = int(time.time() * 1000)
server_socket.send(f"{input_time}|move_up".encode())
```

## Synchronization Issues

### Problem: Clients Display Different Game States

Synchronization problems can occur when the server and clients have inconsistent game states. This is often due to differences in update rates or dropped packets.

**Solution**

1. **Send Regular State Updates:**

Ensure that the server sends regular game state updates to all clients, even if there are no changes. This keeps the clients synchronized:

```python
# Send full game state every 100ms
while True:
    state_message = f"{left_paddle.y},{right_paddle.y},{ball.x},{ball.y}"
    broadcast(state_message.encode())
    time.sleep(0.1)
```

2. **Use a Fixed Update Rate:**

Maintain a consistent update rate on both the server and clients to avoid discrepancies in the game state:

```python
clock.tick(60)   # 60 updates per second
```

3. **Apply State Interpolation:**

Use interpolation to smoothly transition between game states received from the server, reducing the jarring effects of sudden position changes:

```python
# Interpolate between current and received positions
left_paddle.y = 0.9 * left_paddle.y + 0.1 * server_left_paddle_y
```

## Debugging Network Issues

### Problem: Difficulty Identifying the Source of Network Problems

Network issues can be challenging to diagnose, especially when they only occur intermittently or under specific conditions.

## Solution

1. **Enable Detailed Logging:**

Add comprehensive logging to both the client and server to capture detailed information about network events:

```
import logging

logging.basicConfig(level=logging.DEBUG,
filename="network_debug.log", filemode="w")
logging.debug("Client connected from IP: %s", client_address)
logging.debug("Received data: %s", data)
```

2. **Use Network Analysis Tools:**

Utilize tools like `netstat`, `tcpdump`, or `wireshark` to analyze network traffic and identify issues like packet loss or latency spikes:

```
sudo tcpdump -i wlan0 port 5555
```

3. **Simulate Adverse Network Conditions:**

Test your game under different network conditions using `tc` on Linux to add latency or packet loss:

```
# Add 100ms delay
sudo tc qdisc add dev eth0 root netem delay 100ms

# Add 5% packet loss
sudo tc qdisc add dev eth0 root netem loss 5%
```

## Conclusion

In this section, we addressed some of the most common network issues you may face when building a multiplayer game. By following these troubleshooting steps and best practices, you can enhance the stability and performance of your game, providing a smoother and more enjoyable experience for players. Networking challenges are inevitable, but with careful debugging and optimization, they can be overcome.

# Chapter 9: Advanced Graphics and Game Design with PyGame

## Introduction to Sprite Animation

Sprite animation is a core concept in game development that involves changing the appearance of an object (sprite) frame by frame to create the illusion of movement or other visual effects. In PyGame, working with sprite animations can significantly enhance the visual appeal of your game and bring your characters or objects to life.

In this section, we will dive deep into creating sprite animations using PyGame. We'll cover the following topics:

- Understanding sprites and sprite sheets
- Loading and animating sprites
- Creating a basic sprite animation class
- Managing sprite states for complex animations
- Tips for optimizing sprite performance

## Understanding Sprites and Sprite Sheets

A **sprite** is a two-dimensional image or animation that is integrated into a larger scene. Sprites are commonly used for characters, objects, or visual effects in games. A **sprite sheet** is a collection of multiple sprites packed into a single image file. Using sprite sheets helps improve performance by reducing the number of image loads during gameplay.

### Why use sprite sheets?

- Efficient memory usage: Loading one image instead of multiple files.
- Easier animation handling: Organizing frames in a single sheet.
- Faster rendering: Minimizes texture switching.

A typical sprite sheet might look like a grid of small images, where each image represents a frame of the animation.

## Loading and Animating Sprites

To work with sprite animations, the first step is to load the sprite sheet and extract individual frames. In PyGame, you can achieve this by slicing the sprite sheet into separate surfaces.

### Example: Loading a Sprite Sheet

```
import pygame
```

```python
# Initialize PyGame
pygame.init()

# Constants for screen dimensions
SCREEN_WIDTH = 800
SCREEN_HEIGHT = 600

# Load the sprite sheet
sprite_sheet = pygame.image.load('spritesheet.png').convert_alpha()

# Function to extract individual frames from the sprite sheet
def get_sprite_frames(sheet, frame_width, frame_height):
    frames = []
    sheet_width, sheet_height = sheet.get_size()

    for y in range(0, sheet_height, frame_height):
        for x in range(0, sheet_width, frame_width):
            frame = sheet.subsurface((x, y, frame_width, frame_height))
            frames.append(frame)

    return frames

# Example usage
frame_width = 64
frame_height = 64
frames = get_sprite_frames(sprite_sheet, frame_width, frame_height)
```

In the above code:

- We load a sprite sheet image using `pygame.image.load()`.
- We define a function `get_sprite_frames()` to slice the sprite sheet into frames of a specified width and height.
- The `subsurface()` method is used to create a new surface from the sprite sheet, representing a single frame.

## Creating a Basic Sprite Animation Class

To manage animations effectively, it's useful to create a sprite animation class that handles the frame updates and rendering.

**Example: Sprite Animation Class**

```python
class SpriteAnimation:
    def __init__(self, frames, frame_duration):
        self.frames = frames
        self.frame_duration = frame_duration
        self.current_frame = 0
        self.time_accumulator = 0

    def update(self, delta_time):
        # Increment the time accumulator
        self.time_accumulator += delta_time

        # Update the frame if enough time has passed
        if self.time_accumulator >= self.frame_duration:
            self.time_accumulator = 0
            self.current_frame = (self.current_frame + 1) % len(self.frames)

    def draw(self, screen, position):
        # Draw the current frame at the specified position
        frame = self.frames[self.current_frame]
        screen.blit(frame, position)

# Example usage in a game loop
clock = pygame.time.Clock()
running = True
sprite_animation = SpriteAnimation(frames, frame_duration=100)

while running:
    delta_time = clock.tick(60)
    for event in pygame.event.get():
        if event.type == pygame.QUIT:
            running = False

    sprite_animation.update(delta_time)
    screen.fill((0, 0, 0))
    sprite_animation.draw(screen, (100, 100))
    pygame.display.flip()

pygame.quit()
```

**Key points:**

- `SpriteAnimation` handles the frame updates based on the time elapsed.
- The `update()` method manages the transition between frames.
- The `draw()` method renders the current frame on the screen.

## Managing Sprite States

In more complex games, a sprite may have multiple animations (e.g., walking, jumping, attacking). To manage this, you can define a state system within your sprite class.

### Example: Sprite with Multiple States

```
class PlayerSprite:
    def __init__(self, animations):
        self.animations = animations
        self.current_state = 'idle'
        self.animation = animations[self.current_state]

    def set_state(self, state):
        if state in self.animations:
            self.current_state = state
            self.animation = self.animations[state]

    def update(self, delta_time):
        self.animation.update(delta_time)

    def draw(self, screen, position):
        self.animation.draw(screen, position)

# Defining animations
idle_animation = SpriteAnimation(idle_frames, 150)
walk_animation = SpriteAnimation(walk_frames, 100)

animations = {
    'idle': idle_animation,
    'walk': walk_animation
}

player_sprite = PlayerSprite(animations)

# Switching states based on user input
keys = pygame.key.get_pressed()
if keys[pygame.K_LEFT] or keys[pygame.K_RIGHT]:
    player_sprite.set_state('walk')
```

```
else:
    player_sprite.set_state('idle')
```

This approach allows you to easily switch between different animations based on the player's actions or game events.

## Optimizing Sprite Performance

Sprite animations can be resource-intensive, especially if you have many sprites on the screen at once. Here are some tips for optimization:

1. **Use sprite sheets**: This reduces the number of image loads and texture switches.
2. **Limit the frame rate**: Higher frame rates consume more processing power. Stick to a reasonable frame rate (e.g., 30-60 FPS).
3. **Use PyGame's `Sprite` and `Group` classes**: PyGame provides built-in classes for managing sprites more efficiently.
4. **Preload animations**: Load and prepare all animations during game initialization to avoid loading delays during gameplay.

### Example: Using PyGame's Sprite and Group Classes

```python
class AnimatedSprite(pygame.sprite.Sprite):
    def __init__(self, frames, frame_duration):
        super().__init__()
        self.frames = frames
        self.frame_duration = frame_duration
        self.current_frame = 0
        self.image = frames[self.current_frame]
        self.rect = self.image.get_rect()
        self.time_accumulator = 0

    def update(self, delta_time):
        self.time_accumulator += delta_time
        if self.time_accumulator >= self.frame_duration:
            self.time_accumulator = 0
            self.current_frame = (self.current_frame + 1) % len(self.frames)
            self.image = self.frames[self.current_frame]

# Creating a sprite group
all_sprites = pygame.sprite.Group()
player = AnimatedSprite(frames, 100)
all_sprites.add(player)
```

```
# Updating and drawing sprites in the game loop
all_sprites.update(delta_time)
all_sprites.draw(screen)
```

Using `pygame.sprite.Sprite` and `pygame.sprite.Group` can simplify sprite management and provide built-in methods for collision detection and efficient drawing.

## Conclusion

In this section, we covered the basics of sprite animation in PyGame, including how to load and animate sprites, create reusable animation classes, manage sprite states, and optimize performance. Mastering sprite animation will allow you to create dynamic and visually engaging games.

With these concepts, you can now start implementing more complex and polished animations in your own game projects.

# Creating Parallax Backgrounds

Parallax scrolling is a popular technique used in games to create a sense of depth and motion by having different layers of the background move at different speeds. This method mimics the effect you see when you look out of a moving vehicle: objects closer to you appear to move faster than those farther away. In 2D games, parallax scrolling can make your scenes more immersive and visually appealing.

In this section, we will explore how to implement parallax backgrounds using PyGame. We will cover:

- Understanding the concept of parallax scrolling
- Setting up multiple background layers
- Coding a basic parallax background system
- Enhancing parallax effects with different motion techniques
- Optimizing performance for smooth scrolling

## Understanding Parallax Scrolling

Parallax scrolling involves layering several background images (or layers) and moving them at different speeds based on the player's movement. Typically, the layer closest to the camera (foreground) moves the fastest, while the layer farthest away (background) moves the slowest.

**Key points to remember:**

- Foreground: Closest to the player, moves quickly.
- Midground: Intermediate distance, moves moderately.

- Background: Farthest away, moves slowly.

## Setting Up Multiple Background Layers

To create a parallax effect, you need at least two or more background layers. These layers can be images of different elements like clouds, trees, mountains, and the sky. For this example, let's assume we have three layers:

1. **Sky layer** (background)
2. **Mountain layer** (midground)
3. **Tree layer** (foreground)

We can load these images using PyGame and display them on the screen.

### Example: Loading Background Layers

```
import pygame

# Initialize PyGame
pygame.init()

# Screen dimensions
SCREEN_WIDTH = 800
SCREEN_HEIGHT = 600

# Load background images
sky_image = pygame.image.load('sky.png').convert_alpha()
mountain_image = pygame.image.load('mountains.png').convert_alpha()
trees_image = pygame.image.load('trees.png').convert_alpha()

# Scale images to fit the screen (if necessary)
sky_image = pygame.transform.scale(sky_image, (SCREEN_WIDTH, SCREEN_HEIGHT))
mountain_image = pygame.transform.scale(mountain_image, (SCREEN_WIDTH, SCREEN_HEIGHT))
trees_image = pygame.transform.scale(trees_image, (SCREEN_WIDTH, SCREEN_HEIGHT))
```

In this code snippet:

- We initialize PyGame and set up the screen dimensions.
- We load three background images using `pygame.image.load()`.
- The `convert_alpha()` method is used to handle transparency.
- We scale the images to fit the screen using `pygame.transform.scale()`.

## Coding a Basic Parallax Background System

Now, let's implement the parallax effect by defining a `ParallaxBackground` class that handles the movement of each layer based on the player's input or the game's camera movement.

**Example: Parallax Background Class**

```
class ParallaxBackground:
    def __init__(self, layers, speeds):
        self.layers = layers
        self.speeds = speeds
        self.positions = [0] * len(layers)

    def update(self, delta_x):
        # Update the positions of each layer based on their speed
        for i in range(len(self.layers)):
            self.positions[i] -= delta_x * self.speeds[i]

            # Loop the background layer when it moves off-screen
            if self.positions[i] <= -SCREEN_WIDTH:
                self.positions[i] = 0

    def draw(self, screen):
        # Draw each layer twice to create a looping effect
        for i, layer in enumerate(self.layers):
            pos = self.positions[i]
            screen.blit(layer, (pos, 0))
            screen.blit(layer, (pos + SCREEN_WIDTH, 0))

# Define the layers and their respective speeds
layers = [sky_image, mountain_image, trees_image]
speeds = [0.1, 0.3, 0.5]  # Lower speed values for distant layers

# Create the parallax background instance
parallax_background = ParallaxBackground(layers, speeds)
```

In this example:

- `ParallaxBackground` manages the movement of each layer based on the specified speeds.
- The `update()` method shifts the position of each layer, creating the parallax effect.

- The `draw()` method renders each layer on the screen, ensuring a seamless loop by drawing each layer twice.

## Implementing Parallax Scrolling in the Game Loop

Now, we integrate the `ParallaxBackground` class into the main game loop. This will allow the background layers to scroll based on the player's movement or the camera's position.

### Example: Scrolling with Player Input

```python
# Main game loop
clock = pygame.time.Clock()
running = True
player_speed = 5

while running:
    delta_time = clock.tick(60)
    delta_x = 0

    for event in pygame.event.get():
        if event.type == pygame.QUIT:
            running = False

    # Handle player input
    keys = pygame.key.get_pressed()
    if keys[pygame.K_LEFT]:
        delta_x = player_speed
    elif keys[pygame.K_RIGHT]:
        delta_x = -player_speed

    # Update the parallax background
    parallax_background.update(delta_x)

    # Draw everything
    screen.fill((0, 0, 0))
    parallax_background.draw(screen)
    pygame.display.flip()

pygame.quit()
```

In this game loop:

- We check for player input (left and right arrow keys) to determine the direction of movement.
- The `delta_x` value controls the speed and direction of the background scrolling.
- The parallax background is updated and drawn on the screen every frame.

## Enhancing Parallax Effects

To create a more dynamic and realistic parallax effect, consider the following enhancements:

1. **Multiple Scrolling Directions**: Implement vertical scrolling for games where the player can move up and down (e.g., platformers).
2. **Different Speeds for Horizontal and Vertical Scrolling**: Adjust the speed independently for horizontal and vertical movements for finer control.
3. **Dynamic Layer Speeds**: Change the speed of layers based on the player's velocity to create acceleration effects.

### Example: Vertical Parallax Scrolling

```
def update(self, delta_x, delta_y):
    for i in range(len(self.layers)):
        self.positions[i] = (
            self.positions[i][0] - delta_x * self.speeds[i],
            self.positions[i][1] - delta_y * self.speeds[i]
        )

        # Loop the background layer horizontally and vertically
        if self.positions[i][0] <= -SCREEN_WIDTH:
            self.positions[i] = (0, self.positions[i][1])
        if self.positions[i][1] <= -SCREEN_HEIGHT:
            self.positions[i] = (self.positions[i][0], 0)
```

## Optimizing Parallax Performance

Parallax scrolling can be resource-intensive, especially if you have many layers or large images. Here are some tips for optimization:

1. **Limit the Number of Layers**: Use only as many layers as necessary. Too many layers can slow down rendering.
2. **Preload Images**: Load all images at the start of the game to avoid delays during gameplay.
3. **Use Smaller Textures**: Scale down large images to fit the screen dimensions.
4. **Cache Layer Positions**: Store the positions of the layers in memory to reduce recalculation.

## Conclusion

Parallax scrolling is a powerful technique that can significantly enhance the visual appeal of your 2D games. By layering multiple backgrounds and moving them at different speeds, you can create an immersive sense of depth and motion. The `ParallaxBackground` class provides a flexible and reusable framework for implementing parallax effects in your PyGame projects.

Experiment with different layer speeds, textures, and scrolling directions to create unique and engaging environments for your players. With a solid understanding of parallax scrolling, you can now take your game's visuals to the next level.

# Implementing a Scoring and High-Score System

A scoring system is a fundamental part of most games. It provides players with a measurable goal, enhances the game's competitiveness, and adds replay value by encouraging players to beat their high scores. In this section, we will explore how to implement a basic scoring system using PyGame and extend it to include a high-score feature that persists between game sessions.

We will cover the following topics:

- Understanding scoring mechanics
- Implementing a basic score counter
- Displaying the score on the screen
- Saving and loading high scores
- Enhancing the scoring system with multipliers and bonuses

## Understanding Scoring Mechanics

Before we start coding, it is essential to understand the types of scoring mechanics commonly used in games:

1. **Incremental Score**: The score increases as the player progresses, often based on time survived or enemies defeated.
2. **Collectible Score**: Points are awarded when the player collects certain items (e.g., coins, gems).
3. **Achievement-Based Score**: The score increases when the player achieves specific milestones or completes challenges.

We will implement an incremental score that increases based on time, and a collectible score that adds points when the player collects specific items.

## Implementing a Basic Score Counter

The first step is to create a simple score counter that updates as the game progresses. We will use a variable to keep track of the score and increase it over time.

**Example: Basic Score Counter**

```python
import pygame

# Initialize PyGame
pygame.init()

# Screen setup
SCREEN_WIDTH = 800
SCREEN_HEIGHT = 600
screen = pygame.display.set_mode((SCREEN_WIDTH, SCREEN_HEIGHT))
pygame.display.set_caption("Scoring System Example")

# Font for displaying the score
font = pygame.font.Font(None, 36)

# Initialize the score
score = 0
score_increment = 1

# Main game loop
clock = pygame.time.Clock()
running = True

while running:
    delta_time = clock.tick(60) / 1000  # Convert milliseconds to seconds

    # Event handling
    for event in pygame.event.get():
        if event.type == pygame.QUIT:
            running = False

    # Update the score based on time
    score += score_increment * delta_time

    # Render the score on the screen
    screen.fill((0, 0, 0))
    score_text = font.render(f"Score: {int(score)}", True, (255, 255, 255))
    screen.blit(score_text, (10, 10))

    pygame.display.flip()
```

```
pygame.quit()
```

In this example:

- We initialize the score and increase it based on the elapsed time (`delta_time`).
- The score is displayed using PyGame's `font.render()` method.

## Displaying the Score on the Screen

Displaying the score is crucial for providing feedback to the player. We can enhance the display by adding a background box or styling the text.

**Example: Displaying the Score with a Background Box**

```
def draw_score(screen, score, font):
    score_text = font.render(f"Score: {int(score)}", True, (255, 255, 255))
    text_rect = score_text.get_rect()
    text_rect.topleft = (10, 10)

    # Draw a background box
    pygame.draw.rect(screen, (0, 0, 0), text_rect.inflate(10, 10))
    screen.blit(score_text, text_rect)
```

In this function:

- We use `inflate()` to create a slightly larger rectangle around the text for the background.
- The score text is rendered and displayed on top of the background box.

## Saving and Loading High Scores

To make the high-score system more engaging, we need to save the high score even after the game is closed. We can achieve this by saving the high score to a file and loading it when the game starts.

**Example: High-Score Management**

```
import os

# File to store the high score
HIGH_SCORE_FILE = "highscore.txt"
```

```python
# Function to save the high score
def save_high_score(score):
    with open(HIGH_SCORE_FILE, 'w') as file:
        file.write(str(int(score)))

# Function to load the high score
def load_high_score():
    if os.path.exists(HIGH_SCORE_FILE):
        with open(HIGH_SCORE_FILE, 'r') as file:
            return int(file.read())
    return 0

# Initialize the high score
high_score = load_high_score()

# Update the high score if the current score exceeds it
if score > high_score:
    high_score = score
    save_high_score(high_score)
```

In this code:

- We use a text file (`highscore.txt`) to store the high score.
- `save_high_score()` writes the high score to the file.
- `load_high_score()` reads the high score from the file.

## Displaying the High Score

Let's modify our score display function to include the high score.

### Example: Displaying Score and High Score

```python
def draw_scores(screen, score, high_score, font):
    score_text = font.render(f"Score: {int(score)}", True, (255, 255, 255))
    high_score_text = font.render(f"High Score: {int(high_score)}", True, (255, 215, 0))

    # Positioning the text
    score_rect = score_text.get_rect(topleft=(10, 10))
    high_score_rect = high_score_text.get_rect(topleft=(10, 50))
```

```
    # Draw background boxes
    pygame.draw.rect(screen, (0, 0, 0), score_rect.inflate(10, 10))
    pygame.draw.rect(screen, (0, 0, 0), high_score_rect.inflate(10, 10))

    # Blit the text
    screen.blit(score_text, score_rect)
    screen.blit(high_score_text, high_score_rect)
```

## Enhancing the Scoring System with Multipliers and Bonuses

To make the scoring system more dynamic and engaging, consider implementing score multipliers and bonuses. For example:

- **Combo Multipliers**: Increase the score multiplier when the player performs a series of successful actions without failure.
- **Time-Based Bonuses**: Award bonus points based on the player's speed or efficiency.
- **Item Collectibles**: Award additional points when the player collects specific in-game items.

**Example: Implementing a Score Multiplier**

```
combo_count = 0
multiplier = 1

def update_score(points):
    global score, combo_count, multiplier

    # Increase combo count and adjust multiplier
    combo_count += 1
    if combo_count >= 5:
        multiplier += 1
        combo_count = 0

    # Update score with multiplier
    score += points * multiplier
```

In this code:

- The multiplier increases after a series of successful actions.
- The score is updated with the applied multiplier.

## Optimizing the Scoring System

To ensure the scoring system runs efficiently:

- **Update the score less frequently**: Instead of updating every frame, consider updating the score once per second.
- **Avoid excessive file I/O**: Only save the high score when necessary, not every frame.

**Example: Efficient High-Score Saving**

```python
# Save the high score only if it has changed
if score > high_score:
    high_score = score
    save_high_score(high_score)
```

## Conclusion

In this section, we covered the implementation of a basic scoring system and extended it to include a persistent high-score feature. We also explored ways to enhance the scoring system with multipliers and bonuses to make the game more engaging.

By implementing a well-designed scoring system, you can increase player satisfaction and replay value, encouraging players to strive for higher scores and set new records.

# Optimizing Game Performance

Optimizing game performance is essential for creating smooth and responsive gameplay experiences, especially on resource-constrained devices like the Raspberry Pi. Effective performance optimization can reduce lag, prevent frame drops, and extend battery life in mobile environments. In this section, we'll explore several techniques to enhance the performance of a PyGame-based game, covering topics such as:

- Efficient rendering and blitting
- Managing game loop timing
- Memory management and asset loading
- Collision detection optimizations
- Leveraging PyGame's sprite groups for performance

## Efficient Rendering and Blitting

Rendering, or drawing objects on the screen, is often one of the most resource-intensive operations in a game loop. Optimizing the rendering process can significantly impact game performance.

**Minimize Redundant Drawing**

# Chapter 9: Advanced Graphics and Game Design with PyGame

One simple yet effective optimization is to limit drawing only to areas that have changed. For example, if only a small part of the screen changes, it's inefficient to redraw the entire screen.

**Example: Partial Redrawing with Dirty Rectangles**

```
dirty_rects = []  # A list to store areas that need updating

# In the game loop
dirty_rects.clear()

# Update only the parts of the screen that have changed
if player_moved:
    dirty_rects.append(player.rect)

# Use dirty rects to optimize the screen update
pygame.display.update(dirty_rects)
```

In this approach:

- Only modified areas of the screen (stored in `dirty_rects`) are redrawn.
- This optimization works well for games with a static background and minimal movement, as it minimizes the computational load of redrawing the entire screen.

**Use `convert()` and `convert_alpha()`**

Using `convert()` and `convert_alpha()` methods on images can help improve blitting performance by ensuring the images are in a format that matches the display surface.

```
# Load an image with transparency
sprite_image = pygame.image.load("sprite.png").convert_alpha()

# For opaque images, use convert() instead
background_image = pygame.image.load("background.jpg").convert()
```

## Managing Game Loop Timing

The game loop, which controls the execution flow of the game, should ideally run at a consistent frame rate. PyGame provides a `Clock` object to manage this, but you should carefully consider the target frame rate to balance performance and visual smoothness.

**Set a Target Frame Rate**

Setting an appropriate frame rate, such as 30 or 60 FPS, can help maintain smooth gameplay. However, if the game is designed for lower-spec hardware, a lower frame rate might be necessary.

```
clock = pygame.time.Clock()
target_fps = 30

# Game loop
while running:
    # Cap the frame rate
    delta_time = clock.tick(target_fps)
```

Here:

- The `tick()` function limits the frame rate to `target_fps`, which prevents the game from running faster than the specified FPS.

**Use Delta Time for Movement**

Instead of moving objects based on a fixed speed per frame, use delta time (`delta_time`), which adjusts object movement based on the time elapsed. This approach makes the game speed consistent, even if frame rates fluctuate.

```
# Example of delta-time-based movement
player_speed = 200   # pixels per second
player.x += player_speed * (delta_time / 1000)
```

By dividing `delta_time` by 1000, we convert milliseconds to seconds, making the movement speed in pixels per second.

## Memory Management and Asset Loading

Efficient memory management is essential for smooth performance, especially on devices with limited RAM. Here are some strategies for managing memory effectively.

### Load Assets Once

Loading assets like images, sounds, and fonts repeatedly can slow down the game. Load all assets at the start and reuse them as needed.

```
# Load images at the beginning
enemy_image = pygame.image.load("enemy.png").convert_alpha()
```

## Optimize Sound and Music Playback

Sound files, especially large ones, can consume a significant amount of memory. Use `.ogg` or `.mp3` formats for compressed audio and avoid uncompressed `.wav` files. Load sounds with `pygame.mixer.Sound()` for short effects and use `pygame.mixer.music` for background music.

```
# Example of loading sounds efficiently
laser_sound = pygame.mixer.Sound("laser.ogg")
pygame.mixer.music.load("background_music.mp3")
```

## Remove Unused Objects

In games with many objects (e.g., bullets or enemies), create a mechanism to remove objects that are no longer in use to free up memory.

```
# Removing off-screen bullets
bullets = [bullet for bullet in bullets if bullet.rect.x < SCREEN_WIDTH]
```

## Collision Detection Optimizations

Collision detection can be resource-intensive, especially as the number of objects in the game increases. Here are several ways to optimize collision detection:

### Use Rectangular Collision Detection

Rectangular collisions (`pygame.Rect`) are faster than pixel-perfect or circular collisions. Use rectangular collisions for objects that don't require precise collision boundaries.

```
if player.rect.colliderect(enemy.rect):
    # Handle collision
```

### Implement Spatial Partitioning

Spatial partitioning divides the game space into smaller regions and checks for collisions only within those regions. Common methods include grid-based partitioning or a quadtree structure. This technique is particularly useful for games with many moving objects.

### Example: Basic Grid-Based Spatial Partitioning

```python
# Define a 10x10 grid
GRID_SIZE = 10
grid = [[[] for _ in range(GRID_SIZE)] for _ in range(GRID_SIZE)]

# Assign objects to the grid
for obj in game_objects:
    grid_x = int(obj.rect.x / SCREEN_WIDTH * GRID_SIZE)
    grid_y = int(obj.rect.y / SCREEN_HEIGHT * GRID_SIZE)
    grid[grid_x][grid_y].append(obj)

# Check collisions only within nearby cells
for x in range(GRID_SIZE):
    for y in range(GRID_SIZE):
        for obj in grid[x][y]:
            for other in grid[x][y]:
                if obj != other and obj.rect.colliderect(other.rect):
                    # Handle collision
```

This method reduces the number of collision checks significantly by limiting checks to objects in nearby grid cells.

## Leveraging PyGame's Sprite Groups for Performance

PyGame provides built-in classes like `Sprite` and `Group`, which are optimized for handling multiple sprites and can improve game performance.

**Use Sprite Groups for Efficient Updates and Draws**

By using `pygame.sprite.Group`, you can efficiently manage and draw multiple sprites. Groups can also handle bulk updates and have built-in collision detection functions.

```python
# Define sprite groups
all_sprites = pygame.sprite.Group()
enemies = pygame.sprite.Group()

# Add sprites to the groups
player = PlayerSprite()
all_sprites.add(player)
enemy = EnemySprite()
all_sprites.add(enemy)
```

```
enemies.add(enemy)

# Update and draw all sprites
all_sprites.update()
all_sprites.draw(screen)
```

Using `Group` methods like `update()` and `draw()` reduces the need to loop through individual sprites manually, leading to faster execution.

**Sprite Layering with LayeredUpdates**

If your game requires multiple layers of sprites (e.g., background, midground, and foreground), you can use `pygame.sprite.LayeredUpdates` to control the rendering order.

```
# Layered sprite group
layered_sprites = pygame.sprite.LayeredUpdates()

# Add sprites with specific layers
layered_sprites.add(background_sprite, layer=0)
layered_sprites.add(player_sprite, layer=2)
layered_sprites.add(foreground_sprite, layer=3)
```

By defining specific layers for each sprite, `LayeredUpdates` automatically renders them in the correct order, making it easier to manage complex scenes with multiple layers.

## Avoiding Common Performance Pitfalls

Avoiding common pitfalls can also help keep the game running smoothly:

1. **Excessive Event Handling**: Only handle essential events. Avoid continuously polling for unused events.
2. **Unnecessary Loops**: Avoid redundant loops in the game loop. For example, updating every object on every frame may not be necessary.
3. **Complex Physics Calculations**: Only perform physics calculations on objects that require it.

**Example: Limiting Event Handling**

```
for event in pygame.event.get([pygame.QUIT, pygame.KEYDOWN,
pygame.KEYUP]):
    if event.type == pygame.QUIT:
        running = False
```

This example only handles quit and key events, ignoring unnecessary event types to reduce processing.

## Conclusion

Optimizing game performance is a crucial part of game development, particularly for games running on low-powered devices. By managing rendering, timing, memory, and collision detection effectively, you can create smoother and more efficient games.

Each optimization technique in this section can be applied independently or in combination, depending on the specific needs of your game. Implementing these optimizations will help ensure a more enjoyable experience for your players, whether they are playing on a powerful computer or a limited-resource device like a Raspberry Pi.

# Chapter 10: Case Study: Creating a Raspberry Pi Arcade Console

## Designing the Console Hardware

Designing a custom arcade console powered by Raspberry Pi offers a hands-on experience in both hardware and software integration. In this section, we'll explore the fundamental steps for designing the hardware for a Raspberry Pi arcade console, covering everything from selecting components to wiring, housing, and assembling the console. By the end of this section, you'll be equipped with a detailed plan to bring your arcade console to life.

### Choosing the Raspberry Pi Model

The Raspberry Pi serves as the core computing unit of the console. Here are some factors to consider when selecting the model:

- **Processing Power**: For smooth gameplay, especially for more graphics-intensive games, the Raspberry Pi 4 is ideal. It offers better CPU and GPU performance than previous models.
- **Memory**: Depending on the complexity of the games, a model with at least 2GB of RAM is recommended. The 4GB or 8GB versions provide additional memory to support larger games or multitasking.
- **Connectivity**: The Raspberry Pi 4 also supports HDMI output, which is beneficial if you plan on using a larger display screen for the console.

Consider the Pi's form factor, availability, and power requirements to ensure compatibility with your planned design and power supply.

### Selecting a Display Screen

The size and type of display screen you choose will affect the overall feel of the arcade console. Common options include:

- **Small LCD Screens (7-10 inches)**: These are ideal for a compact, tabletop-style arcade. Some touchscreen displays for the Raspberry Pi provide an interactive experience but are not necessary for a classic arcade feel.
- **HDMI-Compatible Monitors**: For larger, standalone arcade consoles, consider an HDMI monitor or TV. Ensure it's compatible with the Raspberry Pi's output resolution for optimal display.
- **CRT Monitors (for Retro Style)**: Although less common, CRT monitors give a nostalgic, retro look to the arcade console. They require special adapters and considerations for power and space.

When installing the screen, ensure it's securely mounted within the arcade cabinet or console frame. You may need a bezel or frame to cover the edges and create a professional look.

## Choosing Controls: Buttons, Joysticks, and Wiring

Classic arcade games typically use a joystick and several buttons for gameplay. For authenticity and durability, arcade-quality components are recommended. Here's a breakdown of the parts and setup:

### Joysticks

- **Single Joystick**: For single-player games, a single 8-way joystick will suffice.
- **Dual Joysticks**: If you plan on designing a console for multiplayer games, consider adding a second joystick.
- **Type of Joystick**: Some players prefer bat-top joysticks, while others prefer ball-top joysticks. Choose based on your preference or the game's aesthetic.

### Buttons

- **Standard Arcade Buttons**: Arcade buttons are larger than typical game controller buttons and provide a satisfying "click" when pressed. Opt for durable, responsive buttons rated for many presses.
- **Layout**: Arrange the buttons in a standard layout for ease of use. For single-player games, a common layout is four to six action buttons plus start, select, and coin buttons. For multiplayer games, duplicate the layout for each player.
- **Additional Controls**: Consider adding extra buttons for game functions such as start, select, coin insert, and menu navigation.

### Wiring and Interfaces

To connect the joystick and buttons to the Raspberry Pi, use a USB encoder. The encoder translates button and joystick movements into signals that the Raspberry Pi recognizes.

1. **USB Encoder**: A USB encoder kit typically includes connectors for each button and joystick, which then connects via USB to the Raspberry Pi.
2. **GPIO Option**: Alternatively, connect the buttons and joystick directly to the Raspberry Pi's GPIO pins. This setup requires knowledge of GPIO programming but avoids the need for additional encoders.

## Designing the Arcade Console Frame

The frame or housing is essential to both the aesthetics and durability of the arcade console. Here are key considerations:

### Material Selection

1. **Wood**: MDF or plywood is often used for DIY arcade cabinets. It's easy to cut and shape, relatively inexpensive, and can be painted or laminated.

2. **Acrylic or Plastic**: These materials give a modern look but require more specialized tools for cutting and assembly.
3. **Metal**: Using metal provides a sleek, industrial look but adds weight and complexity to the build.

**Frame Design**

The frame design should accommodate the display, controls, speakers, and Raspberry Pi while allowing for airflow and easy access to components. Common designs include:

- **Tabletop Console**: Compact and easy to place on a desk or table. Ideal for smaller screens and single-player setups.
- **Full-Size Cabinet**: Resembles a classic arcade machine. It's suitable for larger screens and offers an immersive arcade experience but takes up more space.
- **Portable Console**: Designed to be lightweight and easy to transport. These consoles often use smaller screens and simplified control layouts.

## Assembling the Components

With your components selected and the frame designed, begin assembling the arcade console:

1. **Mount the Display**: Secure the display screen to the frame, ensuring it aligns well with the viewing angle.
2. **Install the Joystick and Buttons**: Drill holes for the joystick and buttons based on your layout. Secure each component firmly to avoid movement during gameplay.
3. **Place the Raspberry Pi**: Install the Raspberry Pi inside the frame. Mount it in a location with good airflow, and ensure the USB and HDMI ports are accessible for easy connection.
4. **Connect the Power Supply**: Use a suitable power adapter for the Raspberry Pi. Route the power cable through the frame for a clean look.

## Wiring and Testing the Setup

With the components installed, it's time to connect everything and test the setup:

1. **Connect Buttons and Joystick to USB Encoder or GPIO**: Follow the instructions for your USB encoder to connect each button and joystick direction to the correct input on the encoder board.
2. **Connect the Encoder to the Raspberry Pi**: Plug the USB encoder into one of the Raspberry Pi's USB ports.
3. **Attach Speakers**: If your design includes speakers, connect them to the Raspberry Pi via the headphone jack or USB.
4. **Power Up and Test**: Turn on the Raspberry Pi and test each control component. Ensure that button presses and joystick movements register correctly in the operating system or within the game environment.

## Finalizing and Refining the Console Design

Once the hardware and connections are functional, consider the finishing touches:

- **Paint or Decorate the Frame**: Add paint, decals, or laminates to give the console a polished look.
- **Install a Bezel Around the Screen**: Use a bezel to cover the screen's edges and enhance the overall appearance.
- **Cable Management**: Use zip ties or adhesive clips to manage cables inside the frame, keeping the internal layout tidy and reducing potential damage to wires.
- **Adding a Marquee**: If creating a larger cabinet-style console, consider adding a marquee with lighting above the screen to replicate classic arcade styling.

## Coding and Testing Your Games on the Console

After the hardware setup, it's time to install and test your games. If you're using RetroPie, follow these steps:

```
# Update and install RetroPie on Raspberry Pi OS
sudo apt update
sudo apt install retropie-setup
cd RetroPie-Setup
sudo ./retropie_setup.sh
```

From here, you can upload games or integrate custom games built with Python and PyGame.

Test each game to ensure smooth operation with the joystick and button inputs. Adjust any settings to improve the gameplay experience.

## Final Thoughts

Building a Raspberry Pi arcade console is a rewarding project that combines hardware and software skills. With careful planning and attention to detail, you can create an arcade console that replicates the experience of classic games and showcases custom game creations.

# Setting Up RetroPie for Classic Games

Setting up RetroPie on your Raspberry Pi allows you to play classic games and use the arcade console with a rich library of retro titles. In this section, we will go through the entire RetroPie setup process, from installation to customization, providing you with a detailed understanding of how to configure and personalize RetroPie for the ultimate arcade experience.

## Overview of RetroPie

RetroPie is a powerful emulation platform that enables your Raspberry Pi to play classic games from a variety of gaming systems, such as Nintendo, Sega, Atari, and PlayStation. With RetroPie, you can turn your arcade console into a multi-platform gaming station. Here are the main features:

- **Multi-System Support**: RetroPie supports emulators for over 50 gaming systems.
- **User-Friendly Interface**: EmulationStation, the graphical interface used by RetroPie, provides an organized and visually appealing way to browse and launch games.
- **Customization Options**: You can add themes, configure controls, and install additional software.
- **Community and Documentation**: RetroPie has extensive community support and documentation, making it accessible for beginners and experts alike.

## Installing RetroPie on the Raspberry Pi

To set up RetroPie on your Raspberry Pi, you need a few essential items:

- Raspberry Pi (preferably a Pi 4 for optimal performance)
- MicroSD card (16GB or larger recommended)
- USB keyboard and/or game controller
- HDMI monitor or display
- Power supply for Raspberry Pi

Once you have these items, follow these steps to install RetroPie:

### Step 1: Download RetroPie

Visit the official RetroPie website and download the latest version of RetroPie for the Raspberry Pi. Select the image appropriate for your Raspberry Pi model (e.g., Pi 4/400).

### Step 2: Flash RetroPie onto the MicroSD Card

After downloading the RetroPie image, you'll need to flash it onto your microSD card. You can use software like **balenaEtcher** or **Raspberry Pi Imager**:

1. Insert your microSD card into your computer.
2. Open balenaEtcher (or Raspberry Pi Imager).
3. Select the downloaded RetroPie image.
4. Choose your microSD card as the target drive.
5. Click "Flash" to start the process. This may take several minutes.

### Step 3: Insert the MicroSD Card and Boot Up

Once the flashing process is complete, insert the microSD card into your Raspberry Pi, connect the necessary peripherals (keyboard, controller, monitor), and power it on. The Raspberry Pi will boot into RetroPie.

## Initial Configuration and Controller Setup

When RetroPie first boots, you'll be prompted to configure your controller. If you're using a USB keyboard, you can also configure it as the primary input device. Follow these steps:

1. On the "Welcome" screen, press and hold a button on your controller to start the configuration process.
2. Go through each button prompt, pressing the corresponding button on your controller. If you do not have a particular button, hold any button to skip it.
3. Once you complete the configuration, you'll be taken to the main RetroPie menu.

If you plan to use multiple controllers, connect each one individually and repeat the setup process.

## Updating RetroPie

Before adding games or making further customizations, it's recommended to update RetroPie to the latest version. To do this:

1. From the main RetroPie menu, navigate to **RetroPie Setup**.
2. Select **Update RetroPie-Setup script** and confirm the update.
3. Once updated, return to the RetroPie Setup menu and select **Basic Install**. This will update the core RetroPie software and emulators.

Updating ensures compatibility with new features, themes, and additional emulators.

## Adding Game ROMs to RetroPie

To play games on RetroPie, you'll need to add game ROMs, which are digital copies of game cartridges or discs. Note that downloading ROMs for games you do not own may be illegal in some regions. Here's how to add ROMs legally or with personal backups:

### Using a USB Drive to Add ROMs

1. Format a USB drive to FAT32 or exFAT (for compatibility).
2. Create a folder named `retropie` on the root of the USB drive.
3. Insert the USB drive into your Raspberry Pi, and RetroPie will automatically create subfolders for each emulator (e.g., `nes`, `snes`, `gba`).
4. Remove the USB drive from the Raspberry Pi and plug it back into your computer.
5. Place the ROM files in the appropriate system folders on the USB drive.
6. Insert the USB drive back into the Raspberry Pi. RetroPie will copy the ROM files to its storage.

### Using Network Transfer to Add ROMs

Alternatively, you can transfer ROMs over your local network:

1. Ensure your Raspberry Pi is connected to the same network as your computer.
2. On your computer, open a file explorer and navigate to `\\retropie` (Windows) or `smb://retropie` (Mac/Linux).

3. Open the roms folder, then drag and drop your ROM files into the respective system folders.

## Configuring Emulators and Video Settings

Once your ROMs are installed, you can customize the emulators and video settings to optimize the gameplay experience. RetroPie uses **EmulationStation** as the front-end, and **RetroArch** as the back-end for many emulators.

### Selecting an Emulator

For each game, you can choose a specific emulator to ensure compatibility and performance:

1. Launch a game and press any button on the controller during startup to access the configuration menu.
2. Choose **Select Emulator for ROM** and select from the available emulator options.
3. Save your choice to use this emulator each time you launch the game.

### Adjusting Video Settings

To ensure the games display correctly on your chosen monitor or display, you can adjust the video settings in RetroPie:

1. Go to the **RetroPie Configuration** menu.
2. Select **Raspberry Pi Configuration** and open **Raspberry Pi Configuration Tool (raspi-config)**.
3. In the raspi-config menu, navigate to **Advanced Options > Resolution** and select a resolution that best fits your display.

For CRT displays, RetroPie offers specific shaders and scanline effects to mimic the original look of classic arcade machines. Access these options in the **RetroArch** menu under **Settings > Video > Shaders**.

## Customizing the RetroPie Interface

RetroPie allows extensive customization of its interface and appearance through themes and other visual options.

### Installing Themes

RetroPie includes several built-in themes, but you can also download additional themes:

1. Go to the **RetroPie Setup** menu.
2. Select **ES Themes**.
3. Browse available themes, select your preferred one, and choose **Install**.
4. After installation, go back to EmulationStation, select **UI Settings**, and choose the installed theme.

Themes allow you to personalize the look and feel of the arcade console, enhancing the retro experience with custom graphics, icons, and layouts.

### Customizing Metadata and Game Artwork

To add box art, descriptions, and other metadata to your games:

1. In the EmulationStation main menu, select **Scraper**.
2. Choose a source for game metadata (e.g., TheGamesDB).
3. Begin the scraping process to automatically download box art and descriptions.

Adding metadata makes browsing through your game library more enjoyable, as each game is displayed with its title, cover art, and additional information.

## Configuring Controllers and Hotkeys

To ensure smooth gameplay and ease of use, configure controller settings and set up hotkeys for RetroPie:

1. From the main RetroPie menu, go to **RetroArch**.
2. Select **Settings > Input** to configure button mappings for each emulator.
3. Set up hotkeys for essential functions like Save State, Load State, and Reset. For example, mapping **Select + Start** to **Exit** allows you to quit games easily.

Hotkeys improve the gaming experience by allowing quick access to RetroArch functions without navigating through multiple menus.

## Testing and Troubleshooting Common Issues

After setup, test your arcade console with a few games to ensure everything works as expected. Here are some common issues and solutions:

- **Game Lag**: If games are lagging, try a lower-resolution video setting, or select a different emulator that runs more efficiently.
- **Controller Input Lag**: Input lag can be caused by incorrect settings or poor-quality USB controllers. Reconfigure the controller in the Input settings or use a higher-quality controller.
- **Audio Issues**: If you experience audio problems, go to the RetroPie Audio settings and adjust the output options.

## Final Thoughts

Setting up RetroPie on your Raspberry Pi arcade console unlocks a world of classic games and customization. By following this guide, you now have a fully functional RetroPie system ready to bring nostalgia and retro gaming to your custom console.

# Integrating Your Custom Games into RetroPie

Integrating custom games into RetroPie enables you to showcase your programming skills by incorporating games you've developed with Python and PyGame. In this section, we'll cover the complete process of preparing, configuring, and launching custom games on your Raspberry Pi arcade console. This includes setting up the RetroPie environment, preparing your PyGame projects, creating launch scripts, and integrating your games into the RetroPie interface.

## Preparing Your Custom Game Files

To integrate a custom game, first ensure that your game files are organized and compatible with the Raspberry Pi environment. Follow these guidelines:

1. **Optimize Code for Raspberry Pi**: Depending on your game's complexity, you may need to optimize your code to ensure smooth performance on the Raspberry Pi. Focus on efficient handling of graphics and sound to reduce lag.
2. **Organize Your Game Assets**: Place all assets (images, sounds, and fonts) in dedicated folders within the main game directory. This will make it easier to manage and troubleshoot issues during integration.
3. **Test on Raspberry Pi**: If possible, test your game directly on the Raspberry Pi to confirm that it runs as expected. Use Python 3 for PyGame projects, as it's the preferred version on recent Raspberry Pi systems.

Your directory structure might look like this:

```
my_game/
│
├── main.py      # Main script file
├── assets/
│   ├── images/
│   ├── sounds/
│   └── fonts/
└── config/
    └── settings.json  # Optional configuration file for game settings
```

Ensure the main script (e.g., `main.py`) serves as the entry point to the game.

## Setting Up Python and PyGame on RetroPie

RetroPie typically runs with RetroArch and pre-configured emulators, but you can manually add Python and PyGame support. Here's how to set it up:

**Install Python**: Most Raspberry Pi systems come with Python pre-installed, but if you need to install or update Python, use the following commands:
bash

```
sudo apt update
sudo apt install python3 python3-pip
```

1.

**Install PyGame**: Use pip to install PyGame, which is required to run your game:
bash

```
pip3 install pygame
```

2.

**Test the Installation**: To verify that PyGame is properly installed, open a terminal and run:
bash

```
python3 -m pygame.examples.aliens
```

3. If the example game runs without issues, PyGame is correctly set up.

## Creating a Launch Script for Your Game

RetroPie requires an executable script to launch custom games. To integrate your game, you'll need to create a launch script that RetroPie can execute directly. Here's a basic example:

In your game directory (`my_game/`), create a new shell script file, `launch_my_game.sh`:
bash

```
nano launch_my_game.sh
```

1.

Add the following lines to the script, replacing `my_game` with the name of your main Python file:
bash

```
#!/bin/bash
cd /home/pi/RetroPie/roms/ports/my_game   # Replace with your actual game path
python3 main.py
```

2.

Save and close the file, then make it executable:
bash

```
chmod +x launch_my_game.sh
```

3.

This script changes the directory to your game folder and runs the main Python file. RetroPie will use this script to launch your game.

## Placing the Game in the Appropriate RetroPie Directory

RetroPie organizes games in specific directories based on system emulation types (e.g., NES, SNES). For custom games, use the `ports` directory:

Move your game folder to the `ports` directory on your Raspberry Pi:
bash

```
mv my_game /home/pi/RetroPie/roms/ports/
```

1.
2. Move the `launch_my_game.sh` script into the same directory, so RetroPie can locate and run it.

Your `ports` folder should now look like this:

```
RetroPie/roms/ports/
├── my_game/
│   ├── main.py
│   ├── assets/
│   └── launch_my_game.sh
```

## Adding Your Game to the RetroPie Menu

To launch your custom game from the RetroPie menu, create a metadata file in the `ports` folder. This file will display your game as an option within RetroPie's graphical interface.

Open a new file in the `ports` directory, using the `.sh` extension (this script will appear as a game entry in RetroPie):
bash

```
nano /home/pi/RetroPie/roms/ports/My_Game.sh
```

1.

In this file, add the following content to point RetroPie to your launch script:
bash

```
#!/bin/bash
/home/pi/RetroPie/roms/ports/my_game/launch_my_game.sh
```

2.

Save and close the file, then make it executable:
bash

```
chmod +x /home/pi/RetroPie/roms/ports/My_Game.sh
```

3.
4. Restart EmulationStation (RetroPie's front end) to load the new entry. From the main RetroPie menu, select **Quit > Restart EmulationStation**. Your game should now appear under **Ports**.

## Configuring Controller Support in PyGame

RetroPie relies on controllers for input, and PyGame supports controller input as well. To integrate controller functionality, use the PyGame `joystick` module. Below is an example of initializing controller input in PyGame:

```python
import pygame
import sys

# Initialize PyGame and the joystick module
pygame.init()
pygame.joystick.init()

# Detect the first connected joystick
if pygame.joystick.get_count() > 0:
    joystick = pygame.joystick.Joystick(0)
    joystick.init()

# Game loop
running = True
while running:
    for event in pygame.event.get():
        if event.type == pygame.QUIT:
            running = False
        elif event.type == pygame.JOYBUTTONDOWN:
```

# Chapter 10: Case Study: Creating a Raspberry Pi Arcade Console

```
            if joystick.get_button(0):  # Example: Button 0 (usually the A button)
                print("Button 0 pressed!")
        elif event.type == pygame.JOYAXISMOTION:
            x_axis = joystick.get_axis(0)  # Horizontal axis
            y_axis = joystick.get_axis(1)  # Vertical axis
            print(f"Joystick moved: x={x_axis}, y={y_axis}")

# Clean up
pygame.quit()
sys.exit()
```

This code detects joystick input and maps it to PyGame's event loop. Test your controller configuration within the RetroPie environment to ensure smooth operation.

## Setting Up Game Metadata and Artwork

Adding custom artwork and metadata to your game improves the RetroPie interface. Here's how to add artwork and descriptions:

1. **Metadata**: In the `/home/pi/.emulationstation/gamelists/ports/` folder, create an XML file named `gamelist.xml`.

Open `gamelist.xml` and add metadata for your game:
xml

```
<gameList>
    <game>
        <path>./My_Game.sh</path>
        <name>My Custom Game</name>
        <desc>An original game developed with Python and PyGame.</desc>
        <image>/home/pi/RetroPie/roms/ports/my_game/assets/artwork.png</image>
    </game>
</gameList>
```

2.
3. **Artwork**: Place an image in the specified path (e.g., `assets/artwork.png`) for a game icon in RetroPie's interface.
4. Restart EmulationStation to load your updated metadata and artwork.

## Configuring Performance Settings

Since custom games may require more resources, it's important to configure RetroPie's settings to optimize performance:

**Overclocking**: For advanced users, overclocking the Raspberry Pi can improve performance. Access the Raspberry Pi configuration:
bash

```
sudo raspi-config
```

1. In the menu, select **Overclock**, but use caution and monitor temperatures to avoid overheating.

**Frame Rate and Resolution Adjustments**: If your game struggles with performance, reduce the resolution or frame rate. This may involve modifying the PyGame display settings:
python

```
# Set a lower resolution for improved performance
screen = pygame.display.set_mode((800, 600))
```

2.
3. **Optimize Game Assets**: Reducing image file sizes and compressing sound files can improve load times and reduce lag.

## Testing and Troubleshooting Your Custom Game

Finally, test your game within the RetroPie environment to ensure everything works as expected:

1. **Launching from RetroPie**: Select your game from the **Ports** menu and confirm that it launches properly.
2. **Debugging Common Issues**:
    - **Game Crashes**: Check for missing dependencies, file path issues, or unsupported PyGame functions.
    - **Controller Mapping Problems**: Verify that the joystick input is mapped correctly within PyGame.
    - **Performance Lag**: Experiment with simpler graphics and lower frame rates if the game struggles to run smoothly.

## Conclusion

Integrating your custom PyGame projects into RetroPie allows you to add unique, personalized games to your Raspberry Pi arcade console. By following the steps outlined in this section, you can seamlessly add, configure, and launch custom games, transforming your console into a showcase of your programming skills.

# Final Assembly and Testing

Completing the final assembly and testing of your Raspberry Pi arcade console involves combining all the components—hardware, software, and custom configurations—into a fully functional unit. In this section, we will walk through the detailed steps for assembling, organizing, and thoroughly testing each part of your console. By following these steps, you'll ensure a smooth, enjoyable gaming experience.

## Hardware Assembly

### Positioning and Securing the Raspberry Pi

The Raspberry Pi is the central processing unit of your arcade console. Here's how to securely position it:

1. **Choose an Accessible Location**: Place the Raspberry Pi inside the cabinet, close to ports for power, HDMI, and USB cables.
2. **Mount the Raspberry Pi**: Use adhesive pads, screws, or a small mounting bracket to secure the Raspberry Pi to the inside wall of the console. Ensure that there's enough ventilation around it to avoid overheating.
3. **Connect Power and HDMI Cables**: Route the power cable and HDMI cable through the frame openings to the outside of the console. Secure these cables to prevent them from disconnecting during use.

### Installing the Display

Mounting the display properly is crucial for a comfortable gaming experience. Follow these steps to securely install the display:

1. **Secure the Screen**: Place the screen at a comfortable viewing angle within the frame. Use screws or brackets to hold it firmly in place, especially if your console will be moved around frequently.
2. **Install a Bezel**: A bezel can help cover the screen's edges for a more polished look. Measure and cut a bezel to fit around the screen, then attach it to the frame.
3. **Connect the Display to the Raspberry Pi**: Use an HDMI cable to connect the Raspberry Pi to the display. If your display requires additional adapters or converters, install them at this stage.

### Attaching Joysticks and Buttons

Now that the core components are installed, focus on the input controls, which are essential for the arcade experience:

1. **Mounting the Joystick**: Drill the necessary holes for the joystick and mount it securely. Make sure it moves smoothly in all directions.
2. **Installing Buttons**: Drill holes for each button, including action buttons, start, select, and special function buttons as required. Secure each button into its designated slot, ensuring it clicks firmly into place.

3. **Connecting to the Encoder**: Use the provided wires to connect each button and joystick direction to the encoder board. If using a USB encoder, plug the encoder into one of the Raspberry Pi's USB ports.
4. **Testing Button Connections**: Once connected, test each button to ensure it's wired correctly. Misconnected buttons can disrupt gameplay.

### Audio and Speaker Setup

Adding speakers enhances the arcade experience. Many displays come with built-in speakers, but if you're using external speakers, here's how to install them:

1. **Mount the Speakers**: Place the speakers inside the cabinet or attach them near the screen. Secure them with screws or adhesive to prevent movement.
2. **Connect to the Raspberry Pi**: Use the headphone jack or a USB audio adapter to connect the speakers. If using Bluetooth speakers, pair them with the Raspberry Pi's Bluetooth module.
3. **Adjust Volume Controls**: Configure the default audio output and test the sound levels to ensure an immersive gaming experience without distortion.

### Power Management

Setting up efficient power management is essential for safe, long-term operation of your console:

1. **Power Strip or Adapter**: If multiple components require power, use a power strip inside the console. This will reduce the need for multiple power outlets.
2. **Add a Power Switch**: For easy on/off functionality, install a power switch between the Raspberry Pi and the power supply. You can use an in-line power switch or a soft shutdown button if your Raspberry Pi OS supports it.
3. **Cable Management**: Use zip ties or cable organizers to keep cables tidy. This not only improves airflow but also reduces the risk of accidental disconnections.

## Software Setup and Configuration

Once the hardware assembly is complete, configure the software for an optimal gaming experience.

### Configuring RetroPie for Optimal Performance

Fine-tuning RetroPie's settings is essential to ensure smooth gameplay:

1. **Overclocking Options**: Overclocking can improve game performance, especially for more resource-intensive emulators. In the `raspi-config` menu, choose a moderate overclocking setting, but monitor temperature closely.
2. **Shader and Filter Adjustments**: RetroPie allows you to add shaders for a retro look or reduce filters for improved speed. Adjust these settings in the RetroArch configuration menu.
3. **Emulator Selection**: Some games perform better with specific emulators. Test different emulators and configure RetroPie to use the best option for each game.

## Testing Custom Games and ROMs

Run each custom game and ROM to ensure compatibility with the hardware:

1. **Launch Games**: Navigate to your custom games or installed ROMs in RetroPie's menu and launch each one. Check for issues with performance, controls, and display.
2. **Troubleshooting**: For any game that experiences lag or crashes, consider using a different emulator or adjusting the display settings.
3. **Save States and Controls**: Configure save states for easy progress saving. Ensure that each game recognizes the controller and that button mappings are accurate.

## Setting Up a Safe Shutdown Script

To prevent data corruption, set up a safe shutdown script for the Raspberry Pi. This will ensure that when you turn off the console, all data is safely saved:

**Install Python GPIO Zero Library**: Install the GPIO Zero library to allow the Raspberry Pi to detect button presses on GPIO pins.
bash

```
sudo apt install python3-gpiozero
```

1.

**Create a Shutdown Script**: Create a Python script that listens for a button press to initiate a safe shutdown.
python

```
from gpiozero import Button
import os

shutdown_btn = Button(17)   # Replace with the GPIO pin number you use

shutdown_btn.wait_for_press()
os.system("sudo shutdown -h now")
```

2.

**Run the Script at Startup**: Add the script to the Raspberry Pi's startup sequence, so it runs automatically when the console powers on.
bash

```
sudo nano /etc/rc.local
```
Add the following line above `exit 0`:
bash

```
python3 /path/to/your/shutdown_script.py &
```

3.

## Final Testing and Quality Checks

### Testing All Controls and Buttons

Conduct thorough testing to confirm that each control functions correctly:

1. **Button Mapping Verification**: Launch multiple games and verify that each button maps correctly. Test the joystick's responsiveness and ensure smooth gameplay.
2. **Multiplayer Testing**: If your console includes multiple controllers, test multiplayer functionality with compatible games to ensure all inputs work as expected.

### Testing Game Performance

Evaluate the performance of each game, especially those with higher graphics demands:

1. **Frame Rate Testing**: For visually demanding games, ensure a stable frame rate by adjusting RetroPie's video settings if needed.
2. **Audio-Visual Sync**: Verify that the audio matches the visual timing, especially in fast-paced games where delays can affect gameplay quality.

### Stability Testing

Run a few games for extended periods to test the console's stability:

1. **Temperature Monitoring**: Use temperature monitoring tools to ensure the Raspberry Pi doesn't overheat, especially if you're overclocking.
2. **Stress Testing**: Run CPU and GPU-intensive games for at least 30 minutes. Check for any system instability, audio issues, or display problems.

### Polishing the Exterior and Interior

Finally, clean up both the exterior and interior of the console for a professional finish:

1. **Exterior Polishing**: Wipe down the cabinet to remove dust and fingerprints. Apply any final decals, labels, or artwork to enhance the appearance.
2. **Interior Organization**: Re-check cable management inside the console, ensuring no wires obstruct airflow or moving parts.

## Adding Final Customizations

Consider adding a few final touches to make the console unique:

1. **LED Lighting**: Add LED strips inside the cabinet for an attractive glow. Connect the lights to a USB power source or control them via GPIO for custom lighting effects.

# Chapter 10: Case Study: Creating a Raspberry Pi Arcade Console

2. **Personalized Marquee**: Design a marquee banner for the top of the console. You can print this or use custom art to match the theme of your console.

**Custom Startup Animation**: Replace the RetroPie splash screen with a custom animation. Save your custom animation as an MP4 file and replace the default RetroPie startup file:
bash

```
sudo cp /path/to/custom_animation.mp4 /opt/retropie/supplementary/splashscreen/
```

3.
4. **Testing Your Final Setup**: Reboot the system multiple times to ensure smooth startup, shutdown, and consistent performance.

## Troubleshooting Common Issues

Even after assembly, you may encounter some common issues. Here are solutions to address potential problems:

**Display Not Recognized**: Ensure HDMI is properly connected. If issues persist, modify the `config.txt` file:
bash

```
sudo nano /boot/config.txt
```
Uncomment the following line:
bash

```
hdmi_force_hotplug=1
```

- 
- **Game Lag or Stuttering**: Reduce the resolution or use a less resource-intensive emulator to improve performance.
- **Audio Issues**: Adjust audio settings in `raspi-config` or RetroPie's configuration to ensure the correct output device is selected.

## Final Thoughts and Reflection

Completing the final assembly and testing of your Raspberry Pi arcade console is an accomplishment that reflects your skills in both hardware and software. By following each of these steps, you've created a fully functional arcade console that combines classic gaming nostalgia with customizations unique to your vision.

This project is also a springboard to future customization, allowing you to explore additional games, emulation settings, and aesthetic modifications.

# Chapter 11: Publishing Your Game: From Raspberry Pi to the World

## Packaging Your Game for Distribution

In this section, we'll explore the final steps for sharing your game with the world, including preparing the game for distribution, uploading it to a public repository, and promoting it effectively. Taking your game from a personal project to something that others can enjoy involves more than just finishing the code; it's about packaging, sharing, and marketing it in a way that maximizes its reach and appeal. Let's dive into the steps required to publish your game, from creating the right file structure to handling licensing.

### Preparing Your Game Files

When sharing your game, you'll want to ensure that it is well-organized, easy to install, and works across different systems. Here are some basic principles for organizing your game files:

**Main Directory Structure**: Create a main folder for your game project. This folder should contain subfolders for assets, source code, documentation, and any libraries that are necessary for the game to run.
css

```
my_game/
├── src/
├── assets/
│   ├── images/
│   ├── sounds/
│   └── music/
├── docs/
└── README.md
```

1.
    - `src/`: Contains all the source code files, such as Python scripts.
    - `assets/`: Houses all images, sounds, and other resources. It's helpful to have subfolders for different types of assets (e.g., images, sounds).
    - `docs/`: This folder should include documentation files, such as installation guides or game instructions.

- README.md: Provides a quick overview of your game and instructions for installation.

**Dependencies**: Make sure to create a `requirements.txt` file listing all Python dependencies for your game, so users can install everything they need by running:
bash

```
pip install -r requirements.txt
```

Example of `requirements.txt`:
makefile

```
pygame==2.0.1
numpy==1.19.4
```

2.

**Configuration File**: Create a configuration file to store settings that users may want to change, like screen resolution or sound volume. Use a format like `.ini` or `.json` for easy parsing. For example, `config.ini` might look like:
ini

```
[GameSettings]
screen_width = 800
screen_height = 600
fullscreen = false
```

3.

**Executable Files**: Package your game as an executable file so that users can play it without needing Python installed. This can be done with tools like PyInstaller:
bash

```
pyinstaller --onefile my_game.py
```

4. PyInstaller will create a standalone executable that includes Python and all necessary dependencies, making it easy for users to run your game with a simple double-click.

## Creating a README File

The `README.md` file is a critical part of your game distribution package. It should provide a clear, engaging description of your game and explain how to install and run it. Here's an example structure for your README:

### Example README Structure

```
# My Game
```

My Game is an exciting arcade-style game where you control a paddle to break bricks.

## Features
- Classic arcade gameplay
- Multiple levels with increasing difficulty
- High-score tracking

## Installation

1. Clone this repository:
    ```bash
    git clone https://github.com/yourusername/my_game.git
    ```

Install dependencies:
bash

```
pip install -r requirements.txt
```

   2.

Run the game:
bash

```
python src/main.py
```

   3.

# Configuration

To change game settings, open `config.ini` and edit the values.

# Contributing

Feel free to open issues and submit pull requests to improve the game.

### Uploading to GitHub

To share your game with the community, consider uploading it to GitHub. GitHub offers version control, visibility, and the chance for feedback and contributions from other developers.

#### Steps to Upload Your Game to GitHub

1. **Initialize Git**: Open your terminal and navigate to the main directory of your game project. Initialize Git with:

    ```bash
    git init
    ```

**Add Files to Git**: Add all files to your repository with:
bash

git add .

2.

**Commit Your Changes**: Create an initial commit with a message describing your game:
bash

git commit -m "Initial commit of My Game"

3.
4. **Create a GitHub Repository**: Log in to GitHub and create a new repository. You can name it after your game and add a short description.

**Push Your Code to GitHub**: Link your local Git repository to the new GitHub repository and push the code:
bash

git remote add origin https://github.com/yourusername/my_game.git
git push -u origin main

5.
6. **Add a License**: Select an open-source license (e.g., MIT, GPL) to specify how others can use, modify, and distribute your code. GitHub provides a tool for this under "Add a license file" when creating a repository.

## Sharing Your Game on Other Platforms

Once your game is on GitHub, consider sharing it on additional platforms to reach a wider audience. Here are some popular options:

1. **itch.io**: A platform tailored to indie game developers. You can upload your game files, add descriptions and screenshots, and connect with a large community of players and developers.
2. **Game Jolt**: Another platform popular with indie developers, providing tools for community engagement and feedback.

3. **Social Media**: Use Twitter, Reddit, and Facebook to announce your game, share screenshots, and provide download links. The Python, Raspberry Pi, and PyGame communities on Reddit are great places to share your work.

## Marketing and Promoting Your Game

Marketing is essential to get people interested in your game. Here are a few marketing tips:

1. **Create a Trailer**: A short video showing the gameplay is an effective way to capture attention. Use screen recording software to capture in-game footage and edit it into a one-minute trailer.
2. **Develop a Website or Landing Page**: A simple site with a description, screenshots, and download links makes your game look professional and accessible. You can use free website builders like Wix or WordPress.
3. **Engage with the Community**: Be active in online forums, participate in game development discussions, and respond to feedback on your game. Engaging with the community can help you find new players and collaborators.
4. **Consider a Press Kit**: A press kit is a collection of media files (like screenshots, logos, and a fact sheet) that you can share with bloggers, YouTubers, and other media outlets.

## Legal Considerations and Licensing

As a game developer, you should consider the legal aspects of sharing your game:

1. **Copyrights and Trademarks**: Ensure that all assets (images, sounds, code) are either original, licensed, or in the public domain. Avoid using copyrighted material without permission.
2. **Licensing Your Code**: Choose a license that fits your goals for the game. The MIT license, for instance, allows others to use, modify, and distribute your code as long as they credit you.
3. **Consider an End-User License Agreement (EULA)**: If you plan to distribute your game commercially, a EULA outlines the terms of use for players. While this is optional for open-source projects, it can be beneficial for paid games.

## Conclusion

By following the steps outlined above, you can take your Raspberry Pi game from a personal project to a polished, distributable product. Preparing your game for distribution, uploading it to GitHub, and sharing it on various platforms will not only make your game accessible to a wider audience but also increase your exposure as a developer. Don't forget to engage with the gaming community, take feedback constructively, and keep iterating on your work.

# Uploading to GitHub and Sharing Code

Sharing your game's code on GitHub offers numerous benefits, from enabling collaboration with other developers to giving you a platform for version control and project management.

This section will walk you through the process of uploading your game to GitHub, managing your repository, and making the project accessible to the broader community. By the end of this section, you'll have a working knowledge of Git and GitHub workflows, making it easier to maintain your project and interact with others who are interested in your game.

## Step 1: Setting Up Git Locally

Before uploading your game to GitHub, you need to set up Git on your local machine if you haven't done so already. Git is a distributed version control system that tracks changes in your code and allows for easy collaboration.

**Installing Git**

If you're using a Raspberry Pi, Git may already be installed. You can check by opening a terminal and typing:

```
git --version
```

If Git is installed, you'll see the version number displayed. If not, you can install it with:

```
sudo apt update
sudo apt install git
```

**Configuring Git**

Once Git is installed, configure it with your name and email address. This information will be associated with your commits and will help identify you as the author.

```
git config --global user.name "Your Name"
git config --global user.email "your.email@example.com"
```

## Step 2: Initializing a Local Repository

Navigate to your game's main directory in the terminal. Initialize a Git repository in this folder:

```
cd path/to/your_game
git init
```

This creates a hidden `.git` folder where Git will store information about your project's history.

### Step 3: Adding Files to the Repository

Now, add all files in your project to the Git repository. You can stage files individually, but using `.` will add all files in the directory:

```
git add .
```

### Step 4: Committing Changes

A commit in Git represents a snapshot of your project at a given time. Create an initial commit with a message describing the changes:

```
git commit -m "Initial commit of My Game"
```

### Step 5: Creating a GitHub Repository

Next, go to GitHub and log in or create an account if you don't have one yet. Once logged in, click the **New** button in the repositories section to create a new repository.

1. **Repository Name**: Name it after your game project (e.g., "my_game").
2. **Description**: Provide a brief description of your project.
3. **Public/Private**: Choose "Public" if you want others to view your code. Select "Private" if you'd prefer it to be accessible only to collaborators.
4. **Initialize with README**: Leave this unchecked, as you've already created a README in your project folder.

Click **Create repository** to proceed.

### Step 6: Linking the Local Repository to GitHub

After creating the GitHub repository, you'll see some setup instructions. Copy the repository URL (it should look like https://github.com/yourusername/my_game.git). Back in the terminal, link your local repository to GitHub using this URL:

```
git remote add origin https://github.com/yourusername/my_game.git
```

You can verify the remote URL with:

```
git remote -v
```

## Step 7: Pushing the Code to GitHub

Now that your local repository is connected to GitHub, you can push your code to the GitHub repository:

```
git push -u origin main
```

This command uploads your code to GitHub, making it accessible online.

## Step 8: Writing a Comprehensive README

The `README.md` file serves as the landing page for your GitHub repository. It should contain a clear description of your game, installation instructions, usage guidelines, and any other relevant information.

### Example of a README File

```
# My Game

Welcome to **My Game**, an arcade-style experience built with Python
and PyGame on Raspberry Pi.

## Features
- Classic gameplay mechanics
- Adjustable difficulty levels
- High-score tracking

## Getting Started

### Prerequisites
- Python 3.x
- Pygame library

### Installation
1. Clone the repository:
   ```bash
   git clone https://github.com/yourusername/my_game.git
```

Install required libraries:
bash
```

```
pip install -r requirements.txt
```

2.

Run the game:
bash

```
python src/main.py
```

3.

# License

This project is licensed under the MIT License.

### Step 9: Adding a License to Your Repository

Licensing your code is essential when sharing it on GitHub. It specifies what others can and cannot do with your code. Here are common open-source licenses:

- **MIT License**: Allows others to use, modify, and distribute your code as long as they give you credit.
- **GPL License**: Requires anyone who distributes your code to make their version open-source.
- **Apache License**: Allows usage with some restrictions, including a limitation of liability.

To add a license, click on **Add file** in your GitHub repository, then select **Create new file**. Name it `LICENSE` and choose your preferred license from the GitHub template options.

### Step 10: Using Branches for Development

GitHub allows you to work with branches, which are separate versions of your code that you can modify without affecting the main codebase. This is helpful for adding new features or fixing bugs.

#### Creating a New Branch

```bash
git checkout -b feature-new-feature
```

### Making Changes and Committing

Make any necessary changes to the code, then stage and commit the changes as usual:

```
git add .
git commit -m "Added new feature"
```

### Merging Changes into Main Branch

Once your feature is ready, switch back to the main branch and merge the changes:

```
git checkout main
git merge feature-new-feature
```

### Pushing Branches to GitHub

To push the new branch to GitHub, use:

```
git push origin feature-new-feature
```

You can then create a **Pull Request** on GitHub to review and merge the branch into the main codebase.

## Step 11: Managing Your Repository with Issues and Pull Requests

GitHub's **Issues** and **Pull Requests** tools are valuable for tracking changes, reporting bugs, and implementing new features.

### Creating Issues

Issues allow you to track bugs and feature requests in your repository. Navigate to the **Issues** tab, then click **New issue**. Provide a title and description to outline the issue.

### Working with Pull Requests

If you're working on a team, pull requests are a way to propose changes to the main codebase. Each pull request can be reviewed, discussed, and modified before being merged.

1. **Create a Pull Request**: Go to the **Pull Requests** tab and click **New pull request**. Select the branches you want to merge and provide a description.
2. **Review and Merge**: Once reviewed, click **Merge pull request** to integrate the changes.

## Step 12: Continuous Improvement with GitHub

Maintaining a GitHub repository means frequently updating the code, adding new features, and refining the project based on feedback. Here are a few practices for maintaining a healthy repository:

1. **Document Changes**: Each time you update your game, add notes to the `README.md` or create a `CHANGELOG.md` file.
2. **Engage with Users**: Respond to comments, answer questions, and listen to suggestions.
3. **Contribute to Other Projects**: If you're using code or assets from another project, consider contributing back to those projects or giving credit in your documentation.

## Conclusion

Uploading and sharing your code on GitHub makes it accessible to others and enables you to receive feedback, collaborate, and grow as a developer. By setting up a structured Git workflow, documenting your project clearly, and using GitHub's tools to manage your repository, you're not only making your game available to others but also building a foundation for future projects and collaborations. Embrace the community aspect of open-source development, and use GitHub as a platform to enhance your game, improve your skills, and connect with other creators.

# Marketing and Sharing Your Game Online

Creating a game is an incredible accomplishment, but sharing it with the world is an equally important step to ensure it reaches an audience. Marketing doesn't have to mean expensive ads or professional campaigns; with a strategic approach and the right tools, you can effectively promote your game and build a community around it. In this section, we'll cover how to leverage social media, create engaging promotional materials, reach out to influencers, and connect with gaming communities. By the end, you'll have a comprehensive guide to bring your game to a larger audience and make a lasting impact.

## Building a Game Website or Landing Page

A website or landing page serves as a central hub for your game where users can learn about it, download it, and stay updated on new features. Here's how to build an effective landing page for your game:

1. **Choose a Website Builder**:
   - Platforms like WordPress, Wix, and Carrd make it easy to create a website without coding. Choose one based on your needs and budget.

- Alternatively, if you're comfortable with HTML and CSS, you can create a custom website hosted on GitHub Pages.
2. **Essential Sections of the Landing Page**:
    - **Hero Section**: At the top of the page, include a captivating image or short video clip from your game, along with the game title and a short description.
    - **Gameplay Overview**: Describe the gameplay mechanics, key features, and objectives. This section can include short video clips or GIFs that showcase interesting gameplay moments.
    - **Download Link**: Ensure there's a prominent button where users can download the game directly or access links to platforms where it's hosted.
    - **Testimonials or Reviews**: If you have any user feedback or reviews, display them to provide social proof and build trust with new players.
    - **Developer Bio**: Include a section about yourself or your team. Sharing your journey can make players feel more connected to the game.
3. **SEO and Analytics**:
    - **SEO**: Use keywords that players might search for (e.g., "Python arcade game" or "indie breakout game"). Optimize page titles, descriptions, and headings to improve search engine visibility.
    - **Analytics**: Use tools like Google Analytics to track website visitors, discover how they're finding your site, and understand their behavior.

## Social Media Marketing Strategies

Social media is an invaluable tool for promoting your game, building a community, and keeping players engaged. Here are some tips for creating an effective social media strategy:

1. **Choose Your Platforms Wisely**:
    - **Twitter**: Great for game developers, as the indie game community is active here. You can share development updates, screenshots, and engage with others.
    - **Instagram**: Visual content works well here. Post images, short gameplay videos, or stories about the development process.
    - **YouTube**: If you can create video content, YouTube is ideal for posting trailers, gameplay highlights, or development logs.
    - **Reddit**: Join subreddits like r/gamedev, r/IndieDev, and r/raspberry_pi to share updates, ask for feedback, and interact with a tech-savvy audience.
2. **Create a Content Plan**: Develop a posting schedule that includes different types of content. For example:
    - **Weekly updates**: Share what's new with the game or development.
    - **Gameplay clips**: Highlight exciting or unique moments.
    - **Behind-the-scenes**: Show the development process, whether it's coding, designing, or debugging.
    - **Community Engagement**: Polls, Q&A sessions, and feedback requests can foster a sense of involvement.
3. **Use Hashtags Effectively**: Hashtags can increase visibility on platforms like Twitter and Instagram. Research popular hashtags like #indiedev, #gamedev, and #raspberrypi. Experiment with a mix of broad and niche hashtags to reach both wide and specific audiences.

4. **Engage with the Community**: Comment on, like, and share other developers' posts, join conversations, and offer help where possible. The more engaged you are, the more likely people will reciprocate by checking out and promoting your game.

## Creating Promotional Materials

Compelling promotional materials can capture potential players' interest. Here are essential elements you should consider:

1. **Game Trailer**:
    - **Length**: Keep it short (around 1–2 minutes) to hold attention.
    - **Content**: Showcase exciting gameplay elements, unique mechanics, or storyline highlights. Start with an action-packed scene to hook viewers right away.
    - **Editing Tips**: Use free software like DaVinci Resolve or iMovie to edit clips and add music or sound effects.
2. **Screenshots**:
    - Capture high-quality screenshots showing key moments and unique visuals. These should highlight different aspects of gameplay, environments, characters, or features.
    - Post screenshots on social media, your website, and any platforms where your game is available. They give potential players a sense of what to expect.
3. **Press Kit**:
    - A press kit is a collection of media and information that you can share with bloggers, reviewers, and influencers.
    - Include screenshots, your game's logo, a short description, key features, and download links. This makes it easy for media outlets to promote your game accurately.
4. **Gameplay GIFs**:
    - Short GIFs of exciting moments can be shared on social media or embedded on your website.
    - Tools like ScreenToGif (Windows) or LICEcap (Windows and Mac) are great for creating GIFs.

## Reaching Out to Influencers and Media Outlets

Influencers, bloggers, and YouTubers can give your game significant exposure if they're interested in covering it. Here's how to reach out effectively:

1. **Identify Relevant Influencers**:
    - Focus on influencers who cover indie games, Raspberry Pi projects, or Python development. They're more likely to appreciate and promote your game.
    - Look for smaller influencers who have a dedicated audience and might be more approachable. Often, micro-influencers (10,000–50,000 followers) have more engaged audiences.
2. **Craft a Professional Email**:

- Start with a friendly introduction that explains who you are and briefly describes your game. Highlight unique aspects that would interest their audience.
  - Offer them a free download code or a press kit and mention that you'd love any feedback they might have.
  - Keep it short, respectful, and to the point, as influencers often receive many similar requests.
3. **Follow Up**:
   - If you don't hear back, it's okay to send a polite follow-up after a week or so. However, don't send multiple follow-ups or pressure them for coverage.

## Engaging with Gaming Communities

Online communities provide invaluable support for indie game developers, offering feedback, encouragement, and, sometimes, new fans. Here are some tips on getting involved:

1. **Join Indie Game Forums**:
   - Indie game development forums like TIGSource, IndieDB, and the GameMaker Community allow you to showcase your game and get advice from other developers.
2. **Post Devlogs**:
   - Devlogs are regular updates about your development journey. Share these on forums and social media to give players insight into your process and struggles.
   - Devlogs can include bug fixes, design choices, or feature updates. Many players enjoy seeing the behind-the-scenes evolution of a game.
3. **Participate in Game Jams**:
   - Game jams are events where developers create games in a short time frame based on a theme. Participating in jams can help you gain exposure, learn new skills, and network with other developers.
4. **Engage on Discord**:
   - Many gaming communities and developer groups have Discord servers. Look for servers focused on Raspberry Pi, Python development, or indie games, and join conversations, ask questions, and offer help.

## Leveraging Online Platforms for Distribution and Exposure

Uploading your game to specific platforms can extend your reach. Here are some popular options:

1. **Itch.io**:
   - Itch.io is an indie game platform with a supportive community. You can host your game here, offer a free or paid version, and engage with players through comments and feedback.
   - Itch.io also allows you to join game jams and participate in events that could give your game more visibility.
2. **Game Jolt**:

- Game Jolt is another platform popular with indie game developers. It has a community-oriented approach and is well-suited for devlogs, screenshots, and updates.
3. **YouTube**:
    - Creating a developer channel on YouTube can give your game a longer shelf life. Post gameplay videos, development updates, and tutorials to engage a broad audience.
    - Consider creating a playlist for your game, making it easy for viewers to follow your journey.

## Analyzing Feedback and Adapting

As you gain exposure, pay attention to player feedback. This feedback can help you understand which features are working and where improvements might be needed:

1. **Read Comments and Reviews**:
    - Whether it's on your website, social media, or a distribution platform, reading comments can help you gauge player satisfaction and identify areas for improvement.
2. **Use Feedback for Iterative Improvements**:
    - After receiving feedback, consider making updates or small changes to the game. Iterative improvements can refine gameplay and demonstrate your responsiveness to the community.
3. **Engage Directly with Players**:
    - Respond to comments, thank users for feedback, and make them feel heard. An engaged audience is more likely to support and promote your work.

## Conclusion

Marketing and sharing your game online is essential for reaching new players and building a community around your project. By creating a professional online presence, engaging with social media, reaching out to influencers, and leveraging distribution platforms, you can successfully launch your game and connect with an audience eager to play it. Remember, marketing is a continuous process, and even small efforts can lead to significant rewards if done consistently.

# Legal Considerations and Licensing

When publishing your game, it's crucial to understand the legal landscape to protect your work and comply with regulations. Legal considerations encompass licensing, copyright, trademarks, and user agreements. This section will guide you through the essentials of licensing your game, avoiding copyright issues, and ensuring that your game is legally sound. Understanding these aspects can prevent potential legal disputes and safeguard your project as it grows.

## Copyright Basics

Copyright law grants the creator of an original work exclusive rights to its use and distribution. For game developers, copyright covers the code, artwork, music, and other creative elements. Here's what you need to know:

1. **Ownership of Assets**:
   - If you created all the assets (code, graphics, music) yourself, you own the copyright for those elements.
   - If you used third-party assets (e.g., stock images, sounds), make sure you have the proper license to use them. Many assets come with specific usage terms, such as "personal use only" or "commercial use allowed."
2. **Public Domain and Creative Commons**:
   - Assets in the **public domain** are free to use without restriction. However, it's important to verify that the asset is truly public domain.
   - **Creative Commons** licenses are often used for free assets. These licenses specify the terms under which you can use the asset. For example, a **CC BY** license allows you to use the asset as long as you provide attribution to the creator.
3. **Avoiding Copyright Infringement**:
   - Be cautious about using recognizable elements from other games (e.g., character names, music, logos). Even small references can lead to legal issues if they are protected by copyright or trademark law.
   - If you want to use popular songs or well-known images, you must obtain explicit permission or a license from the copyright holder.

## Choosing the Right License for Your Game

Selecting a license for your game is one of the most important legal decisions you'll make. The license dictates how others can use, modify, and distribute your game. Here are some common licenses used in the game development community:

1. **MIT License**:
   - The MIT License is simple and permissive, allowing others to use, modify, and distribute your code as long as they provide attribution to you.
   - This license is popular in the open-source community because it places minimal restrictions on users.

**Example MIT License**:
text

```
MIT License

Copyright (c) 2024 Your Name

Permission is hereby granted, free of charge, to any person
obtaining a copy of this software and associated documentation files
(the "Software"), to deal in the Software without restriction,
including without limitation the rights to use, copy, modify, merge,
```

```
publish, distribute, sublicense, and/or sell copies of the Software,
and to permit persons to whom the Software is furnished to do so,
subject to the following conditions:

The above copyright notice and this permission notice shall be
included in all copies or substantial portions of the Software.

THE SOFTWARE IS PROVIDED "AS IS", WITHOUT WARRANTY OF ANY KIND,
EXPRESS OR IMPLIED, INCLUDING BUT NOT LIMITED TO THE WARRANTIES OF
MERCHANTABILITY, FITNESS FOR A PARTICULAR PURPOSE AND
NONINFRINGEMENT. IN NO EVENT SHALL THE AUTHORS OR COPYRIGHT HOLDERS
BE LIABLE FOR ANY CLAIM, DAMAGES OR OTHER LIABILITY, WHETHER IN AN
ACTION OF CONTRACT, TORT OR OTHERWISE, ARISING FROM, OUT OF OR IN
CONNECTION WITH THE SOFTWARE OR THE USE OR OTHER DEALINGS IN THE
SOFTWARE.
```

2.
3. **GPL (General Public License)**:
    - The GPL requires that any derivative work must also be open-source and distributed under the same license. This is known as a "copyleft" license.
    - If you choose the GPL, anyone who uses your code must share their modifications with the community.
4. **Key Consideration**: The GPL is ideal if you want to ensure that your game and any derivative projects remain open-source.
5. **Apache License 2.0**:
    - The Apache License provides a balanced approach, allowing commercial use while protecting your code from being used without attribution.
    - This license includes a clause that explicitly grants users the right to patent use.

**Example Apache License Clause**:
text

```
Licensed under the Apache License, Version 2.0 (the "License");
you may not use this file except in compliance with the License.
You may obtain a copy of the License at

http://www.apache.org/licenses/LICENSE-2.0
```

6.
7. **Proprietary License**:
    - If you want full control over your game and prefer not to share the source code, a proprietary license might be the best option.
    - This type of license restricts users from modifying, distributing, or using the game in any way not explicitly allowed by you.

# End-User License Agreement (EULA)

A **EULA** is a legal contract between you (the developer) and the player, outlining the terms of use for your game. While optional for open-source projects, a EULA is essential for commercial games or any project where you want to limit user actions (e.g., reselling or reverse engineering).

## Basic EULA Components

1. **Grant of License**:
    - Specify what the user is allowed to do with the game (e.g., play for personal use only).

text

```
This game is licensed, not sold. You are granted a non-exclusive,
non-transferable license to use the game for personal entertainment
purposes only.
```

2.
3. **Restrictions**:
    - List activities that are prohibited, such as modifying the game code or distributing copies without permission.

text

```
You may not:
- Decompile, reverse engineer, or modify the game.
- Distribute or sell copies of the game without explicit permission.
```

4.
5. **Limitation of Liability**:
    - Limit your liability in case the game causes any issues on the user's system.

text

```
The game is provided "as is" without any warranties. The developer
is not liable for any damages arising from the use of the game.
```

6.
7. **Termination**:
    - Specify the conditions under which the license can be terminated (e.g., if the user violates the terms).

text

```
This license is effective until terminated. It will automatically
```

terminate if the user fails to comply with any terms of this agreement.

8.

## Protecting Your Game with Trademarks

A **trademark** is a recognizable sign, design, or expression that distinguishes your game from others. Trademarking your game's title or logo can protect your brand and prevent others from using similar names or symbols.

1. **Conduct a Trademark Search**:
    - Before you settle on a game title, perform a trademark search to ensure it isn't already in use. This can prevent legal conflicts and help you establish a unique brand identity.
2. **Registering a Trademark**:
    - In most countries, you can register a trademark through a national trademark office (e.g., the USPTO in the United States or the UK Intellectual Property Office).
    - Registering a trademark gives you exclusive rights to use the name or logo in connection with your game.
3. **Using the Trademark Symbol**:
    - Use the ™ symbol if you claim a trademark but haven't registered it. Use the ® symbol only after your trademark is officially registered.

## Handling Player Data and Privacy

If your game collects any form of player data (e.g., high scores, user profiles), you must comply with privacy laws such as the **General Data Protection Regulation (GDPR)** in Europe or the **California Consumer Privacy Act (CCPA)** in the United States.

1. **Data Collection Policy**:
    - Be transparent about what data you collect and why. Include a **Privacy Policy** on your website or within the game that explains this clearly.

text

```
We collect user data solely to improve the gameplay experience. This
includes high scores, preferences, and settings. We do not share
your data with third parties.
```

2.
3. **Obtaining Consent**:
    - Before collecting personal data, ask for the user's consent. This can be done through a simple pop-up when the game starts.

text

By continuing to play, you consent to the collection of your high scores for leaderboard purposes.

4.
5. **Right to Delete Data**:
    - Allow users to request the deletion of their data. This is a requirement under GDPR.

text

If you wish to have your data deleted, please contact support@yourgame.com.

6.

## Conclusion

Legal considerations and licensing are critical aspects of game development that should not be overlooked. By understanding copyright, selecting the right license, drafting a clear EULA, and complying with privacy laws, you can protect your work and build trust with your players. These steps not only help you avoid legal issues but also lay the groundwork for a successful and professional game release. Make sure to revisit these legal aspects as your project evolves, especially if you plan to monetize or expand your game.

# Chapter 12: Conclusion and Next Steps in Game Development

## Reflecting on What You've Learned

As you reach the conclusion of this book, it's essential to take a moment to reflect on your journey. By now, you've gained a comprehensive understanding of game development fundamentals, specific techniques for programming and designing games on the Raspberry Pi, and have seen how Python, PyGame, and the Raspberry Pi's hardware capabilities can come together to create unique gaming experiences. This reflection is not only to celebrate your progress but also to help you solidify the skills and concepts you've learned, setting you up for continued success in game development.

### Reviewing Your Progress

Let's break down some of the significant achievements you should be proud of:

1. **Understanding the Basics of Game Development**: You started by learning what game development is and how it works, with an introduction to Python and PyGame. These basics provided the foundation for all the concepts and projects that followed.
2. **Setting Up and Exploring the Raspberry Pi**: Configuring your Raspberry Pi for game development was an essential step. You familiarized yourself with this unique, flexible hardware platform and learned how to install and configure Python and PyGame. Additionally, you explored using the GPIO (General Purpose Input/Output) pins, which are a distinctive feature of the Raspberry Pi, giving it an edge in creating custom game controls and interactive hardware setups.
3. **Building and Programming Games with PyGame**: From creating a simple "Hello World" game to coding a more complex arcade-style game like Breakout, you delved into PyGame's core functionality. This journey included setting up game loops, managing graphics and animations, adding sound effects, and handling user inputs, all of which form the core of game development.
4. **Applying Game Physics and Enhancements**: As you progressed, you added depth to your games by integrating physics and gameplay enhancements. You learned how to make gameplay more dynamic and engaging by adjusting object speeds, implementing power-ups, and creating smooth animations.
5. **Exploring Custom Controls and Multiplayer Functionality**: With your knowledge of GPIO, you developed custom game controllers and created multiplayer games. You learned the fundamentals of networking in Python and how to enable local multiplayer experiences, adding an entirely new dimension to your games.
6. **Case Study of a Raspberry Pi Arcade Console**: Creating a dedicated Raspberry Pi arcade console was a unique experience that blended hardware design with software implementation. You assembled the console, installed RetroPie for classic games,

and integrated your custom games, turning your Raspberry Pi into a personal arcade machine.

## What Each Chapter Brought to Your Skillset

Each chapter aimed to build upon the previous ones, introducing you to new skills and techniques that were immediately applicable to real game development projects. The following are the core skills you can now carry forward:

- **Programming**: Your Python programming skills have likely improved dramatically. You worked with fundamental programming constructs and expanded to more advanced concepts such as object-oriented programming, which is crucial in game development.
- **Game Design Principles**: While this book focused on the technical aspects, you also gained an understanding of game design, including creating engaging experiences, planning game flow, and considering player feedback.
- **Problem Solving**: Game development is a continuous process of overcoming obstacles. Each chapter presented unique challenges, from debugging code to troubleshooting hardware connections, helping you sharpen your problem-solving skills.
- **Project Planning and Execution**: Creating a game, especially one with both software and hardware components, requires good planning and a methodical approach. By following the projects in this book, you learned how to plan, organize, and execute projects systematically.

## Key Takeaways for Continued Learning

As you move forward, here are some essential takeaways and suggestions that can help you on your journey:

1. **Experiment with More Complex Games**: You've created basic games; now consider experimenting with more complex genres, such as platformers, puzzle games, or RPGs (role-playing games). These genres often involve more advanced programming techniques and game design concepts.
2. **Learn About Advanced Game Physics**: Physics can play a significant role in making your games feel realistic and enjoyable. Consider diving deeper into topics like particle physics, rigid body dynamics, and collision resolution.
3. **Explore Advanced Graphics Techniques**: Working with PyGame gives you a good foundation, but there are advanced graphics libraries and engines you may want to explore. Libraries such as OpenGL and engines like Unity or Unreal provide more powerful graphics capabilities, enabling you to create 3D games or visually stunning 2D games.
4. **Focus on Optimization**: Game performance is crucial, especially when working with resource-limited devices like the Raspberry Pi. Practice optimizing your code, managing memory, and ensuring your games run smoothly, even with more complex elements and graphics.
5. **Networked Multiplayer and Online Games**: Creating local multiplayer games was a great start, but you can also explore creating networked multiplayer games that allow

players to connect and play over the internet. While this requires a good understanding of networking and server management, it's a highly valuable skill in game development.
6. **Experiment with Other Platforms and Languages**: Although Python and Raspberry Pi are excellent starting points, don't hesitate to experiment with other languages, platforms, and game engines. Platforms like Unity, Godot, and Unreal Engine use different languages (C#, GDScript, and C++), but they offer extensive documentation and tutorials, making them accessible for new developers.

## Example Project Ideas

To further develop your skills, here are some example projects you could tackle. Each of these ideas builds on the concepts you've learned but also introduces new challenges:

1. **Platformer Game with Parallax Scrolling**: Create a simple platformer game where the background layers move at different speeds, giving the impression of depth. This will allow you to practice animation, physics, and collision detection.
2. **Top-Down Shooter Game with Custom Controller**: Design a top-down shooter where the player controls a character with a custom joystick or button controller. Add features like enemy AI, scoring systems, and power-ups to enhance gameplay.
3. **Multiplayer Maze Game**: Build a multiplayer game where players navigate a maze and compete to reach the end. You can implement networking code to allow players on different Raspberry Pi devices to play together.
4. **Retro Arcade Collection**: Using the Raspberry Pi and RetroPie, create a collection of classic arcade-inspired games. Include games like Snake, Tetris, and Asteroids, and add your unique twists to each game to make them stand out.
5. **Raspberry Pi Adventure Game**: Adventure games often involve puzzles and exploration, providing an excellent opportunity to explore advanced game logic, inventory systems, and save/load functionality.

## Code Example for a Final Reflection Project

Let's say you want to create a simple final project to consolidate your skills: a top-down shooter where the player controls a character that shoots at moving targets. Here's a small sample of what part of the code might look like.

```
import pygame
import random

# Initialize Pygame
pygame.init()

# Screen setup
screen_width, screen_height = 800, 600
screen = pygame.display.set_mode((screen_width, screen_height))
pygame.display.set_caption("Top-Down Shooter")
```

```python
# Colors
WHITE = (255, 255, 255)
BLACK = (0, 0, 0)
RED = (255, 0, 0)

# Player setup
player_size = 50
player_pos = [screen_width // 2, screen_height - player_size]
player_speed = 5

# Enemy setup
enemy_size = 50
enemy_pos = [random.randint(0, screen_width - enemy_size), 0]
enemy_speed = 5

# Game loop
running = True
while running:
    screen.fill(BLACK)

    # Move player
    keys = pygame.key.get_pressed()
    if keys[pygame.K_LEFT] and player_pos[0] > 0:
        player_pos[0] -= player_speed
    if keys[pygame.K_RIGHT] and player_pos[0] < screen_width - player_size:
        player_pos[0] += player_speed

    # Move enemy
    enemy_pos[1] += enemy_speed
    if enemy_pos[1] >= screen_height:
        enemy_pos[1] = 0
        enemy_pos[0] = random.randint(0, screen_width - enemy_size)

    # Draw player and enemy
    pygame.draw.rect(screen, WHITE, (player_pos[0], player_pos[1], player_size, player_size))
    pygame.draw.rect(screen, RED, (enemy_pos[0], enemy_pos[1], enemy_size, enemy_size))
```

```
    # Update the display
    pygame.display.flip()

    # Event handling
    for event in pygame.event.get():
        if event.type == pygame.QUIT:
            running = False

pygame.quit()
```

This example is a basic framework but demonstrates the foundational concepts of player movement, collision handling, and screen updates, which are essential in many game genres.

## Embracing the Community and Expanding Your Network

Finally, as you continue learning, remember that the game development community is vibrant and supportive. Joining forums, participating in online groups, or attending game jams can provide you with valuable feedback, inspiration, and connections with other developers.

# Exploring Advanced Game Development Topics

The journey in game development doesn't stop with mastering the basics. This section will delve into some advanced topics that can significantly elevate your games. We will explore more sophisticated techniques that can be applied using Python and PyGame, as well as potential tools and concepts that you may want to integrate into future projects. These topics will help you push the boundaries of what you can create, turning your games from simple prototypes into polished, professional-level experiences.

## Advanced Game Physics

Physics is a cornerstone of realistic game mechanics. While we've touched upon basic collision detection and movement, there are more advanced physics topics that can make your games more engaging.

### Rigid Body Dynamics

Rigid body dynamics deals with the motion and collision of objects that do not deform. This is essential in many games, especially those involving vehicles or any type of solid object. Although PyGame doesn't have a built-in physics engine, you can use libraries like **PyMunk** or **Box2D** for Python to implement realistic physics.

Here's an example using PyMunk for a basic physics simulation:

```python
import pygame
import pymunk

# Initialize Pygame
pygame.init()
screen = pygame.display.set_mode((800, 600))
clock = pygame.time.Clock()

# Initialize PyMunk
space = pymunk.Space()
space.gravity = (0, 900)

# Create a ball
ball_body = pymunk.Body(1, pymunk.moment_for_circle(1, 0, 30))
ball_body.position = (400, 50)
ball_shape = pymunk.Circle(ball_body, 30)
ball_shape.elasticity = 0.8
space.add(ball_body, ball_shape)

# Game loop
running = True
while running:
    for event in pygame.event.get():
        if event.type == pygame.QUIT:
            running = False

    screen.fill((0, 0, 0))
    space.step(1 / 60.0)

    # Draw the ball
    pygame.draw.circle(screen, (255, 255, 255),
(int(ball_body.position.x), int(ball_body.position.y)), 30)
    pygame.display.flip()
    clock.tick(60)

pygame.quit()
```

In this example, we create a simple simulation of a bouncing ball using PyMunk. The ball has elasticity, which makes it bounce off the ground. Libraries like PyMunk can handle complex physics calculations, freeing you from implementing them manually.

**Particle Systems**

Particle systems are used for simulating effects like smoke, fire, and explosions. A particle system involves many small particles that move and change over time, creating fluid-like visual effects. In PyGame, you can create a basic particle system by managing a list of particles.

Example code for a basic particle system:

```python
import pygame
import random

pygame.init()
screen = pygame.display.set_mode((800, 600))
clock = pygame.time.Clock()

particles = []

def emit():
    if len(particles) < 100:
        pos = pygame.mouse.get_pos()
        particles.append([pos[0], pos[1], random.randint(-10, 10), random.randint(-10, 10)])

def update_particles():
    for particle in particles[:]:
        particle[0] += particle[2]
        particle[1] += particle[3]
        particle[3] += 0.5  # gravity
        if particle[1] > 600:
            particles.remove(particle)

def draw_particles():
    for particle in particles:
        pygame.draw.circle(screen, (255, 255, 255), (particle[0], particle[1]), 5)

running = True
while running:
    screen.fill((0, 0, 0))
    emit()
    update_particles()
    draw_particles()
    pygame.display.flip()
```

```
        clock.tick(60)

        for event in pygame.event.get():
            if event.type == pygame.QUIT:
                running = False

pygame.quit()
```

This code creates a simple particle system where particles are generated at the mouse position and fall due to gravity. The particles are removed once they fall off the screen. This is a basic example, but particle systems can be expanded to include more complex behaviors, such as color changes, varying sizes, or interactions with other objects.

## Artificial Intelligence (AI) in Games

Artificial Intelligence can make your games feel more dynamic and challenging. There are many types of AI you can implement in games, ranging from simple behaviors like random movement to complex algorithms like pathfinding.

**Pathfinding with A***

The A* (A-star) algorithm is a popular pathfinding technique used in games. It finds the shortest path between two points on a grid, which is useful for enemy AI that needs to navigate around obstacles.

Here's a basic outline of how A* works:

1. Initialize a list of open nodes (nodes to be evaluated) and a list of closed nodes (nodes already evaluated).
2. Start with the initial node and add it to the open list.
3. For each node, evaluate its neighbors and calculate the cost to move to each neighbor.
4. Choose the node with the lowest total cost (distance traveled + estimated distance to the target).
5. Repeat until the target node is reached or there are no nodes left to evaluate.

While implementing A* fully can be complex, libraries like **Pathfinding** in Python can simplify this process.

Example using the Python Pathfinding library:

```
from pathfinding.core.grid import Grid
from pathfinding.finder.a_star import AStarFinder

matrix = [
```

```
        [0, 1, 0, 0, 0],
        [0, 1, 0, 1, 0],
        [0, 0, 0, 1, 0],
        [1, 1, 0, 0, 0],
        [0, 0, 0, 0, 0]
]

grid = Grid(matrix=matrix)
start = grid.node(0, 0)
end = grid.node(4, 4)

finder = AStarFinder()
path, _ = finder.find_path(start, end, grid)

print(path)
```

In this example, we define a matrix where 0 represents a walkable tile and 1 represents an obstacle. The A* algorithm finds the shortest path from the top-left corner to the bottom-right corner, avoiding obstacles.

## Procedural Generation

Procedural generation is a technique where content is generated algorithmically rather than manually. It's commonly used in games for creating random levels, landscapes, or even characters.

### Generating Random Mazes

One classic example of procedural generation is a random maze generator. There are many algorithms for generating mazes, such as Prim's algorithm or depth-first search (DFS).

Here's a basic maze generator using DFS:

```
import pygame
import random

pygame.init()
width, height = 800, 600
screen = pygame.display.set_mode((width, height))
clock = pygame.time.Clock()

cols, rows = 20, 15
cell_size = 40
```

```python
maze = [[1 for _ in range(cols)] for _ in range(rows)]

def carve_maze(x, y):
    maze[y][x] = 0
    directions = [(0, 1), (1, 0), (0, -1), (-1, 0)]
    random.shuffle(directions)
    for dx, dy in directions:
        nx, ny = x + dx * 2, y + dy * 2
        if 0 <= nx < cols and 0 <= ny < rows and maze[ny][nx] == 1:
            maze[ny-dy][nx-dx] = 0
            carve_maze(nx, ny)

carve_maze(0, 0)

def draw_maze():
    for y in range(rows):
        for x in range(cols):
            color = (255, 255, 255) if maze[y][x] == 0 else (0, 0, 0)
            pygame.draw.rect(screen, color, (x * cell_size, y * cell_size, cell_size, cell_size))

running = True
while running:
    screen.fill((0, 0, 0))
    draw_maze()
    pygame.display.flip()
    clock.tick(60)

    for event in pygame.event.get():
        if event.type == pygame.QUIT:
            running = False

pygame.quit()
```

This script creates a random maze using depth-first search. It carves passages by visiting each cell and randomly exploring its neighbors. The result is a randomly generated maze that can be used as a level in your game.

## Conclusion

These advanced topics barely scratch the surface of what's possible in game development. By exploring physics, AI, procedural generation, and other complex systems, you can significantly enhance your games. Don't be afraid to experiment and push your limits. The skills you develop by tackling these challenges will make you a more versatile and capable game developer.

# Joining the Game Development Community

The game development community is a vibrant and supportive ecosystem filled with individuals who share a passion for creating games. Whether you are a hobbyist or aspiring professional, engaging with the community is a vital step in your journey. Connecting with others can provide you with valuable feedback, resources, mentorship, and even opportunities for collaboration. In this section, we'll explore how to get involved in the game development community, the benefits of doing so, and practical steps you can take to build your network and skills.

## The Benefits of Community Involvement

Before diving into the specifics of joining the community, it's important to understand why being an active participant is beneficial:

1. **Access to Resources**: The game development community is a goldmine of resources, including tutorials, open-source code, and tools. Many experienced developers share their knowledge through blog posts, YouTube channels, forums, and GitHub repositories. By engaging with the community, you gain access to a wealth of information that can help you solve problems and learn new techniques.
2. **Networking and Collaboration**: One of the biggest advantages of joining the game development community is the opportunity to meet other developers. Whether you're looking to collaborate on a project, find a mentor, or seek career advice, networking with others in the industry can open doors to new opportunities. Collaborative projects can also be a great way to gain experience, especially if you're new to game development.
3. **Feedback and Peer Review**: Sharing your work with the community can provide you with valuable feedback. Other developers can help you identify bugs, suggest improvements, and offer constructive criticism that can help you refine your games. Peer review is an essential part of growing as a developer, and it can be especially helpful when you're stuck on a particular issue.
4. **Staying Up to Date**: The game development landscape is constantly evolving, with new tools, technologies, and techniques emerging regularly. By engaging with the community, you can stay up to date on the latest trends and innovations, ensuring that your skills remain relevant.
5. **Motivation and Inspiration**: Game development can be challenging, and it's easy to feel discouraged when working on a complex project. Engaging with the community can be a great source of motivation and inspiration. Seeing what others are creating and sharing in their successes and challenges can help reignite your passion for game development.

## Online Communities and Forums

There are numerous online communities and forums where game developers gather to share ideas, ask questions, and showcase their projects. Here are some popular platforms you can join:

### Reddit

Reddit has several active game development communities, including:

- **r/gamedev**: This is one of the largest game development communities on Reddit. It's a great place to ask questions, share your projects, and get feedback from other developers. The community covers a wide range of topics, from programming and design to marketing and publishing.
- **r/pygame**: If you're using PyGame, this subreddit is a great resource for finding tutorials, sharing your work, and discussing Python-based game development.
- **r/indiedev**: This community is focused on independent game development. It's a great place to connect with other indie developers, share your progress, and find resources related to indie game production.

### Discord

Discord is home to many game development communities, where you can join channels dedicated to specific topics, engines, or programming languages. Some popular Discord servers include:

- **Game Dev League**: This server is one of the largest game development communities on Discord. It has channels for general game development, specific game engines, and programming languages. It's a great place to ask for help, find collaborators, and showcase your work.
- **PyGame Community Server**: If you're working specifically with PyGame, the PyGame Community Server is an excellent place to connect with other Python developers. You can ask questions, share code snippets, and discuss Python-related game development topics.

## Game Jams

Game jams are events where developers come together to create a game within a short timeframe, typically 24 to 72 hours. Participating in game jams is one of the best ways to learn, challenge yourself, and meet other developers. Some of the most popular game jams include:

- **Ludum Dare**: One of the oldest and most well-known game jams, Ludum Dare runs three times a year. Developers create a game from scratch based on a theme announced at the start of the event.
- **Global Game Jam**: This is a large international event where participants create games over a weekend. It's a great opportunity to connect with local developers, as many cities host in-person jam sites.

- **PyWeek**: PyWeek is a game jam specifically for Python developers. It's a fantastic way to practice your Python skills, learn new techniques, and showcase your work to the Python game development community.

## Contributing to Open-Source Projects

Another excellent way to get involved in the game development community is by contributing to open-source projects. Many game engines, libraries, and tools are open-source, and they often rely on community contributions for improvements and bug fixes.

### How to Get Started with Open-Source Contributions

1. **Find a Project**: Look for open-source projects that align with your interests and skill level. Websites like **GitHub** and **GitLab** are great places to start. You can search for tags like `#gamedev`, `#pygame`, or `#python` to find projects that need help.
2. **Read the Documentation**: Before contributing, make sure you understand the project's goals, coding standards, and contribution guidelines. Most projects have a `CONTRIBUTING.md` file that outlines the process for submitting changes.
3. **Start Small**: If you're new to open-source contributions, start with small issues like fixing bugs or updating documentation. This will help you get familiar with the project's codebase and build confidence.
4. **Submit a Pull Request**: Once you've made your changes, submit a pull request. Be sure to provide a clear description of what you've done and why. The project maintainers will review your changes, and they may provide feedback or request modifications.

## Attending Conferences and Meetups

Attending game development conferences and meetups is a great way to connect with others in the industry. Many events offer workshops, talks, and networking opportunities that can help you learn new skills and meet potential collaborators.

### Notable Conferences

- **Game Developers Conference (GDC)**: GDC is the largest annual event for professional game developers. It features talks, panels, and workshops from industry leaders and is a great place to learn about the latest trends in game development.
- **IndieCade**: IndieCade is an event focused on independent game developers. It showcases innovative indie games and provides opportunities for developers to connect and share ideas.
- **PyCon**: If you're a Python enthusiast, PyCon is the premier conference for Python developers. It often features talks and tutorials related to game development with Python.

### Local Meetups

In addition to large conferences, local meetups can provide a more personal way to connect with other developers. Websites like **Meetup.com** can help you find game development groups in your area. These events are often less formal than conferences, making them a great place to practice networking and get to know others in your local community.

## Sharing Your Work

Once you've created a game, sharing it with the community is an excellent way to get feedback and recognition. There are many platforms where you can showcase your projects:

- **Itch.io**: Itch.io is a platform for independent game developers to share their games. It's particularly popular among indie developers and is a great place to get feedback on your work.
- **GitHub**: If you're comfortable sharing your code, GitHub is a great platform to host your projects. It allows others to view your source code, suggest changes, and even collaborate on your project.
- **YouTube and Twitch**: Creating video content about your game development process can be a great way to build an audience. You can share tutorials, live stream your development process, or create videos showcasing your games.

## Conclusion

Joining the game development community can be one of the most rewarding aspects of your journey as a developer. By engaging with others, you can learn new skills, find inspiration, and make meaningful connections that can help you grow both personally and professionally. Whether you choose to participate in online forums, contribute to open-source projects, attend game jams, or showcase your work on social media, the key is to stay active and continue learning. The game development community is filled with people who share your passion, and by becoming a part of it, you open yourself up to a world of opportunities and experiences.

# Final Thoughts and Resources for Continued Learning

As you reach the end of this book, it's time to look back on your journey and consider the next steps. Game development is a vast and continuously evolving field, and your learning should never stop here. Whether you plan to develop games as a hobby, seek a career in the industry, or aim to release your own indie projects, there are countless resources and strategies you can use to continue growing your skills.

## Embrace a Growth Mindset

The key to success in game development—or any creative field—is a growth mindset. This mindset involves embracing challenges, learning from feedback, and persisting through setbacks. Game development is a complex process, and you will inevitably face problems that seem insurmountable at first. However, each challenge is an opportunity to learn something new. By maintaining a positive, resilient attitude, you can continually improve your skills and create better games.

### Learning Through Failure

One of the most valuable aspects of game development is that it allows you to experiment and fail in a safe environment. In fact, failure is often a crucial part of the learning process. By trying out new ideas, testing different mechanics, and pushing the limits of your skills, you gain a deeper understanding of what works and what doesn't.

For example, let's say you're developing a platformer game and you implement a new jumping mechanic that feels awkward to play. Rather than viewing this as a setback, analyze why it feels off. Is the jump arc too steep? Is the player control too stiff? By iterating and refining the mechanic, you learn valuable lessons about game physics and user experience.

## Keep Practicing and Building Projects

The best way to continue learning game development is by building more projects. The more games you create, the more experience you gain. Each project doesn't have to be a full-fledged game; small prototypes and experiments can be just as valuable.

### Example Project Ideas for Continued Practice

1. **Physics-Based Puzzles**: Create a physics-based puzzle game where players need to use objects and mechanics to solve challenges. This will help you practice implementing realistic physics and collision detection.
2. **AI Experiments**: Build a game that focuses on artificial intelligence, such as an enemy that learns from player actions or a cooperative AI teammate.
3. **Procedural Generation**: Experiment with procedural content generation. Create a dungeon crawler where the levels are generated randomly each time the player starts the game.
4. **Complex UI Systems**: Design a game with a complex user interface, such as a strategy game with multiple menus, inventories, and HUD elements. This will help you learn about user experience design and efficient UI implementation.

By setting small, achievable goals for each project, you can steadily build your skills without feeling overwhelmed. Remember, even the simplest game can teach you something new.

## Learn New Tools and Technologies

While you've learned the fundamentals of Python and PyGame in this book, the world of game development offers many more tools and technologies worth exploring. Diversifying your skill set can make you a more versatile developer and open up new possibilities for your projects.

### Explore Other Game Engines

- **Unity**: Unity is one of the most popular game engines in the world, known for its ease of use and strong community support. It uses C# as its primary programming language and offers extensive resources for both 2D and 3D game development.
- **Unreal Engine**: Unreal Engine is another powerful game engine, favored for its high-quality graphics and robust toolset. It primarily uses C++, making it a good choice if you want to dive deeper into low-level programming and optimization.

- **Godot**: Godot is an open-source game engine that is gaining popularity due to its flexibility and ease of use. It supports both 2D and 3D game development and uses GDScript, a language similar to Python.

**Learn Advanced Programming Concepts**

As you continue learning, consider studying more advanced programming concepts that can enhance your game development skills:

- **Design Patterns**: Design patterns, such as the Singleton, Observer, and Factory patterns, can help you write more efficient, maintainable code.
- **Algorithms and Data Structures**: Understanding algorithms and data structures is crucial for optimizing your games. Topics like pathfinding (e.g., A* algorithm), sorting algorithms, and data management are essential for complex game logic.
- **Multithreading**: For more advanced games, especially those with complex physics or AI, multithreading can help distribute processing tasks across multiple CPU cores, improving performance.

## Utilize Online Learning Platforms

There are many online platforms that offer courses and tutorials in game development. These resources can be invaluable for learning new skills, especially if you prefer structured learning environments.

**Recommended Learning Platforms**

- **Coursera and edX**: These platforms offer courses from top universities on various topics, including game development, programming, and computer science. Look for courses related to graphics programming, AI, and software design.
- **Udemy and Skillshare**: These platforms provide a wide range of game development courses, often created by industry professionals. You can find tutorials on Unity, Unreal Engine, Godot, and more.
- **YouTube**: YouTube has countless free tutorials covering every aspect of game development. Channels like Brackeys, GameMaker's Toolkit, and The Cherno offer high-quality content on programming, game design, and engine-specific tips.

## Engage in Continuous Learning

The field of game development evolves rapidly. New tools, libraries, and best practices emerge frequently, making it essential to stay up to date. Here are some strategies to help you keep learning:

1. **Follow Industry News**: Websites like Gamasutra (now GameDeveloper.com) and Polygon often publish articles on industry trends, new technologies, and game development insights.
2. **Read Books**: There are many excellent books on game development and programming. Some recommended titles include:
    - "Game Programming Patterns" by Robert Nystrom
    - "The Art of Game Design: A Book of Lenses" by Jesse Schell

# Creating Games with Python, PyGame, and Raspberry Pi

- "Clean Code" by Robert C. Martin
3. **Participate in Game Development Challenges**: Websites like Codewars and LeetCode offer coding challenges that can help you practice your programming skills. Game jams, as mentioned in the previous section, are also a great way to challenge yourself and learn quickly.

## Code Example: Expanding Your Skills

Here's a more advanced Python code example that demonstrates a basic implementation of a pathfinding algorithm using breadth-first search (BFS). This type of problem-solving skill is essential as you tackle more complex game mechanics.

```python
from collections import deque

def bfs(start, goal, grid):
    queue = deque([start])
    visited = set()
    visited.add(start)

    while queue:
        current = queue.popleft()
        if current == goal:
            print("Path found!")
            return True

        x, y = current
        for dx, dy in [(-1, 0), (1, 0), (0, -1), (0, 1)]:
            neighbor = (x + dx, y + dy)
            if neighbor not in visited and 0 <= neighbor[0] < len(grid) and 0 <= neighbor[1] < len(grid[0]) and grid[neighbor[0]][neighbor[1]] == 0:
                queue.append(neighbor)
                visited.add(neighbor)

    print("No path found.")
    return False

# Example grid (0 = walkable, 1 = obstacle)
grid = [
    [0, 1, 0, 0, 0],
    [0, 1, 0, 1, 0],
    [0, 0, 0, 1, 0],
```

```
        [1, 1, 0, 0, 0],
        [0, 0, 0, 0, 0]
]

start = (0, 0)
goal = (4, 4)

bfs(start, goal, grid)
```

This simple pathfinding example can be expanded and incorporated into your games, especially if you plan to implement AI that needs to navigate complex environments.

## Conclusion

You have taken the first steps on an exciting and rewarding path in game development. By continuing to learn, experiment, and connect with others in the community, you can achieve great things. The skills you've developed are just the beginning, and there is a whole world of knowledge and creativity waiting for you to explore. Keep pushing the limits of your abilities, stay curious, and most importantly, enjoy the process of making games. Your journey as a game developer is just beginning, and the possibilities are endless.

# Chapter 13: Appendices

## Glossary of Terms

This section provides a comprehensive glossary of key terms used throughout the book. Whether you're a beginner or an experienced developer, these definitions will help clarify important concepts in game development, Python programming, and Raspberry Pi hardware. The glossary is organized alphabetically for quick reference.

### Algorithm

An algorithm is a step-by-step procedure or set of rules used to solve a problem or perform a task. In game development, algorithms are used for everything from AI pathfinding to rendering graphics.

### API (Application Programming Interface)

An API is a set of functions and protocols that allow software components to communicate with each other. In Python, libraries like PyGame provide APIs for creating games, handling input, and managing graphics.

### Argument

An argument is a value provided to a function when it is called. For example, in Python, if you have a function `print(message)`, the `message` passed to `print()` is the argument.

**Example:**

```
def greet(name):
    print(f"Hello, {name}!")

greet("Alice")  # 'Alice' is the argument
```

### Array

An array is a data structure that stores a collection of items, typically of the same type. In Python, arrays can be represented using lists or the `array` module.

**Example:**

```python
numbers = [1, 2, 3, 4, 5]
print(numbers[0])  # Outputs: 1
```

## Bit

A bit is the smallest unit of data in computing, representing a value of either 0 or 1. Bits are used to encode binary data in digital systems.

## Boolean

A Boolean value is a data type that can be either `True` or `False`. It is commonly used in conditional statements.

**Example:**

```python
is_game_over = False

if not is_game_over:
    print("Game is still running!")
```

## Class

A class is a blueprint for creating objects in object-oriented programming. It defines a set of attributes and methods that the objects created from the class will have.

**Example:**

```python
class Player:
    def __init__(self, name, score):
        self.name = name
        self.score = score
```

```python
    def display(self):
        print(f"{self.name}: {self.score}")


player1 = Player("Alice", 100)
player1.display()
```

## Collision Detection

Collision detection is the process of determining when two or more objects in a game intersect. It is a critical part of gameplay mechanics, used in actions like hitting a ball or detecting player contact with obstacles.

## CPU (Central Processing Unit)

The CPU is the main processor of a computer, responsible for executing instructions. It performs the calculations necessary for game logic, physics, and AI.

## Debugging

Debugging is the process of identifying and fixing errors in your code. Tools like print statements, logging, and debuggers help in finding the root cause of issues.

**Example:**

```python
for i in range(5):
    print(f"Loop iteration: {i}")
```

## Dictionary

A dictionary is a Python data structure that stores key-value pairs. It is useful for storing data that can be looked up using a unique key.

**Example:**

```python
game_settings = {
    "resolution": "1920x1080",
    "fullscreen": True,
    "volume": 75
}
print(game_settings["resolution"])   # Outputs: '1920x1080'
```

## Event Loop

The event loop is a core component of game development that continuously checks for user inputs, updates the game state, and redraws the screen. In PyGame, this loop is essential for maintaining game flow.

**Example:**

```python
import pygame

pygame.init()
screen = pygame.display.set_mode((800, 600))

running = True
while running:
    for event in pygame.event.get():
        if event.type == pygame.QUIT:
            running = False

pygame.quit()
```

## FPS (Frames Per Second)

FPS is a measure of how many frames (images) are rendered per second in a game. A higher FPS results in smoother animations.

## GPIO (General-Purpose Input/Output)

GPIO pins are a feature of the Raspberry Pi used to control electronic components. These pins can be programmed to read input or send output signals, making them ideal for custom game controllers.

**Example:**

```
import RPi.GPIO as GPIO


GPIO.setmode(GPIO.BCM)

GPIO.setup(18, GPIO.OUT)

GPIO.output(18, GPIO.HIGH)   # Turns on the connected component
```

## Library

A library is a collection of pre-written code that can be used to perform common tasks. PyGame is a popular library for game development in Python.

## Object

An object is an instance of a class in object-oriented programming. It has attributes (data) and methods (functions) defined by the class.

**Example:**

```
ball = {"x": 100, "y": 200, "speed": 5}
print(ball["x"])   # Outputs: 100
```

## Pixel

A pixel is the smallest unit of a digital image, typically a single point in a grid. The resolution of a screen is determined by the number of pixels it displays.

## Python

Python is a high-level, interpreted programming language known for its readability and versatility. It is widely used in various domains, including web development, data analysis, and game development.

## Sprite

A sprite is a 2D image or animation integrated into a game. Sprites are used for characters, objects, and backgrounds.

**Example using PyGame:**

```
import pygame

pygame.init()

sprite_image = pygame.image.load("player.png")

screen.blit(sprite_image, (50, 100))

pygame.display.update()
```

## Variable

A variable is a named storage location in a program that holds a value. Variables can store different types of data, such as numbers, strings, and lists.

**Example:**

```
score = 0

player_name = "Alice"

print(f"{player_name} has a score of {score}")
```

## Vector

A vector is a mathematical object used to represent direction and magnitude. In game development, vectors are used for movement and physics calculations.

**Example:**

```
position = [0, 0]
velocity = [5, 3]

# Update position based on velocity
position[0] += velocity[0]
position[1] += velocity[1]
print(position)  # Outputs: [5, 3]
```

## IDE (Integrated Development Environment)

An IDE is a software application that provides tools for software development. Common Python IDEs include PyCharm, Visual Studio Code, and Thonny (often used for Raspberry Pi).

## Loop

A loop is a programming construct that repeats a block of code multiple times. The most common types are `for` and `while` loops.

**Example:**

```
for i in range(10):
    print(i)
```

## Module

A module is a file containing Python code that can be imported and used in other Python programs.

**Example:**

```
import math

print(math.sqrt(16))    # Outputs: 4.0
```

This glossary should serve as a quick reference throughout your game development journey, helping you understand the key concepts and terminology involved in creating games with Python and Raspberry Pi.

## Resources for Further Learning

As you continue your journey in game development with Python and Raspberry Pi, it is essential to have access to quality resources that can help expand your knowledge, provide solutions to common problems, and inspire you to try new projects. This section provides a curated list of resources, including books, online courses, tutorials, forums, and useful libraries, to help you become a proficient game developer.

### Books

#### 1. Python Crash Course by Eric Matthes

This book is an excellent starting point for beginners who want to learn Python. It covers the basics of Python programming and then dives into project-based learning, including a section on developing simple games using PyGame.

#### 2. Invent Your Own Computer Games with Python by Al Sweigart

A classic book for beginners that focuses on game development with Python. It provides step-by-step instructions for creating several simple games and is a great introduction to Python and PyGame.

#### 3. Raspberry Pi User Guide by Eben Upton and Gareth Halfacree

Written by the co-creator of the Raspberry Pi, this book offers an in-depth look at the hardware and software of the Raspberry Pi. It includes sections on GPIO programming, which is particularly useful for creating custom game controllers.

#### 4. Making Games with Python & PyGame by Al Sweigart

This book is tailored specifically for game development with PyGame. It guides you through creating several games, covering essential topics like game loops, graphics, sound, and animation.

## Online Courses

### 1. Coursera – Python for Everybody

This course series is one of the most popular Python courses available online. It covers Python from the basics to advanced topics, with a focus on practical application. It's a great foundation for those new to programming.

### 2. Udemy – Python Game Development using PyGame

Udemy offers various courses on Python game development, including specific courses focused on PyGame. These courses typically include video lectures, downloadable resources, and interactive coding exercises.

### 3. edX – Introduction to Python Programming

This course from edX is an excellent resource for learning Python. It covers basic Python syntax, data structures, and includes projects that involve creating simple games.

### 4. Raspberry Pi Foundation – Projects Hub

The Raspberry Pi Foundation's Projects Hub is a fantastic resource for hands-on projects. It includes a variety of game development projects using Python and the Raspberry Pi, with detailed instructions and source code.

## YouTube Channels

### 1. The Coding Train

This channel is hosted by Daniel Shiffman and features tutorials on creative coding with Python and JavaScript. The channel has a series on creating games with Python and PyGame.

### 2. Tech With Tim

Tim is a YouTube creator who covers Python programming and game development. His channel includes tutorials on building games with PyGame and other Python libraries.

### 3. Raspberry Pi

The official Raspberry Pi YouTube channel offers tutorials and project ideas for Raspberry Pi enthusiasts. It includes videos on setting up your Raspberry Pi, using GPIO pins, and creating custom controllers for games.

## Tutorials and Blogs

## 1. Real Python

Real Python is one of the best online resources for Python programming. It offers in-depth tutorials on a wide range of topics, including game development with PyGame. The tutorials are well-written and include code examples and exercises.

## 2. PyGame Official Documentation

The PyGame documentation is an essential resource for any game developer using Python. It provides a detailed overview of the PyGame modules, functions, and classes, along with examples and best practices.

## 3. Raspberry Pi Blog

The Raspberry Pi blog features tutorials, project ideas, and updates on the latest Raspberry Pi hardware and software. It's a great place to find inspiration for your next game development project.

## 4. Stack Overflow

Stack Overflow is a question-and-answer site for programmers. It has a large community of Python and Raspberry Pi developers who can help answer your questions about game development, debugging, and performance optimization.

# Libraries and Tools

## 1. PyGame

PyGame is the primary library used for game development in this book. It provides modules for handling graphics, sound, and user input. The official website includes comprehensive documentation and a community forum.

## 2. NumPy

NumPy is a powerful library for numerical computing in Python. It is particularly useful in game development for handling complex mathematical calculations, such as vector operations and collision detection.

**Example:**

```python
import numpy as np


vector1 = np.array([1, 2])

vector2 = np.array([3, 4])
```

```
dot_product = np.dot(vector1, vector2)
print(dot_product)   # Outputs: 11
```

### 3. Pillow (Python Imaging Library)

Pillow is a library for working with images in Python. It can be used in game development to manipulate and display images, create sprites, and handle image-based animations.

### 4. PyOpenGL

PyOpenGL is a Python binding for OpenGL, a powerful graphics library. It can be used to create more complex and visually impressive 3D games, although it has a steeper learning curve than PyGame.

### 5. RPi.GPIO

RPi.GPIO is the standard Python library for working with the GPIO pins on the Raspberry Pi. It allows you to control hardware components like LEDs, buttons, and joysticks, making it essential for custom game controllers.

**Example:**

```
import RPi.GPIO as GPIO
import time

GPIO.setmode(GPIO.BCM)
GPIO.setup(17, GPIO.IN, pull_up_down=GPIO.PUD_UP)

while True:
    input_state = GPIO.input(17)
    if input_state == False:
        print("Button Pressed")
        time.sleep(0.2)
```

## Communities and Forums

### 1. PyGame Community

The PyGame community is an active and helpful group of developers who share their projects, ask questions, and provide feedback on the official PyGame Discord server and forums.

### 2. Raspberry Pi Community

The Raspberry Pi community includes enthusiasts and developers who are passionate about using the Raspberry Pi for projects like game development. The Raspberry Pi forums and subreddit are excellent places to ask for help and share your projects.

### 3. GitHub

GitHub is a platform for hosting and sharing code. It's a great resource for finding open-source game projects, contributing to other developers' projects, and hosting your own game code.

**Example:**

```
# Clone a PyGame project from GitHub
git clone https://github.com/username/pygame-project.git
cd pygame-project
python main.py
```

## Conferences and Events

### 1. PyCon

PyCon is the largest annual conference for Python developers. It includes workshops, talks, and tutorials on a wide range of Python-related topics, including game development with PyGame.

### 2. Raspberry Pi Jam

Raspberry Pi Jams are community events where enthusiasts gather to share projects, learn new skills, and collaborate on projects. It's a great place to showcase your game development projects and get feedback.

### 3. Game Developers Conference (GDC)

GDC is one of the largest conferences for game developers. While it primarily focuses on professional game development, it includes sessions on indie game development, Python programming, and educational games.

## Final Tips for Continuous Learning

1. **Keep Experimenting:** Don't be afraid to experiment with different game mechanics, graphics, and sounds. Learning through experimentation is one of the best ways to improve your skills.
2. **Join a Community:** Becoming part of a developer community can provide support, feedback, and inspiration. Consider joining online forums, Discord servers, or local Raspberry Pi and Python meetups.
3. **Contribute to Open-Source Projects:** Contributing to open-source projects on GitHub can help you learn from other developers and gain experience working on larger codebases.
4. **Stay Updated:** The world of game development and Python programming is constantly evolving. Follow blogs, subscribe to newsletters, and keep an eye on updates for PyGame and Raspberry Pi.

This list of resources should provide you with a solid foundation for further learning and exploration in game development with Python and Raspberry Pi. Happy coding!

# Sample Projects and Code Snippets

This section showcases a variety of sample projects and code snippets designed to help you apply what you've learned throughout the book. These projects range from simple beginner-level games to more complex examples that incorporate advanced features like custom controls using Raspberry Pi's GPIO pins. The code snippets provide practical examples that you can integrate into your own projects or use as a foundation for creating new games.

## Project 1: Simple Snake Game

The classic Snake game is a great beginner project for learning game development. It involves controlling a snake that grows in length each time it eats food. The goal is to keep the snake from colliding with the walls or itself.

### Code: Snake Game with PyGame

```
import pygame

import random


pygame.init()
```

```python
# Screen settings
width, height = 600, 400
screen = pygame.display.set_mode((width, height))
clock = pygame.time.Clock()
font = pygame.font.Font(None, 36)


# Game variables
block_size = 20
snake = [(100, 100)]
snake_dir = (block_size, 0)
food = (random.randint(0, (width - block_size) // block_size) * block_size,
        random.randint(0, (height - block_size) // block_size) * block_size)
score = 0
game_over = False


def draw_snake():
    for block in snake:
        pygame.draw.rect(screen, (0, 255, 0), (*block, block_size, block_size))


def draw_food():
    pygame.draw.rect(screen, (255, 0, 0), (*food, block_size, block_size))
```

```python
def update_snake():
    global game_over
    new_head = (snake[0][0] + snake_dir[0], snake[0][1] + snake_dir[1])
    if (new_head in snake) or (new_head[0] < 0 or new_head[0] >= width) or (new_head[1] < 0 or new_head[1] >= height):
        game_over = True
    snake.insert(0, new_head)
    if new_head == food:
        return True
    snake.pop()
    return False


while not game_over:
    screen.fill((0, 0, 0))
    for event in pygame.event.get():
        if event.type == pygame.QUIT:
            game_over = True
        elif event.type == pygame.KEYDOWN:
            if event.key == pygame.K_LEFT and snake_dir != (block_size, 0):
                snake_dir = (-block_size, 0)
            elif event.key == pygame.K_RIGHT and snake_dir != (-block_size, 0):
                snake_dir = (block_size, 0)
```

```python
            elif event.key == pygame.K_UP and snake_dir != (0, block_size):
                snake_dir = (0, -block_size)
            elif event.key == pygame.K_DOWN and snake_dir != (0, -block_size):
                snake_dir = (0, block_size)

    if update_snake():
        score += 1
        food = (random.randint(0, (width - block_size) // block_size) * block_size,
                random.randint(0, (height - block_size) // block_size) * block_size)

    draw_snake()
    draw_food()
    score_text = font.render(f"Score: {score}", True, (255, 255, 255))
    screen.blit(score_text, (10, 10))
    pygame.display.flip()
    clock.tick(10)

pygame.quit()
```

This simple Snake game teaches basic concepts like handling user input, updating game state, and collision detection.

## Project 2: Pong Game with Multiplayer Support

Pong is one of the earliest arcade games, and it's a great project for learning about game physics and multiplayer functionality. In this project, you will create a two-player Pong game using PyGame.

**Code: Pong Game**

```python
import pygame

pygame.init()

# Screen settings
width, height = 800, 600
screen = pygame.display.set_mode((width, height))
clock = pygame.time.Clock()
font = pygame.font.Font(None, 36)


# Game variables
ball_speed = [5, 5]
ball = pygame.Rect(width // 2 - 15, height // 2 - 15, 30, 30)
paddle1 = pygame.Rect(50, height // 2 - 60, 10, 120)
paddle2 = pygame.Rect(width - 60, height // 2 - 60, 10, 120)
paddle_speed = 10
score1, score2 = 0, 0


def draw_objects():
    pygame.draw.ellipse(screen, (255, 255, 255), ball)
    pygame.draw.rect(screen, (255, 255, 255), paddle1)
```

```python
    pygame.draw.rect(screen, (255, 255, 255), paddle2)

    score_text = font.render(f"{score1} - {score2}", True, (255, 255, 255))

    screen.blit(score_text, (width // 2 - 50, 10))


def move_ball():

    global score1, score2

    ball.x += ball_speed[0]

    ball.y += ball_speed[1]

    if ball.top <= 0 or ball.bottom >= height:

        ball_speed[1] = -ball_speed[1]

    if ball.colliderect(paddle1) or ball.colliderect(paddle2):

        ball_speed[0] = -ball_speed[0]

    if ball.left <= 0:

        score2 += 1

        ball.center = (width // 2, height // 2)

    elif ball.right >= width:

        score1 += 1

        ball.center = (width // 2, height // 2)


while True:

    screen.fill((0, 0, 0))

    for event in pygame.event.get():

        if event.type == pygame.QUIT:

            pygame.quit()
```

```
            exit()

    keys = pygame.key.get_pressed()

    if keys[pygame.K_w] and paddle1.top > 0:

        paddle1.y -= paddle_speed

    if keys[pygame.K_s] and paddle1.bottom < height:

        paddle1.y += paddle_speed

    if keys[pygame.K_UP] and paddle2.top > 0:

        paddle2.y -= paddle_speed

    if keys[pygame.K_DOWN] and paddle2.bottom < height:

        paddle2.y += paddle_speed


    move_ball()

    draw_objects()

    pygame.display.flip()

    clock.tick(60)
```

This Pong game introduces more advanced topics like multiplayer controls, game physics, and score tracking.

## GPIO-Controlled LED Game

In this project, we use the GPIO pins on the Raspberry Pi to create a simple game that involves pressing a button to toggle an LED on and off. This is a fun way to learn about hardware programming with the Raspberry Pi.

### Code: GPIO LED Game

```
import RPi.GPIO as GPIO
```

```python
import time

# GPIO setup
GPIO.setmode(GPIO.BCM)
GPIO.setup(18, GPIO.OUT)
GPIO.setup(17, GPIO.IN, pull_up_down=GPIO.PUD_UP)

try:
    while True:
        button_state = GPIO.input(17)
        if button_state == False:
            GPIO.output(18, not GPIO.input(18))
            print("LED Toggled!")
            time.sleep(0.2)
except KeyboardInterrupt:
    GPIO.cleanup()
```

This project teaches you how to read input from a button and control an LED, making it a great starting point for custom game controllers.

## Final Thoughts

These sample projects and code snippets should give you a strong foundation to build upon. Experiment with modifying the code, adding new features, and combining elements from different projects to create your own unique games. With practice and creativity, you'll be well on your way to mastering game development with Python and Raspberry Pi.

## Reference Guide

This reference guide serves as a comprehensive overview of the key concepts, functions, modules, and techniques covered in this book. It is designed to be a quick lookup resource for game developers working with Python, PyGame, and Raspberry Pi. This guide includes important Python syntax, essential PyGame functions, GPIO programming tips, and troubleshooting advice.

## Python Basics

### Variables

Variables are used to store data in Python. They can hold different data types such as integers, floats, strings, and lists.

**Example:**

```
score = 0
player_name = "Alice"
high_scores = [100, 200, 150]
```

### Data Types

Common Python data types include:

- **Integer:** Whole numbers (e.g., `10`, `-5`)
- **Float:** Decimal numbers (e.g., `3.14`, `-0.99`)
- **String:** Text data (e.g., `"Hello, World!"`)
- **List:** Ordered collection of items (e.g., `[1, 2, 3]`)

**Example:**

```
pi = 3.14159
message = "Welcome to the game!"
colors = ["red", "green", "blue"]
```

### Control Flow

Control flow statements include `if`, `for`, and `while` loops, which control the execution of code based on conditions.

**Example:**

```
for i in range(5):
    if i % 2 == 0:
        print(f"{i} is even")
    else:
        print(f"{i} is odd")
```

## PyGame Reference

PyGame is a Python library for game development that includes modules for handling graphics, sound, and input.

### Setting Up PyGame

To use PyGame, you first need to initialize it and create a display surface.

**Example:**

```
import pygame

pygame.init()

screen = pygame.display.set_mode((800, 600))

pygame.display.set_caption("My Game")
```

### Game Loop

The game loop is the core of any PyGame application, handling events, updating game state, and drawing frames.

**Example:**

```
running = True

while running:

    for event in pygame.event.get():

        if event.type == pygame.QUIT:

            running = False


    screen.fill((0, 0, 0))    # Clear the screen with black

    pygame.display.flip()     # Update the display


pygame.quit()
```

## Drawing Shapes

PyGame provides functions to draw basic shapes like rectangles, circles, and lines.

**Example:**

```
pygame.draw.rect(screen, (255, 0, 0), (50, 50, 100, 50))   # Red rectangle

pygame.draw.circle(screen, (0, 255, 0), (400, 300), 50)    # Green circle

pygame.draw.line(screen, (0, 0, 255), (0, 0), (800, 600), 5)   # Blue line
```

## Handling User Input

PyGame allows you to capture keyboard and mouse input.

**Example:**

```
keys = pygame.key.get_pressed()

if keys[pygame.K_LEFT]:

    print("Left arrow key pressed")

if keys[pygame.K_RIGHT]:

    print("Right arrow key pressed")
```

**Loading and Playing Sounds**

PyGame can load and play sound files using its `mixer` module.

**Example:**

```
pygame.mixer.init()

sound = pygame.mixer.Sound("beep.wav")

sound.play()
```

## Raspberry Pi GPIO Reference

The GPIO (General-Purpose Input/Output) pins on the Raspberry Pi allow you to control hardware components like LEDs, buttons, and sensors.

**Setting Up GPIO**

To use GPIO pins in Python, you need the `RPi.GPIO` module.

**Example:**

```
import RPi.GPIO as GPIO


GPIO.setmode(GPIO.BCM)

GPIO.setup(18, GPIO.OUT)
```

## Controlling an LED

You can turn an LED on and off using a GPIO pin.

**Example:**

```
GPIO.output(18, GPIO.HIGH)   # Turn on the LED
time.sleep(1)
GPIO.output(18, GPIO.LOW)    # Turn off the LED
```

## Reading Button Input

Buttons can be connected to GPIO pins and used to control game actions.

**Example:**

```
GPIO.setup(17, GPIO.IN, pull_up_down=GPIO.PUD_UP)

while True:
    if GPIO.input(17) == GPIO.LOW:
        print("Button Pressed!")
```

# Troubleshooting Tips

## Common PyGame Errors

**Display Surface Error:** If you encounter `pygame.error: display Surface quit`, ensure that your game loop handles the `QUIT` event correctly.
python

```
if event.type == pygame.QUIT:
    running = False
```

1.

**Sound Not Playing:** If sounds aren't playing, check if you've initialized the mixer module.
python

```
pygame.mixer.init()
```

2.

**Frame Rate Issues:** If your game is running too fast or too slow, control the frame rate using `pygame.time.Clock`.
python

```
clock = pygame.time.Clock()

clock.tick(60)   # Limit to 60 frames per second
```

3.

## GPIO Troubleshooting

**GPIO Pin Not Responding:** Make sure you've set the pin mode correctly (`GPIO.BCM` or `GPIO.BOARD`).
python

```
GPIO.setmode(GPIO.BCM)
```

1.

**Debouncing Button Input:** If your button input is erratic, add a delay or use software debouncing.
python

```
time.sleep(0.2)   # Add a small delay
```

2.

**Permission Error:** If you get a permission error, try running your script with `sudo`.
bash

```
sudo python3 my_script.py
```

3.

# Python Modules and Libraries

Below is a list of useful Python modules and libraries you can use in your game projects:

- **NumPy:** For complex mathematical calculations.
- **Pillow:** For advanced image handling and manipulation.
- **PyOpenGL:** For 3D graphics rendering.
- **RPi.GPIO:** For controlling the GPIO pins on the Raspberry Pi.

**Example of Using Pillow:**

```
from PIL import Image


image = Image.open("sprite.png")
image.show()
```

## Game Design Tips

1. **Plan Your Game Mechanics:** Before you start coding, outline the core mechanics of your game. Define how the player interacts with the game world, the objectives, and the rules.
2. **Start Small:** Begin with a simple prototype to test your game's mechanics. Avoid feature creep by focusing on core gameplay first.
3. **Use Incremental Development:** Build your game in small, manageable pieces. Test each feature as you add it to ensure everything works correctly.
4. **Optimize for Performance:** Use techniques like sprite batching, reducing draw calls, and controlling frame rates to optimize your game's performance.
5. **Playtest Frequently:** Get feedback early and often. Playtesting helps you identify issues with game mechanics and balance before they become difficult to fix.

### Final Reference

- **Python Official Documentation:** https://docs.python.org/3/
- **PyGame Official Site:** https://www.pygame.org/
- **Raspberry Pi GPIO Guide:** https://www.raspberrypi.org/documentation/usage/gpio/

This reference guide should serve as a helpful resource throughout your development process, providing quick access to key information, functions, and tips to make your game development experience smoother and more enjoyable.

# Frequently Asked Questions

This section addresses common questions and issues you may encounter while working with Python, PyGame, and Raspberry Pi for game development. It provides solutions, tips, and code examples to help you overcome challenges and understand key concepts.

## 1. How do I install PyGame on my Raspberry Pi?

Installing PyGame on Raspberry Pi is straightforward with Python's package manager, `pip`. Open your terminal and use the following command:

```
sudo pip3 install pygame
```

If you encounter issues, ensure your Python installation is up to date:

```
sudo apt update
sudo apt upgrade
sudo apt install python3-pip
```

To verify the installation, open Python and try importing PyGame:

```
import pygame
print(pygame.ver)
```

If you see the version number, the installation was successful.

## 2. How can I fix the 'display Surface quit' error in PyGame?

This error usually occurs when your game loop doesn't handle the `QUIT` event properly. Make sure to include the following code snippet in your game loop:

```
for event in pygame.event.get():
    if event.type == pygame.QUIT:
        pygame.quit()
        exit()
```

This ensures the PyGame display is closed correctly when the user exits the game.

## 3. My game is running too fast or too slow. How do I control the frame rate?

You can control the frame rate in PyGame using `pygame.time.Clock`. This allows you to set a consistent frames per second (FPS) for your game.

**Example:**

```
clock = pygame.time.Clock()

while True:
    clock.tick(60)  # Limit the game to 60 FPS
    # Your game code here
```

Setting a frame rate helps synchronize the game speed across different devices.

## 4. How do I handle keyboard input in PyGame?

In PyGame, you can handle keyboard input using the `pygame.key.get_pressed()` function. This function returns a list of boolean values representing the state of each key.

**Example:**

```
keys = pygame.key.get_pressed()
if keys[pygame.K_LEFT]:
    print("Left key pressed")
if keys[pygame.K_RIGHT]:
    print("Right key pressed")
```

Alternatively, you can use the `KEYDOWN` and `KEYUP` events:

```
for event in pygame.event.get():
    if event.type == pygame.KEYDOWN:
        if event.key == pygame.K_SPACE:
            print("Space key pressed")
```

## 5. How do I connect a button to my Raspberry Pi for use in a game?

To connect a physical button to your Raspberry Pi and use it in a PyGame application, you need to use the GPIO pins.

**Example:**

```
import RPi.GPIO as GPIO
import time

GPIO.setmode(GPIO.BCM)
GPIO.setup(18, GPIO.IN, pull_up_down=GPIO.PUD_UP)

while True:
    button_state = GPIO.input(18)
    if button_state == GPIO.LOW:
        print("Button pressed!")
        time.sleep(0.2)  # Debounce delay
```

This code sets up the button on GPIO pin 18 and prints a message when the button is pressed.

## 6. How can I optimize my game's performance in PyGame?

Here are some tips to optimize your game's performance:

- **Limit the frame rate:** Use `pygame.time.Clock()` to control the FPS.
- **Use efficient drawing methods:** Avoid redrawing the entire screen every frame. Use `pygame.display.update(rect)` to update only specific areas.
- **Preload assets:** Load images, sounds, and other assets at the start of your game rather than during the game loop.
- **Reduce image size:** Smaller images consume less memory and processing power.

**Example:**

```
rect = pygame.Rect(100, 100, 50, 50)
pygame.display.update(rect)
```

This updates only the specified rectangle, reducing the amount of drawing required.

## 7. How do I play background music in PyGame?

PyGame's `mixer` module allows you to easily play background music.

**Example:**

```
import pygame

pygame.mixer.init()
pygame.mixer.music.load("background.mp3")
pygame.mixer.music.play(-1)  # Loop the music indefinitely
```

To stop the music:

```
pygame.mixer.music.stop()
```

Ensure the music file is in a supported format like MP3 or WAV.

## 8. My GPIO input is inconsistent. How do I handle button debouncing?

Button debouncing is necessary when using physical buttons with GPIO pins, as mechanical switches can generate multiple signals for a single press. You can solve this using software debouncing with a small delay.

**Example:**

```python
import RPi.GPIO as GPIO
import time

GPIO.setmode(GPIO.BCM)
GPIO.setup(18, GPIO.IN, pull_up_down=GPIO.PUD_UP)

try:
    while True:
        if GPIO.input(18) == GPIO.LOW:
            print("Button pressed!")
            time.sleep(0.3)  # Debounce delay
except KeyboardInterrupt:
    GPIO.cleanup()
```

Alternatively, you can use the `event_detected()` method:

```python
GPIO.add_event_detect(18, GPIO.FALLING, bouncetime=200)
```

## 9. How do I create an executable file from my Python game?

To distribute your game as an executable, you can use `PyInstaller`.

**Installation:**

```
pip install pyinstaller
```

**Creating an Executable:**

```
pyinstaller --onefile --windowed my_game.py
```

This command creates a standalone executable file that can be shared without requiring Python to be installed on the user's machine.

## 10. Can I use a joystick with PyGame?

Yes, PyGame supports joysticks and game controllers through its `pygame.joystick` module.

**Example:**

```
import pygame

pygame.init()
pygame.joystick.init()

joystick = pygame.joystick.Joystick(0)
joystick.init()

while True:
```

```
    pygame.event.pump()

    axis = joystick.get_axis(0)

    print(f"Joystick axis 0 value: {axis}")
```

This code initializes the first joystick and prints the value of its first axis.

## 11. How do I update PyGame to the latest version?

You can update PyGame using `pip`.

```
sudo pip3 install --upgrade pygame
```

To check the installed version:

```
python3 -m pygame --version
```

Ensure you're using the latest version to access new features and bug fixes.

## 12. Why isn't my game responding to events immediately?

If your game is lagging in processing events, make sure you are using `pygame.event.pump()` or handling events correctly within your game loop. Avoid blocking code like `time.sleep()` unless necessary.

## 13. How can I handle multiple button presses in PyGame?

Using `pygame.key.get_pressed()` allows you to detect multiple key presses simultaneously.

**Example:**

```
keys = pygame.key.get_pressed()

if keys[pygame.K_LEFT] and keys[pygame.K_UP]:
```

```
print("Moving diagonally left and up")
```

This method provides better control for games requiring complex input handling.

## 14. How do I resize the game window in PyGame?

You can resize the PyGame window using `pygame.display.set_mode()` with the `RESIZABLE` flag.

**Example:**

```
screen = pygame.display.set_mode((800, 600), pygame.RESIZABLE)
```

Handle the `VIDEORESIZE` event to update your game objects when the window is resized.

## 15. What is the best way to package and share my Python game?

For packaging Python games, consider using `PyInstaller` or `cx_Freeze`. Host your project on GitHub to share the source code, and use a platform like Itch.io or Steam for distribution.

This FAQ section aims to cover the most common issues and provide you with the information you need to troubleshoot and enhance your game development projects. Keep experimenting, learning, and building new games!

www.ingramcontent.com/pod-product-compliance
Lightning Source LLC
Chambersburg PA
CBHW071018240526
45469CB00006BD/1966